RUSSIA
&
POSTWAR EUROPE

BY

DAVID J. DALLIN

TRANSLATED BY
F. K. LAWRENCE

NEW HAVEN
YALE UNIVERSITY PRESS

To my son Alexander

PREFACE

THIS book deals with Soviet Russia's foreign policy now and in the postwar years to come; yet it does not set itself the aim of making prophecies or of indulging in guesswork.

The policy of every country has its roots in that country's history, traditions, and its fundamental concepts. Therefore the political course any nation can be expected to follow in the postwar years will represent an application of these fundamental principles and traditions to a new international situation, unless a general transformation in its political system and political aims takes place.

Thus, the first section of this book takes up the problems underlying Soviet policy, its principles, ideas, and theories: the so-called "New Nationalism," its relation to Communism, and its forms of expression during the course of this war.

Elucidation of the main trends of Soviet foreign policy, as it has appeared in the last decades, is the subject of the second section. The scope of this discussion is necessarily restricted to Soviet relations with Great Britain and Germany, since these have held the central place in the international relations of Soviet Russia.

Conclusions drawn from the prewar history of Soviet Russia, as well as their application to the near future, are the theme of the last two sections: Russia in Postwar Europe.

It was necessary to confine the discussion to the problem of Soviet relations with Europe rather than with the entire postwar world, thus by-passing Russia's Far Eastern policy. While I am fully aware of the interdependence of the European and Asiatic policies of the Great Powers, Russia included, and while I realize that disseverance of these policies is often artificial, the problems of the Far East, i.e., of Russia's relations with China and Japan during the concluding stages of this war and after it, constitute so vast a subject that it was impossible to compress them into a few pages or into a single section. The Far Eastern triangle will be the subject of a separate volume.

The conclusions formulated in this book may appear to many as none too optimistic. They may especially upset the rosy hopes of those who expect the present war to end in an era of universal peace, harmony, and happiness. But it is better to foresee the difficulties lying ahead than to entertain wishful illusions which in the days to come may once again be shattered.

D. J. D.

New York City

CONTENTS

RUSSIA & POSTWAR EUROPE

I. CONSTANTS AND VARIABLES

1. FROM CIVIL WARS TO INTERNATIONAL WARS

SOME day, perhaps, geologists will resolve the age-old controversy between the theory of gradual evolution and the theory of sudden catastrophes. The social sciences likewise will resolve the controversy between catastrophes and evolution in the history of humanity.

The theory of catastrophes divides the history of the earth into epochs, periods, and eras, sharply separated from one another by geological catastrophes of such prodigious force that fundamental changes were wrought in the appearance of the earth and the character of all living matter, changes which were preserved in the new epoch for millions of years. Within the span of each geological period natural evolution is restricted to narrow limits, and species of animal and plant life undergo but slow and limited change, until the next catastrophe. The ichthyosaur, the dinosaur, the mastodon, were characteristic forms of life in their respective eras, and all of them perished in subsequent catastrophes. In the history of mankind, revolutions and wars have frequently performed the same role that catastrophes played in the history of the earth.

The political world of the European continent, as it emerged from the catastrophe of 1914–18, provides a striking analogy. In the course of a few years the political fauna of the prewar period underwent a thorough change and new, unfamiliar organisms and strange plants suddenly emerged on the political surface.

The fauna and flora that vanished in Europe included some of the huge empires and old monarchies, the splendor of autocracy and semi-autocracy, enlightened conservatism and conservative liberalism, economic strength, stability of currencies, and security of savings and fortunes. But political formations heretofore unknown arose out of the catastrophe and persisted, almost without change, during the following quarter of a century.

There sprang up states which the world had never known, and other states which had perished long ago in some former

catastrophe came to life again. In the south of Europe there
appeared a new species of political fauna, fascism, which was
able to preserve itself throughout the period. In the early
'twenties the future leader of Germany wrote his new gospel,
which in its basic features has retained its importance to this
day. France, regarded as the strongest European power, held
this position until the new catastrophe. After 1918 the formerly revolutionist parties of Europe became moderate, and
socialist governments were often governments of Their
Majesties. Among the new organisms born in this catastrophe
was Bolshevism, both the Russian and the world varieties.
When the waters of the cataclysmic flood subsided Bolshevism
was already installed as one of the most formidable forces of
the period that followed. Though it has since changed in many
ways and has undergone an evolutionary development, this
new species of fauna has remained basically the same. *Plus
ça changeait, plus c'était la même chose.*

It is important to comprehend the wholeness of this historical period of about a quarter century. This wholeness is
seen in the interdependence of the elements of the period,
their complementariness, their architectonic unity—the stability of the states, parties, and intellectual movements of
the period. History is a record of eternal flux, of myriad
changes, of daily evolution. But he would be a poor historian
who could not see the forest for the trees, who, absorbed in
the study of kaleidoscopic detail, overlooked the constancy of
political species.

Regarded as a whole, Soviet policy was a characteristically
individual combination of elements, which on superficial examination was called by some democratic and by others a
return to traditional Russian autocracy. The verbal democratic embellishments, such as "self-determination of peoples," "liberation from foreign oppression," or "liberty," did
not make democratic an international activity which set itself
widely expansionist aims. The concept of a "democratic
foreign policy" (the accuracy of the term itself is open to
some doubt) is rather vague, but taken, as it usually is, to
imply self-limitation within the confines of a national state
and renunciation of expansionist aims, it cannot, certainly,
be applied to the policy of the Soviet Government.

It would be as much an error, however, to regard that policy as a return to the ideas of imperial nationalism. It is perfectly true that the past decade witnessed a constant display of nationalist trends in the Soviet press, propaganda, and ideology, and that every month, especially since the war, marked the growth of these sentiments. It is also true that the attitude of the Soviet Government toward some of its neighbors in Europe, as well as in Central Asia, somewhat resembled the attitude of the old Russian imperialism. Nevertheless, there is a profound and important difference between the two policies.

The first point of difference appears in the treatment of neighboring nations. As soon as they are brought within the Soviet Union they are subjected to a process of complete social break-up, directed by a small minority within each national unit, in accordance with Moscow plans. The old Russian Empire never conducted, or had reason to conduct, such a thorough and wholesale attack on traditional social relations.

The second point of difference lies in the fact that Soviet foreign policy (until the particular expansionist aim is realized), supports and stimulates local revolutionary movements. It regards the latter not merely as a means of bringing the enemy countries to a state of disintegration (every power resorts to this means) but as a political medium for developing tendencies akin to its own. No other Russian regime was able to support its foreign policy with a network of its own organizations throughout the world.

The third point of difference is seen in the far greater reach of expansionist tendencies during the Soviet period than was ever true of the old regime. The imperialism of the Czarist era, even at the moments of its most violent outbursts, was always an imperialism of limited aims. Turning its face now to the west, now to the east, it saw the objects of its expansionist desires always in the nearest territories. Its ambitions did not extend to China, Germany, or France, and it stretched out its hands toward India only in a fit of mad adventure. Soviet revolutionism, on the other hand, has not set itself any limits, at least in principle. The outward resemblance to the ways of the old imperialism is due to geography, not ideology. If the Balkans, Poland, and Finland are in the forefront of

Russian policy today, as in former days, this is because the Arctic Ocean and the Black Sea have remained where they were, despite wars and revolutions.

The fourth point of difference is the product of the first three—Soviet policy does not and cannot recognize lasting alliances with other, capitalist, powers, but only agreements of limited content. Her former collaboration with Germany and her present alliance with the United Nations are no more than maneuvers which have limited and temporary application.

There is another widespread but mistaken interpretation of Soviet foreign policy. It is said that this is the same old policy of prerevolutionary Russian nationalism, but turned, although not for the first time, toward the east. It does not set itself aims in Europe, it is asserted, other than restoration of the Soviet frontiers of 1941, and has no thought of engineering popular movements and revolutions. On the contrary, it is directed toward those regions where it will meet less resistance and where the backward population regards Soviet Russia as a bearer of progress and culture. This theory has no basis in fact. Contrary to what the theory asserts, Moscow is primarily interested in the European west, the cradle of modern culture, of material power, and of military might. Europe is not struck off the list, as a matter of a priori reasoning. Quite the reverse—almost all attention is centered upon it.

No greater mistake can be made than to see Soviet policy as moderate, conciliatory in spirit, and limited to narrow objectives, while failing to realize its potentially vast scope and dazzling goals. Moscow is not to be blamed for such shortsightedness. As Karl Radek, one of the best interpreters of Soviet foreign policy, once remarked, Bolshevism is not an umbrella which can be opened or closed at will; nor a bath whose temperature can be raised or lowered to suit one's convenience. Bolshevism is a single unified system and must, Radek justly demanded, be considered as a whole.

Despite some considerable changes, the policy of the Soviet Government was and has remained to this day a Russian application of the policy of Communism. The Anglo-Soviet antagonism, the collaboration with Germany, the rapprochement with the United States, the pacts and treaties with France due to the growth of the menace of Germany, the participation in the grand military alliance against Germany, the neutral attitude toward Japan, and, finally, the waging of a separate war within the united front of the Allies—all these twists and turns are but natural manifestations of the consistent policy of Communism.

What is usually referred to as the national movement in today's Russia was not so much the government policy as the widespread, if vague, sentiments of non-Communist circles, which embraced far greater numbers of people than the Communist party. These were oppositionist sentiments, unclarified, not reduced to any system, undiscussed among any organized groups, committees, or editorial offices. These were sentiments, not a program; emotions, not a policy. The old parties with their ready-made concepts have long since vanished from Soviet life and, naturally, no new parties have been able to arise. Hence political movements other than the official one can exist only in the form of vague public opinion.

Nonetheless, up to 1941 "national" feeling remained in opposition to the official course. To Russians "national" means something involving the entire nation, uniting all classes. Communism, on the contrary, has always borne the traits of exclusiveness, of a minority. The national feeling directs all its power against the external, militant, anti-Russian forces; the Communist, against the property-owners, down to the last remnants of them, and those who appear as their "agents." To the Communist mind, economic transformation is the alpha and omega of all wisdom. The national attitude is to center attention upon aspects of the state in its relations with other states. The difference is brought out not only in the fat volumes of the theorists but in the live, primitive feeling which inspires thousands of people to fight for their native land and thousands of others to live for the coming of the socialist millennium.

National sentiment, when developed to its logical conclusion, may be of two kinds. First, it may represent tendencies of the whole nation, as opposed to class politics. Second, it may mean a belief in the superiority of one's own nation over other nations, in which case it turns into nationalism. A differentiation of both kinds of national sentiment has not yet taken place in the Soviet national movement.

To the Russian Communist, even after all his changes, economic property is the source of all evil. He is prepared to put up with differences in income and living conditions of various social strata (from which some observers of Russia are prone to deduce a resurgence of "capitalism"), but he is adamantly opposed to individual economy. Everything else in the world, whether it be foreign policy or war, is, in this concept, bound up with some particular aspect of the question of property and private economy.

The past fifteen years have been a disappointment to those who believed in evolutionary change from one political type to another, in a transformation, imperceptible to the naked eye, of Communism into a national movement. It was during this last period that the Soviet Government carried out an operation of social wrecking on the largest scale ever known in the history of recent centuries—the transformation of private peasant economy into the system of collective farms. Expropriation of roughly 20 million peasants—with their families about 100 million people—was an operation which in the vastness of its scope surpassed anything done by the English or French revolutions, and even the great social overturn which took place in Russia in the years between 1918 and 1921. The enforcement of collective farming, which took millions of peasants away from their homesteads, was spread over several years and, as estimated by the statisticians, cost the lives of 5 to 8 million people. It was pushed through to its goal without compromise. Not a single spot in Russia was spared. Exceptions made one day were wiped out the next.

This policy had a political aspect which is pertinent to our theme. The campaign was carried through, from beginning to end, by the huge administrative machinery of the Communist party. Not less than a million people worked to bring about the collectivization. They had to be ruthless in their task. By 1936 private peasant economy was dead. Party Communists who brought the collectivization campaign to a successful conclusion were living evidence of the tenacious vitality of the old Communist type and the deadly slowness of the evolution toward a national unity rising above class divisions.

The history of the kolkhoz (collective farms) is but one illustration of this fact. The same recent period of Soviet history provided another example in the five-year plans of industrialization. There was feverish activity in the building of new plants and particularly in the development of war industries. Simultaneously, and in apparent contradiction to these aims, all foreign "concessions" were wound up and foreign capital was being driven out of Russian economy. The shortage of consumer goods resulting from the industrialization inflicted great hardships on the population and caused much discontent. But this was disregarded, and whatever relief could have been obtained from abroad was ruled out by the deliberate policy of avoiding investment of foreign capital in Russia in any shape or form.

In the annals of Soviet Russia several occasions are recorded when a national tendency seemed momentarily to take the upper hand in the inner life of the ruling party. It was sometimes referred to as "sliding toward the peasantry with the brakes on." In every case, however, the tendency was short-lived and was firmly checked. In the years 1923–25 Leonid Krassin insisted on a rapprochement with Britain and on concessions to capitalist economy in industry and trade. His influence was completely and effectively checked by Stalin. Later, Nikolai Bukharin advocated compromise with the peasants by urging them "to enrich themselves," and Ambassador Sokolnikov recommended a policy of concessions to the opposition parties. But this "rightist opposition" was first removed from active politics and then, in 1937–38, finally "liquidated." The hard, inflexible nature of Soviet policy revealed itself on these occasions with the utmost clarity.

Taking what they wished to see for reality, foreign reporters and political writers have on occasions tried to prove that the Soviet Government has already gone through a great evolutionary change—from the old that was evil to the new that is good. These efforts usually coincided with certain requirements of the foreign political situation, such as attempts to obtain recognition of the Soviet Government, conclusion of a new treaty, and similar friendly acts. They were always backed up with appropriate quotations from Soviet leaders, official declarations, and statistics. But after some time had passed all these elaborate constructions disappeared. Among the Russians, too, faith in the salutary evolution of Bolshevism periodically seized considerable non-Communist groups, especially outside of Russia. As early as twenty years ago a number of influential non-Communist Russian politicians and scholars abroad formed a group under the name of *Smena Vekh* (Change of Landmarks) united in the conviction that Bolshevism had renounced its old aims and was taking Russia back to her national ways. The following statements made twenty years ago have an oddly contemporary ring:

"The revolution, like Antaeus, is being filled with new power. Revival of the soviets, increased activity of the peasants, democratization of trade-unions . . . efforts to restore the rule of law—all these are political facts of the first order." [1]

Or this:

"The early stages of Lenin's activity have created a false impression of him as a fanatic of Communism. Now this impression has been dispelled. If the revolution inevitably led to ruin and excesses, the evolution which is replacing it will act as an antidote." [2]

These notions were widespread among different movements and parties throughout the world. They swept over some socialist parties in Europe, creating naïve illusions inside the moderate British Labor party, and moving such men as Otto Bauer, leader of the Austrian Socialists, to elaborate theoretical constructions on Soviet evolution. These notes of deceptive optimism, perhaps natural in the N.E.P. (New Economic Policy) period fifteen years ago, continue to this day, and in even greater volume.

There is no denying the fact that during the past twenty-five years Bolshevism has not remained stationary. It has traveled far on the road of evolution. It has developed as has everything in the world—states, nations, parties, individuals. In the history of mankind there have been few generations that have gone through so many sweeping and violent changes and have witnessed so many world-shaking events as this one has. Bolshevism is no exception in this changing

---

1. Professor N. Ustryalov, "Under the Emblem of Revolution," in *Smena Vekh*, p. 213.
2. A. P. Bobrischev-Pushkin, in *Smena Vekh*, p. 113.

world. But its evolution proceeded in its own direction, followed its own path. It has not turned either to democracy or nationalism, or any other "ism" except its own. Now and then it has made advances to one or another hostile movement, only to turn its back upon it before long. It remained true to the policy of maneuvers throughout the past quarter century.

In one of their aspects, the theories of Soviet evolution have touched upon an important problem. Twenty-five years after the advent of Bolshevism to power there are practically no important non-Communist parties left either in Russia or among Russian émigré groups in other countries. The political police and the ravages of time have destroyed all the big organizations, militant as well as moderately oppositionist. Further development of Russian political life is therefore impossible outside the official ruling organizations. In these organizations, in their millions-strong mass of humanity, united for the time being by a community of leadership and program, there lie hidden the germs of different, mutually opposed, ideas which are destined to come to the fore in public life under certain conditions. Not from without, but from within, is Bolshevism threatened by the greatest hazards. Its inevitable differentiation is probably more dangerous for it than the German guns.

But even this path—the germination, the branching out from a single stem of new elements and forces—will not be a simple evolution proceeding without conflicts or crises. History knows no evolution of one kind of government authority into another taking place smoothly, imperceptibly, gradually, and without crises. The transition to a new political system represents a stupendous reconstruction not only in practical activities but in ideology, and this can at no time and nowhere occur without heavy conflicts. In some cases the crises take the form of vast popular upheavals. In other cases they are confined to small ruling circles. But the transformation never occurs with the smoothness and gradualness with which night turns into day or a child into a youth. On the contrary, at some point there is a break in the gradual development and the process of evolution takes a leap. In politics the elements of a new system accumulate slowly, sometimes secretly, within the framework of the old. After the inevitable crisis, these new elements become the ruling elements.

In the Russian national sentiment, deeply rooted and at times deeply hidden, there emerge the beginnings of a new political mentality. During the past ten years they have grown much in strength, due to a number of reasons but mainly to foreign politics. At the basis of this process lies the change in the historical situation of Russia, the transition from civil wars to international wars.

Civil war is the acknowledged domain of Communism. International war is the domain of national movements. For fifteen to twenty years after 1917 Russia went through a process of revolutionary reconstruction, the process of intense and ruthless civil war. The entire internal regime, as well as the foreign policy, was adjusted to the aim of this civil war—the building of socialism in Russia. Popular education, literature, peace with the neighbors, the machinery of administration—everything was a means to this end. A great degree of coördination was accordingly achieved between the system of government (the dictatorship of the Communist party) and the functions of the Communist machinery of socialization.

Since the middle 'thirties, however, as the danger of war increased, much has changed. A national war, involving clash and contact with different nations, was on the agenda of history. As this war drew nearer, and when it finally broke out, the divergence between the old system of ideas and the necessity for a new one became strongly felt. The government, which knew how to conduct revolutions, i.e., to wage civil wars—which nursed them, relied on them, promised them to all countries—this government was obliged to seek out new political ways. It did not switch over to a new track —this, as has been pointed out, is impossible in politics—but it was obliged to implant and cultivate national sentiments, to encourage their public profession, to yield, if only in words, to the new "world outlook." It tolerated a non-Communist way of thinking, where necessary and useful for the purposes of foreign policy. Thanks to all this, the "national," which was frequently non-Communist, grew in strength and assumed an increasing importance. From the Communist interpretation, the aims of war could not be anything but realization of Communism. But the waging of war required a unity of the people, a strong Russian national movement. According to Communist theory, war was to transform itself inevitably into a series of revolutions. But the actual waging of war was found possible only with the term "revolution" deleted from the vocabulary.

National tendencies began to make increasing inroads into the orthodox Soviet ideology as early as the middle 'thirties. The leaders and the leading political organs made reluctant concessions to them, but they were given free play in the army and the schools, and they found their way into everyday life in the revival of old Russian fashions in clothes, furniture, and other articles of daily use. Before the war broke out, however, all these manifestations of nationalism often bore the stamp of something artificial and made to order.

For that matter, not everything changed at once even after the outbreak of war. The present war between Russia and Germany is certainly a national war. The unquestionably defensive character of this war, on the Russian side, the German intention to erase Russia as a state, the German attitude toward Russian culture—all these combine to make this war a doubly national one for Russia. But history entrusted the direction of this national war to a small minority of the Russian people, to a government that had been conducting its most sweeping purge on the very eve of the war, and was keeping millions of its citizens in concentration camps and in exile. This was a patent contradiction. To get out of it the Soviet Government appealed to national sentiment.

During the first months of the war the appeal brought no more than a lukewarm response. To be sure, everything that recalled the traditional Communist slogans, such as "class war," "revolution," "the building of socialism," disappeared from the official vocabulary. But the population was slow to grasp the significance of the new situation and its attitude toward the war lacked clarity. Everything was too sudden. The wounds inflicted by the Germans were still too fresh. A halo of invincibility seemed to crown the German Army. Public speeches and articles on national defense grew in numbers, but they were not yet the voice of the people.

Gradually there came a change. German successes and German failures, as well as the behavior of Germans in Russia, raised the national temperature. A new sentiment began to grow—an emotion, not a theory—which spread ever wider and gained in strength. The struggle against the invaders was assuming a national character. The artificially roused national breeze swelled into a national hurricane. It was a spirit which those who evoked it were almost unable to control.

These moods revealed themselves first of all in the attitude toward Germany. It appears to be the same controversy about the German people which is now being argued out in England and America: Is the ruling clique or is the entire German people to be held responsible for the war? Placing the blame on the rulers of Germany accords with Communist traditions and the phraseology of the last World War. This point of view was most sharply expressed in Lenin's statement: "Hatred of the German, beat the German—such was and still is the motto of the ordinary, i.e., bourgeois patriotism. But we will say: Hatred of imperialist plunderers, hatred of capitalism, death to capitalism." [3] This was a natural sequence to the differentiation of classes which Lenin applied to the policies of all countries.

The second point of view, which can be called the national one, takes peoples as integral wholes irrespective of the social structure under which they live.

The profound difference in these two sentiments leads to different foreign policies. If the blame lies only with the German bourgeoisie and its government, then the main object of the war is to remove that government and give the people the possibility of freely arranging their future. The self-determination of the German people becomes a decisive and favorable factor in the life of future Europe. The so-called "democratic peace" with Germany is a logical requirement emanating from this position, as is also hostility to the Treaty of Versailles which was the crux of Soviet foreign policy down to 1934.

The strongly expressed condemnation of Germany and of the entire German people in the war years 1914–16, prior to the revolution, could not have appeared in Soviet literature or policy from 1917 down to 1941. But during the second half of 1941 new notes began to be sounded in Russia. Statements were made and reiterated that during the past seventy-five

---

3. Lenin, *Izvestiya*, March 11, 1918.

years Germany, as a country, was responsible for five European wars; and, although strictly forbidden before, it was now openly asserted that she was to blame for the war of 1914–18. Moreover, the responsibility for the present war was placed on the Germans and on Germany, not merely on "German fascists." Accompanying these utterances the contemptuous "Fritz," analogous to the French "Boche," came into general use.

The most prominent literary figure representative of this national movement has been Ilya Ehrenburg, who has become the most widely read author in Russia since the war, surpassing all other more gifted writers. After Stalin, Ehrenburg has the widest reading public. He has become an outstanding political figure.

A former hater of Communism, a stern critic of wholesale equalization and regimentation, a worshiper of individualism, Ehrenburg in the early 'thirties found his way into the Communist party, although for a long time afterward he remained an onlooker, a stranger. He wrote many interesting novels and short stories, avoiding purely political writing and occupying a place far from the front ranks in the Soviet literary world. Then, as the war broke out, Ehrenburg, of all Russian writers, acquired a wholly sensational popularity. He was sought after by the editors of all the army newspapers. Huge editions were published of several volumes of his collected articles. Official *Pravda* welcomed him to its pages, and even *Bolshevik*, the most authoritative Communist organ of all, did not disdain to publish him. Soldiers who deluge Soviet editors with their naïve effusions (apparently a familiar phenomenon throughout the world) have striven to write "after Ehrenburg" or have often signed themselves "Not-Ehrenburg," or "Regretfully, not-Ehrenburg."

Thus Ehrenburg has become a political writer. But his politics is confined to very narrow limits—his attitude toward the Germans and toward Germany. One looks in vain in his writings for programs, for tactical or political directions. Their only motif is a burning hatred of the German aggressor, not merely of the German Nazi or the German capitalist. Deviating from Lenin's precepts, Ehrenburg preaches war and vengeance on everything German because it is German. With Ehrenburg the national is ascendant over the social. "In the 'twenties," he wrote, in what may be described as his programmatic article,

> we followed with sympathy the drama of Germany. We shared our bread with the starving Germans. We entertained many illusions. . . .
> When Germany attacked us, our people were far from hating the Germans. Many still tried to find righteous people in Sodom. "Have a cigarette," we offered goodheartedly.
> We did not mature to our present hatred all at once. We came to see that we were not dealing with humans; and then the character of the war changed. Our hatred brought us wisdom. It lifted our army.
> War without hatred is immoral, as cohabitation without love is.[4]

In these words Ehrenburg drew a true picture of the evolution of public sentiment during the first stage of the war— that transition from a rationalistic attitude toward Germans to the impassioned bellicose one. On another occasion he approvingly quoted from a letter sent him by an officer, Lieutenant Morozov: "We have been cured of the sweet illusion that the German people 'will wake up and understand.'" To this Ehrenburg adds: "This is true . . . The German is not a human being, he is an automaton."

As the war progressed these sentiments spread among increasingly wider circles. Reports of German plunder and cruelty, of lost relatives, of hangings and shootings, multiplied. The martyrdom of besieged Leningrad where thousands died of sheer exhaustion engendered strong feeling. "Hatred of the Germans" was becoming a passion. Spreading ever wider and growing in intensity, it began to assume the character of a craving for pitiless revenge. "Dream of Revenge" might have been the title of innumerable poems and short stories in the Soviet press.

Here are a few characteristic examples.

In the almanac, *The Youth of Leningrad,* Elena Victorova wrote in a poem entitled "No Mercy":

> Hurl the grenade, thrust the bayonet,
> Plunge the knife into his throat, and then
> Turn it over inside.
> Tear the heart from the beast's breast,
> Burn, be ready to cause such agonies
> That our losses, our sacred blood
> Will be redeemed.

---

4. *Bolshevik,* 1942, Nos. 19–20.

Or here are the words of a song composed on the Northern front, and called simply "Kill!"

> Comrade, remember the fascist isn't human.
> Kill the bandit-wild beast. Don't let him off.
> Let your blow be like a terror-spreading lightning.
> Strike! Destroy! Avenge! [5]

Another poem, the work of Alexander Prokofiyev, is distinguished for its style, which can but inadequately be conveyed in this English rendering:

> Strike with the bayonet, strike with grenade,
> Strike with what you can, but kill.
> For the Soviet land
> Strike the German wild beasts.
> Glory to everyone who'll kill,
> Who'll shed German blood.
> Strike with the rifle butt, strike with grenade,
> Everywhere destroy the rat.
> If there be no grenade, strike with a spade,
> If there be no spade, strangle with your hand.
> Strike so these violent beasts
> Forget the way to our land,
> Strike till the whole horde roar,
> Strike till they are no more. [6]

Similar sentiments are voiced in prose. A commander of a guerrilla force writes:

For every drop of my children's blood shed by the fascist cannibals, I have already drawn a bucket of enemy blood. . . . But that is not enough. . . . I will fill the whole River Dvina with black blood—and this, too, will be too little. . . . The time will come and we'll square the accounts.[7]

These are merely illustrations. It would be impossible to list the poems and stories of hatred of the Germans, of thirst for revenge, of avengers—they number thousands, they fill the magazines and newspapers. Their authors, however, perhaps have never realized that their utterances were the result of an entirely new set of feelings that had gradually taken shape

---

5. *Literaturnaya Gazeta,* 1942, No. 42.
6. *Zvezda,* 1942, Nos. 1–2.
7. *Izvestiya,* November 15, 1942.

in them, completely different from everything they were taught at school, at meetings, in newspaper articles, during the past quarter century. Nor have they realized that these emotions must lead to a wholly different policy from the one followed theretofore.

Occasionally Ehrenburg was able to arrive at significant political conclusions. He pictured the war as a military alliance of all the currents and sentiments existing in Russia:

"One will say, 'For the Soviet Union,' another, 'For Russia,' a third, 'For the Altai,' a fourth, 'For our village Russky-Brod,' a fifth, 'For Natasha,' but they all feel the same thing —this difficult summer when they are defending their country and their kinsfolk from German death."

Of the five motives listed by Ehrenburg, the last three have no political significance. Only the first two really matter. The people's war, as Ehrenburg pictures it, is a coalition of Communist Russia which fights for Soviet socialism ("For the Soviet Union") and of non-Communist Russia, whose fight is prompted by the elementary reaction of resisting the invader ("For Russia"). Such a coalition, if it were to find its expression in politics, would have highly important consequences for the entire political system of Russia. It is possible that Ehrenburg did not fully realize the political implications of his views. In politics situations sometimes arise when authors of ideas must not see farther than one step ahead.

But the Soviet Government, suffering under no such handicap, was able to form a perfectly clear idea of the problem. It was obvious that hatred of the Germans, desire for vengeance, and militant nationalism were powerful levers capable of moving the people on in the war, and as such were necessary.[8] But these were welcome only until such time as they would again be proclaimed reactionary chauvinism and the Ehrenburgs would be purged. The government dismissed the very thought of the political conclusions which were suggested by the alliance of the Soviet Union with Russia. On the

---

8. Wendell Willkie has this to say of his conversations with Stalin: "He told me again and again that his propaganda was deliberately designed to make his people hate the Nazis, but it was obvious that he himself had a certain bitter admiration for the efficiency by which Hitler had transplanted to Germany as much as ninety-four per cent of the working populations from some of the conquered Russian territory, and he respected the completely professional training of the German Army, particularly its officers." (*One World*, p. 34).

contrary, Stalin deemed it necessary to dissociate himself from a too candid nationalism. What he had to say of Germany and the Germans rang in tones of a firm retort and a return to the Lenin traditions. He repeatedly stated that the Soviet Union was not waging war against the German people:

The Red Army has to annihilate the German invaders not because of their German origin but because they seek to enslave our motherland. . . . The strength of the Red Army lies in the fact that it has been brought up in the spirit of *equality of all peoples and nations.*

Statements appear from time to time in the foreign press to the effect that the Red Army aims at the destruction of the German people. This is a wicked, foolish libel. . . . History teaches that Hitlers come and go but the German people and the German state remain. . . .[9]

Stalin was so strict a follower of Lenin in the early stages of this war that he would not even declare the destruction of Hitlerism to be the goal of his war, suggesting that it was for the Germans themselves to accomplish this destruction. The aim Stalin was setting himself was only "to drive Hitler's armies out of the Soviet Union." Over and over again he stated, "It is not our aim to destroy Germany." [10] He was very cautious: "It is *probable* that this war will bring about the end of Hitler's clique." But neither Soviet Russia nor the United Nations was mentioned as having anything to do with that end. Everything was staked on the German people.

Later, under the influence of various circumstances, Stalin changed his formulas, but in all essential points he and the Soviet Government held to their old positions. Stalin's views were reiterated in the authoritative War and the Working Class, in July 1943: "There exists a school of thought which believes that the German people has proved its complete depravity and inability to collaborate peacefully with other nations. . . . This school forgets that the German people must not be identified with the Hitler Clique."

It was in another branch of the Soviet political system that the new national sentiments gained the strongest hold and inevitably came into conflict with the traditional habits of thought. This occurred within the Red Army, and the story of the growth of the national sentiment there will claim our special attention.

---

9. Stalin, Order of the Day to the Red Army, February 23, 1943.
10. Stalin, speech, November 7, 1942.

2. NATIONALISM, COMMUNISM, AND THE RED ARMY

The rivalry between the party-Communist position and the national tendencies is nowhere so clearly revealed as in the inner life of the Red Army. The history of the Red Army, particularly during the past twelve to fifteen years, has been one continuous struggle of these opposing tendencies, a silent struggle carried on beneath the surface, the parties to it often not fully realizing what it was about. At times growing more bitter, at times subsiding, this struggle is a historical fact of supreme importance.

The Red Army in this war is not a reflection of the Russian people. It *is* the Russian people—in helmets and uniforms, carrying rifles, driving tanks, flying fighter planes and bombers. It is the whole Russian people which has brought to the battlefields—together with the smell of its native soil—its joys and sorrows, its ways of life, its politics, its ancient habits, its new demands. The army represents the Russian people more truly than does the country itself. At the same time that the new masters clicked their heels and raised their right hands to hail their Fuehrer in the streets of Novgorod, Kiev, or Odessa, tens of thousands of natives of Novgorod, Kiev, and Odessa stood in the trenches on the Soviet side of the front line where every province, every district, every nook and corner of both parts of the severed land were represented. During the course of the war the army has become the biggest of the mass organizations of Soviet Russia, exceeding in size the largest political organization of peacetime— the Communist party—although nowhere is it as influential. In this lies the substance of one of the problems of wartime.

In this war the Red Army contains, proportionately, more peasants than does the country as a whole. In peacetime there were sufficient reserves of young men—even of special social groups, such as workers, for example—to make it possible to reduce the peasant percentage in the army, or, as was done for many years, to keep members of the former propertied classes out of the army. But the exigencies of war have put an end to all this. The situation today is reversed. Since hundreds of thousands of workers employed in war industries and transport must work on the home front, the percentage of peasants in the army is increasing and today, despite the great strides in industrialization in recent years, not less than 75 to 80 per cent of the Red Army are peasants. This is directly reflected in the Red Army's present political moods. Formerly, members of the Communist party made up a large part of the army, at times and in certain areas representing as much as half of it. Since the war the army has been expanded by drawing on the older age groups, particularly men from the countryside. The number of regular party members is now comparatively small, despite the official effort to maintain it at a high figure. The reason for this is obvious. To have sent into the army the hundreds of thousands of party members who were employed in the administrative and economic institutions of the Soviet system would have wrecked these institutions. Many of them had to be kept in the rear.

The great Red Army has thus come to be what it is—a predominantly peasant army, more conservatively minded and with fewer Communists in it than before. This applies in the first place, to the several millions of the rank and file, the "fighters," as soldiers are called in Soviet Russia.

The officer personnel has passed through a similar process of development. The officer group leaves its impress on every army and in every epoch, except during periods of revolutionary turmoil. For this reason in Soviet Russia, too, the ranks of regular officers, who are authoritative spokesmen for the army, have been built up by a process of careful and cautious selection carried on for two decades. One layer has grown over the other like the rings of a growing tree: there were the officers, veterans of the civil war; there was the generation of the N.E.P. era; still surviving here and there were the oppositionists of the "rightist deviation"; to take the place of those purged in the stern years 1937–39 there came the younger generation. And so, sifted through military schools, the Communist Youth organization, and the Communist party, there was formed an officer corps three quarters of whose personnel, at one time before the war, were members of the party, while in the highest ranks, among the generals, a full 100 per cent were party-Communist.

Here, too, however, things have changed since the war. Tens of thousands of new officers have been poured into the ranks of the regular officers, and there was no time for care-

ful inquiry regarding their party or social status. To an over-
whelming degree the newer recruits represented the new Soviet intelligentsia, students and Soviet employees. A portion
from this social stratum was no doubt drafted to serve in the
ranks, but another large section, after rapid training courses,
replaced the thinning ranks of the old regular officers. It must
also be borne in mind that even before the war an officer's
membership in the party did not always mean that he supported the Communist movement with all his heart and soul.
Army Communists were always in a class by themselves. But
when a mass of new officers began to pour into the ranks of
the old regulars, the old and new became mixed, forming new
characteristic amalgams.

Growing, maturing, training, and fighting, there has developed a new officer corps, representing the cream of Russia's manhood in our era. To a major extent it is a corps of the
new, young intelligentsia, with a traditionally broad outlook
upon life, serious intellectual interests, and fair general education. Although only a minority of them are tied up with the
Communist party, in the mass these officers are not devoid of
political emotions. Their great grandfathers, many of them
serfs, had lived through the era of great social changes of the
'sixties and 'seventies. Their fathers had carried through two
revolutions and elected democratic delegates to the Constit-
uent Assembly. And they themselves, the heirs of great traditions, saw pass before their eyes during the last decades the
collectivization experiment, the purges of the 'thirties, the
rise of Hitler, the friendship with Germany, and finally the
war with Germany. Today they stand along a battlefront two
thousand miles long, at the head of their armed people, and
wage their people's war for survival. Whatever may be the
course that the inner life of Russia will take in the future,
whatever may be the transformations in the country's regime, these officers are and will remain a firm element of
Russia's public life, and Russia will have no grounds to feel
ashamed of them.

"Gentlemen, these are the men who will some day rule Russia!" writes Ksawery Pruszyński, a Polish writer-officer,
after a long stay in Russia: "There are no others. Bravery,
culture, education, habit of organized action, understanding,

energy, even experience—everything is on their side." [11]

Every army is a political weapon in the hands of its government, in time of peace as well as in time of war. In this respect the ideal is an absolutely submissive army. A dissatisfied army, with a tendency to oppose the government, is dangerous. The sentiments of the army, especially of its officer corps, must be closely tied, even identical, with the policies of the government. What are the relations between the government and the army in Soviet Russia?

Some years before the outbreak of the present war, Trotsky had asserted that the Soviet Government dared not place arms in the hands of its people. Trotsky was wrong. But he clearly foresaw the difficulty which would inevitably face the Soviet Government in time of war.

The situation was relatively simple during the civil war, when the whole system of Soviet warfare—the army ranking system, habits, and ideology—were taking shape. Across the front line there stood another Russian Army, and to fight it successfully the slogans of internal Russian politics had to be raised to the highest pitch possible—for the poor against the rich; for revolution—against counterrevolution; for leaders from the people against czars; for radiant socialism in the future against the unrelieved darkness of the past. Civil war could be waged in no other way, and the ideology of the newly organized Red Army was built on the same foundations as those of the new government and its party. There were close ideological ties between the army and the government. The only difficulty experienced by the government related to the role of the former Czarist officers in whom full trust could not be placed. This difficulty was more or less overcome by means of the institution of political commissars attached to army units.

Entirely different, sometimes quite opposite, methods are demanded in waging an international war. The history of the Red Army between the early 'twenties and the late 'thirties —a period of about fifteen years—is a process of adapting the army of civil war days to the requirements of international war. There was a reason for the long duration of this

---

11. *Wiadomości Polskie* (London, 1942), No. 134.

process and for the fact that it was never fully completed.
The reason lay within the government itself which, while it
tried to reform the army for the future international war,
continued to live in the ideological world of the civil war, carried on with the job of destroying the old class society, and
pinned its hopes for the future on world class cataclysms. It
was building up a national army—whether against Japan, or
England, or Germany—but it continued to believe in the coming of a distinctly civil war situation—a war in which it
would march arm in arm with the Japanese, British, or German masses against their respective upper classes. It strove
to build a strongly united army, which in time of war could
not fail to consist largely of peasants, while it continued to be
inspired by hatred of property and suppressed the numerous
opponents at home. The ideas of civil war driven out through
the front door rushed back through the windows of domestic
and foreign policies. This was the basic contradiction in the
situation as it shaped up on the eve of the war.

In the 'twenties Soviet leaders harbored some flattering if
odd theories about the special "proletarian military science"
which was held to be infinitely superior to its bourgeois counterpart; about revolutionary armies whose artillery fire of a
small weight of metal was more destructive than the heavier
artillery fire of its bourgeois opponents; about the new form
of relations between officers and soldiers. Many Soviet enthu-
siasts were infected by these naïvetés before they learned to
be practical and realistic. But time did tell, and gradually certain obvious facts gained recognition. With the restoration of
war industry, the vexing problems of every armed nation—
guns, airplanes, destroyers—claimed immediate attention. In
some things Russia was catching up with western Europe,
and she was developing some new methods of her own. But
the structure and the ideological foundation of the Red Army
were slow to change, for reasons already indicated. The time
was one of stabilization on all home fronts. The army—growing gradually in strength from half a million effectives to a
million—was by then a permanent element of national life,
and regular officer personnel was being trained. Alongside
the army, to act as a controlling force over it, there were
formed: a special army of 60,000 men under authority of the
G.P.U. (it rose to 250,000 in the 'thirties), for purposes of

political surveillance and as border guards; and a network of sections and functionaries of the Political Administration of the Red Army, performing the functions of propaganda and police control.

In the 'thirties, the era of collectivization and five-year plans, the new officers, in their majority members of the Communist party, held a central position between the rank and file of the army and the party machine. There were many things about which they were not in complete sympathy with the government. They were irked by the strict and unremitting control of the organs of surveillance. A number of officers, including some of the army leaders, sided with the "oppositions" inside the Communist party. These men observed with their own eyes the effect that banishment of millions of "kulaks" to Siberia and liquidation of the independent peasantry had on army morale. Marshal Mikhail Tukhachevsky was the most outstanding but by no means the only one of the military leaders who for some time sided with the "rightist opposition," that nucleus of the national movement within the membership of the ruling party.

The army Communist, as he took shape in that period, was a special type. Although loyal to the program, ideology, and philosophy of Communism, he was distinguished in practical life by his antagonism to the political police (the G.P.U., the N.K.V.D.), to the obligatory and overinsistent training in Communist catechism instead of military subjects, to the continued expansion of revolution, particularly in the villages.

By that time all earlier popular movements had completely subsided. But when peoples grow silent, political life assumes new forms. It takes cover inside comparatively small groups nearest to the government, behind the scenes of public opinion. The struggle of parties is replaced by a struggle among government departments. This time the struggle between deeply rooted political attitudes found expression in the rivalry of the four main units of governmental machinery: the army, the general administration, the party, and the secret police. Each one of these units was an organized body of men and women, tens or hundreds of thousands strong, specially picked, trained, and conditioned for the work of their special branch of the Soviet regime. At times the leading personnel at the head of each section were inclined to seek a compromise between the official ideology and the sentiments of their subordinates, or were ready to beat a retreat, to make concessions, to "slide down with the brakes on."

Among these human machines certain departments of civil administration, such as those dealing with economics, education, finance, trade-unions, and similar matters, employed the bulk of the old and new intelligentsia, including large numbers not affiliated with the Communist movement, and many discontented and even oppositionist elements. In a sense these departmental machines voiced the needs of the Soviet people, acting as a counterweight to the party machine and the secret police. To a still greater extent this was true of the army machine. The latter gradually developed into a great political force, and those who headed it, although loyal Communists, found themselves, with increasing frequency, in conflict with the party and police machine as a result of the military needs of the army.

Voroshilov, an orthodox Communist, held to the end to the primitive view that to achieve victory the most important thing was to fill the army with disciples of Leninism. "The enemy will be quickly swept away and destroyed. The guarantee of this is the Marxist-Leninist ideology by which our army lives." [12] In actual fact, of course, what is needed in training a soldier and in preparing for war is not indoctrination with Leninism but the acquired ability to handle the complicated mechanized weapons of modern war. The role of Communist ideology as an instrument of war is negligible in an international war, while police control over officers and generals, exercised by a political machine ignorant of military science, only irked, roused resentment and opposition, and led to serious conflicts. As a natural result there developed in the Red Army during the 'thirties a semiconscious tendency toward an *emancipation of the army from the political party machine.*

A critical, sometimes slightly derisive, attitude began to manifest itself in military circles with regard to the role of ideology. Military practice demanded that the country proceed in the same direction as the rest of the world, while a

12. Voroshilov, speech at the Eighteenth Congress of the Communist party, 1939.

spirit of realism was permeating the huge army mechanism. Absorbed in the problems of new techniques and of military training, the army was cutting loose from the militant Communist sentiments, and the new spirit, spreading in military circles, penetrated even the Political Administration of the Red Army, an institution especially created to safeguard the party's hold over the military.

Since political control was not abolished, no genuine emancipation of the army eventuated nor could it eventuate in the conditions that prevailed in Soviet Russia in the 'thirties.

Every army unit from the company upward, had, as it still has, a Communist "cell." Every regiment had a party committee with its own secretariat, and a similar organization of the Communist Youth. "Clubs" of a strictly Communist character, libraries with picked staff, and similar educational organizations existed everywhere. In addition to the central organ of the army, many regiments and battalions published their own newspapers and "wall papers," often typewritten, sometimes even in long hand. Frequent reports and lectures on political subjects and obligatory classes in "political grammar" were a part of army training.

When the trends toward army professionalism and emancipation from politics became too pronounced, there began the trials and purges of 1937–39. Thousands of purged and executed officers were neither spies, nor traitors, nor even out-and-out opponents of the Soviet Government. But among the Communist officers and generals there was widespread dissatisfaction with the system of incompetent, extra-military, political coercion which injured personal feelings and undermined prestige as well as hampered the necessary military work. After a few years in high army posts the most loyal Communists began to look for new solutions of the difficult problems. They did not cease to be Communists, nor did they cease to denounce democracy. But the logic of their work produced conflicts with various party institutions and the Soviet Government. From the latter's point of view a mass purge was absolutely necessary to prevent a crisis of the regime under army pressure.

"Purges were a new bolshevization of the entire army," Mekhlis, new chief of the Political Administration of the Red Army, stated at the last congress of the Communist party

(1939). The expelled and executed officers "*attempted to set up army Communists against the territorial party organizations.*" The reappointed "commissars and political workers" were "the eyes and ears of the party inside the army. Nothing *could be allowed to escape* the watchful Bolshevik eyes of the commissars. They had *to know everything* that was going on in every little corner of the Red Army and to *nip* political treason in the bud."

The army mutiny was suppressed before it began. The G.P.U. played the most active part in the suppression. All this left its mark.

Such was the condition and the ideological equipment of the Red Army when it entered a period of wars. The Finnish campaign was the first war in Europe since 1920 in which the Red Army took part. It was a test and the test, in the opinion of Moscow, revealed numerous defects. People's Commissar Voroshilov resigned, and the government launched a series of reforms.

Official organs voiced the opinion that the new officers did not prove to be up to the mark. Undoubtedly as a result of the purges they did not show enough initiative, they waited for orders and directions from superior officers and commissars, they felt they had too little authority of their own and were too much at the mercy of others. In the Finnish War the technical equipment of the Russian Army was superior to that of the enemy—Russian artillery and air force were ample. But the human side of the Red Army left much to be desired.

The war with Finland aroused long and heated debates and discussions among high Soviet military leaders about the "lessons of the Finnish campaign." Charges were made that the Red Army was lax in discipline, that political commissars interfered in purely military matters undermining the authority of the regular commanders, that the training of privates was overloaded wtih "political instruction," and that officers in battle displayed a lack of independence of judgment and of resourcefulness.

Reforms were instituted to eradicate these glaring shortcomings. Essentially these comprised an attempt to Europeanize and nationalize the Soviet military machine—to abolish customs and methods which were organically linked to the revolutionary tradition and heritages of the Red Army —to recreate it on the traditional west European pattern modeled primarily after the German Army. Although the decision to reorganize the Red Army emanated from the Kremlin, it was Marshal Semyon Timoshenko, a rising star on the Soviet military horizon, who was credited with initiating these reforms.

Timoshenko summarized the new program as follows:

Experience during the Finnish War teaches us that our method of training Red Army men and commanders was altogether wrong. Our Red Army is equipped with a first-class technique; our people are loyal to their country to the very end. But we shall be able to win battles with a minimum sacrifice of blood only when we learn to master our technique. It is necessary to learn, to size up each situation individually. We are against an abstract approach! We are for individual initiative! [13]

In the matter of training men Timoshenko believed in teaching them first of all the things that they would have to know on the actual battlefield. This principle was directed primarily against the top-heavy political machine—the Political Administration of the Red Army. Timoshenko sought to reduce "political instruction" to a minimum without, however, running afoul of the orthodox leadership.

The most radical reform in the Red Army linked with the name of Timoshenko was the abolition of the political commissars, their second abolition in the history of the Red Army. Fearing treachery on the part of its officer personnel, the majority of them former Czarist officers, the Soviet Government in 1918, taking a leaf from the French revolutionary armies of the eighteenth century, attached to each non-Communist commander a party commissar who exercised complete control, including the power of veto. This strict Communist control probably forestalled a great deal of treachery in Red Army ranks. Eventually, however, it resulted in intrigues, in spying upon non-Communist officers, and in serious conflicts between the commissars and the commanders. It lowered the prestige of the commanding personnel and destroyed that initiative and daring which are

13. *Pravda*, October 15, 1940.

essential for the proper prosecution of military operations.

The years of peaceful reconstruction after the civil war induced Frunze, who was then People's Commissar of War, to abolish the political commissars in 1924. There remained, however, the Political Administration, whose main task was to foster Communist morale among the soldiers. For a number of years the Red Army functioned without political commissars. They were re-introduced on August 15, 1937, in connnection with the purge of the Red Army. This time their function was to check on the activities of officers who were members of the Communist party but whose loyalty to Stalin was suspect.

It was these commissars whom Soviet public opinion and even some high Kremlin dignitaries blamed for the fiasco in the early stages of the Russo-Finnish War. In many respects this blame was justified.

Timoshenko's first step, then, in his attempt to reorganize the Red Army, was to abolish the institution. By a decree of the Presidium of the Supreme Soviet of August 12, 1940, all political commissars were removed "in the interest of creating a unified Red Army command and to emphasize the authority of the commanders who are the sole leaders of the military forces." To be sure, the "political education" of the Soviet troops was not neglected. Instead of political commissars there were now "assistant commanders," trusted Communists who, while without authority to hamper the decision of the commander in any way, were entrusted with the political administration of the Red Army units. For the Soviet military machine this removal of political commissars was a serious and vital step. As *Pravda* stated editorially, "the commander is the sole leader of the fighting forces. His authority is supreme. Any attempt to detract from the authority of the commander inevitably leads to laxity in discipline and the destruction of the fighting efficiency of the unit." [14]

Another radical reform was the introduction of special insignia for officers. The old ranks such as general, admiral, major, and others, which were discarded soon after the revolution as symbols of Czarist oppression, were reëstablished (reform of this kind had begun in 1935). Saluting of superior officers "in formation and out of formation," which

14. *Idem*, August 13, 1940.

had been abolished more than two decades before as degrading to the common soldier, became compulsory. Moreover, the officers were instructed to adhere strictly to this regulation and to punish all soldiers for failure to salute. Special military commissions were stationed in parks and on city streets to report both officers and men who failed to obey this regulation.

On September 3, 1940, a special "marshal's star" was created which was in many respects reminiscent of the splendor of the old Czarist generals. It was a five-point star made of gold, with ends of platinum studded with small diamonds; a large "diamond of 2.62 carats was mounted in the center; the rays of the star were studded with twenty-five diamonds weighing about 1.25 carats; the grooves contained five diamonds weighing about 3.06 carats." [15]

Two months later President Kalinin presented these stars to the five marshals of the Soviet Union in the order of their importance. First came Voroshilov, then Budenny, Timoshenko, Kulik, and Shaposhnikov. Describing this ceremony, the Soviet press waxed rapturous on how "in Comrade Kalinin's hands the glare of the golden stars merged with the glow of the diamonds." Hundreds of lesser Red Army officers were also decorated with all sorts of medals during 1940.

"Iron discipline" in the Red Army now became the daily cry of the Soviet press. Echoing the Kremlin, the press demanded severe measures against those guilty of breach of discipline. The discipline of the Red Army, said *Pravda, Izvestiya,* and *Red Star,* must not be lower than the discipline of the German Army. Hence, fraternization between officers and privates must be stopped at once. No weakness must be shown, no "liberalism."

Red Star, official organ of the army, commented as follows:

Without discipline there is no army. Discipline is a powerful weapon for victory. All victorious armies from ancient times to our day were distinguished by their iron discipline. . . . It is a crime to weaken discipline through fraternization, by patting the offender condescendingly on the shoulder. An unquestioned discipline is required. . . .

Commanders must be strict.

The popularity of a liberal commander is cheaply bought. A com-

---

15. *Idem,* August 13, 1940.

mander who seeks to gain favor with his subordinates by being soft-hearted is a useless man in the army. He who hasn't the courage to punish severely for a breach of discipline is not a commander but a rag.[16]

According to the new regulations a soldier in the ranks no longer had the right to complain about his immediate superior to a higher officer; orders were no longer subject to discussion by the lower ranks, and a commanding officer could be brought up on charges only upon an order of the People's Commissar of Defense. The former regulations (since 1925) had demanded execution of all orders of one's commander except those deemed "criminal." Those regulations gave the commander the right to employ force against a recalcitrant Red Army man only in time of battle and only for failure to execute a military order. The new regulations adopted in the summer of 1940 prescribed:

A commander is not accountable for the consequences if, in order to punish insubordination and to restore order in the ranks, he is obliged to employ force or arms. A commander who fails to act in a decisive manner in such cases and who fails to follow the regulations will be tried before the Military Tribunal.

The new code of military regulations as well as the comments of the Soviet press were replete with references to "severe and iron discipline," "pitiless measures," and so on. "Red Army discipline must be . . . more severe and ruthless than the discipline in other armies which is based on class submission. . . . Insubordination must be punished pitilessly." [17]

If we were to translate all these reforms of 1940 into the language of politics we would have to say: This was the army's return match in its struggle with the party, after all the purges, offenses, and coercions it had suffered. This was, in a measure, a victory of national principles over party principles. Marshal Semyon Timoshenko accomplished much. But much more still was left unchanged. Despite the support of the army, his work of reform could not overstep the boundaries set by the political regime. The consequences were not slow to show themselves.

---

16. *Red Star*, July 5, 1940.
17. *Idem*, No. 242.

3. THE ARMY IN WARTIME

With the opening of hostilities against Germany, the Soviet Government armed the people and created tens of thousands of new, nonparty officers. Realizing the danger of this situation, however, it took a number of precautionary measures.

The measures constituted a step backward—from the national to the party principle. The reformer Timoshenko was removed from the post of Commissar of Defense. The old system of political commissars (given the name of "military commissars") was restored by the decree of July 16, 1941. No officer or general was now able to issue an order, not even a battle order, unless it was approved by the military commissar. The decree was a vote of no confidence in the new officers.

Yet in one respect the Soviet Government broke sharply with the old traditions. The entire ideology of the war was cleared of all elements of class struggle, Communism, world revolution, and similar political planks. The war was declared to be a patriotic war of liberation, i.e., essentially a national war. Questions of imperialist, capitalist, revolutionary or counterrevolutionary wars were no longer raised. From among the theoretical constructions of Lenin, only the division into just and unjust wars was retained, and accordingly the war of Britain, America, and the smaller allies was pronounced a just war. The Communist party's philosophy and propaganda were adapted to the nonparty elements in the army, and everything that they would resent was methodically suppressed while everything that would appeal to them was emphasized and pushed to the front. In theory, Communism no doubt continued to regard itself as a higher and more progressive system of ideas than "primitive nationalism." But the "higher" system yielded its place to the "lower" one. During the whole period of the war the Soviet press has printed less about capitalism, Communism, and socialism than the publicity apparatus of the tiny Communist party of Britain prints about them in a single day.

The same atmosphere marked the action of the churches in giving their blessing to the patriotic war and in proclaiming Stalin a "God-chosen leader." The number of open churches barely increased, but the telegrams sent by the four Russian metropolitans, the Armenian exarch, a Baptist minister, the Jewish Chief Rabbi, and the Moslem Chief Mufti, conveying the Lord's blessing on the army's efforts, were taken hurriedly into the Kremlin through that gate over which an inscription proclaims that "religion is the opium of the people." Through the same gates, probably, went the Metropolitans of the Russian Orthodox Church on their visit to Stalin last September, when the Soviet Premier gave his approval to the restoration of the Holy Synod and the election of the All-Russian Patriarch of the Orthodox Church.

The ideological basis for the conduct of the war was therefore planned as follows: in the first place, propaganda, press, and speeches were to avoid all questions which might create a division in the Red Army; in the second place, the Red Army was to be kept under strict control with the help of party organizations within the companies, regiments, and armies, as well as of the many thousand-strong organization of military commissars and political workers.

The progress of military events made a radical correction of these plans necessary. Concessions in the field of ideology were of little help in solving practical problems, and the friction between the army and the party organizations, instead of diminishing, grew more and more serious.

We do not yet know what plan of strategy was followed by the Soviet General Staff at the beginning of the war. We do not know, for example, to what extent and along what strategic lines the Soviet retreat was voluntary, and where and how far it was forced by the Germans. But neither did the Red Army, with the exception of a few persons in it, know this. In the eyes of an army a long retreat is always bound up with the idea of defeat. Moreover, Soviet military schools have always taught that the Red Army "will beat the enemy on his territory." An explanation of the continuous reverses was therefore sought, with more and more insistence, by the army, and the army's thought naturally turned to the system and organization of the Soviet military forces and war industry. Criticism was growing. One of its butts was Russian aviation, which was found to be inferior to the German. It was recalled that plants rushed deliveries of large numbers of airplanes without paying enough attention to their quality and speed and that this was done under orders of the Commissariat of Defense. German successes seemed natural in the circumstances.

The failure of military operations was often seen to be due to defective intelligence and reconnaissance work, resulting in false information about the disposition and numbers of the enemy troops, the enemy's strength in tanks, and similar data. Errors of this kind were made repeatedly.[18] Incompetence or negligence, which were taken to be the reasons, were, of course, seen as part and parcel of the entire system.

Again, it was brought out that contrary to everything taught in military schools, radio signaling at the front was often completely paralyzed, thus seriously affecting the success of operations. The mail service, civil and military, was bad, with letters taking several months to reach the front and sometimes failing to arrive at all.[19]

Expressing the mounting discontent, *Red Star* wrote: "It is better to prepare for four hours and fight for half an hour, than to prepare for half an hour and fight for four."[20]

Requirements were eased for enrollment of army men in the Communist organization, and in 1942 the number of new members reached 1,340,000 (including, of course, a certain number of civilians). Many of these men were subsequently killed or wounded. But even apart from this, as the ranks of the army increased with the addition of reserves, the party organization grew relatively smaller. Yet the party machine whose core was made up of specially appointed paid functionaries retained its full power. These party functionaries dominated the entire intellectual life of companies, regiments, and divisions, and it must be said, to their credit, that they displayed great activity. This system neither appealed to the army men nor even conciliated them. The army resented the fact that many of the party members were not obliged to fight but only to talk and write; that very many of them were not educated enough to provide ideological guidance; that

18. *Idem*, February 7 and 10, 1942.

19. In the early part of 1942 the authorities brought criminal charges against a number of post office officials for delaying mail addressed to the front. Sentences of two to ten years' imprisonment were imposed on those found guilty.

20. *Idem*, February 3, 1942.

without their consent no officer had the right to issue orders; that they were in a position to deal out punishment; and much else besides.

As an illustration, one may quote *Red Star* for a picture of the life of a regiment on the eve of an attack:

> . . . The X regiment had a whole day to prepare for the attack. During the day the following tasks were carried out: a conference of political instructors, a conference of the Communist Youth members, a meeting of propagandists to receive instructions, a conference of party organizers. As a result, active Communists were absent from their army units all day.

In despair *Red Star* exclaimed: "What a chase after conferences and meetings . . ." [21]

The state of equilibrium between the party and the army was consequently of brief duration. About October, 1941, only three or four months after the war broke out, friction, conflicts, and all the symptoms of a crisis began to be manifest behind the scenes. Now abating, now suddenly growing in intensity, they filled the political life of the Red Army, finding their expression in the press, in government decrees, in appointments and dismissals. They provided some of the most important events in the internal life of Russia during the first year of the war.

It is worth noting that despite all the subsurface turmoil there were no striking collisions, no proclaimed purges, no programmatic declarations.

The changes resembled not so much avalanches as slow landslides. Masses of soil slid down, almost unseen to the eye. But the forces that pushed them never stopped acting. The landslide was going on everywhere—down the ideological line, down the party line, down the organizational line. Altogether it marked a chapter in the Red Army's struggle for emancipation.

Marshals, generals, colonels left their posts. Beginning with the sensational resignations of Voroshilov and Budenny on October 22, 1941, changes in command came thick and fast. New figures rose to the surface, new uniforms came into the limelight only to vanish into the darkness again. Dozens

---

21. *Idem*, 1942, No. 26.

came and went. There were changes in nearly all the highest posts.

In this sweeping, if quiet, purge, an ideological change was apparent. It was accomplished under the pretense of ridding the army of the officers of the civil war era, as incapable of appreciating modern technical developments and of adjusting themselves to new demands. The new attitude was a concession on the part of the government to the sentiments of the army. Men responsible for the reverses were sought among the old-line Communist leaders. The implication was that the party regime in itself was not wrong but that those party military leaders who failed to adapt themselves to the new conditions were. And such was actually the interpretation that the army placed on the resignation of the first Titans and the dozens of minor figures that followed them. Encouraged by Moscow, a struggle was waged in the army against old commanders, holders of titles and decorations, who were exposed and ridiculed. For their part, the old commanders, proud of their past achievements and their patriotism, denounced their critics as "defeatists" and threatened naïvely, as they went into retirement: "We shall yet see how you will fight without us!"

The longer the struggle continued the greater it grew. "Proletarian origin" began to be less appreciated in the army, while men whose parents belonged to the intelligentsia were promoted to higher posts. The word "comrade" ceased to be obligatory as a form of address. In the army it was often replaced by the rank—"Comrade Petrov" or "Lieutenant Petrov"—sometimes even between officers who were Communists. The slogan "Proletarians of all countries, unite!" which adorned the front pages of all the Bolshevik periodicals without exception, disappeared from the front page of the army and navy newspapers in January, 1942, and was replaced in the same spot and in the same type by the nonparty national slogan of "Death to the German invaders!" The most nationalistic of the new slogans of Red Army Day were proclaimed now:

"Let's get even with the German Fascist rats!"

"Blood for blood! Death for death!"

The old decorations such as the Red Banner, the Order of Lenin, and even the Hero of the Soviet Union had a distinct

Communist flavor. Therefore, in the summer of 1942, new decorations were instituted—for the officers the orders of Suvorov, of Kutuzov, and of Alexander Nevsky, and for the soldiers the orders of Excellent Miner, Excellent Engineer, and others. This was an innovation of notable significance which was further emphasized by the fact that military commissars and political instructors were ruled out as recipients of these new decorations, which were to be conferred only on men in fighting service.

Another characteristic sign of the changing times was the increasing frequency with which reports and articles in the military press spoke of "Russia" instead of "the U.S.S.R.," of "Russian" instead of "Soviet." The landslide was gaining such momentum that within a few months the new terms were dominant in army organs, and old military writers had to learn new ways in quick order. An interesting example of this resurgence of national consciousness is a poem, "A Letter of a Red Army Man to His Friend," by Constantine Simonov, author of the famous war play, *The Russian People*. The poem, first published in *Red Star*, is likewise one of the most popular pieces of war poetry in Soviet Russia. We quote its concluding lines:

> Having sternly scorched, in the Russian way,
> The Russian earth they left behind,
> Our comrades died before our eyes
> Baring their chests, in the Russian way.
>
> Bullets have spared your life and mine,
> Yet, trebly certain that my life is over
> I swell with pride for the dearest gift—
> For the Russian land where I was born.
>
> I swell with pride that its fight is mine,
> That a Russian mother gave us birth,
> That a Russian woman, bidding us goodbye,
> Embraced me thrice, in the Russian way.

In harmony with this the army no longer sang the Soviet revolutionary "Carmagnoles" but the traditional soldier's songs, "Clouds Have Risen Over the City," or "The Sea Is Big and Wide."

"He fights as he can."

"As he can? How soon will he fight as he should?"

"When, O Lord, will this country of ours be at last rid of fools, ignoramuses, time-servers, lickspittles? We must beat these self-enamored incompetents, beat them black and blue, crush them to pieces, and without losing time replace them with other men, men who are new, young, and talented. If we don't we may ruin our great cause. . . . You didn't fight in the civil war? Have few decorations? One is sorry to say this is still the principal consideration among the officers of our high command. If you did not take part in the civil war you are no good."

In this bit of dialogue from Alexander Korneichuk's sensational play *Front*, the old commanding personnel of the Red Army was witheringly characterized by a representative of the younger generation. As a play *Front* was a pretty mediocre piece of work. But as a political pamphlet boldly declaring a new faith and proposing a complete program for reorganization of the Red Army, it represented an event of profound significance. A number of remarkable facts relating to its publication and production shed light on the significance of the play. *Front* was first published in the pages of official *Pravda* during a week in August, 1942, when the Soviet Armies were in full retreat before the Germans. Its blast against the old army command was immediately acclaimed throughout the country. The official benediction of the government was expressed in editorial comments of the Soviet press and, an unprecedented fact, in the special effort of the Government Art Affairs Committee (practically equivalent to a ministry of art) in organizing and supervising the production of the play all over the country. Moreover, Alexander Korneichuk was awarded the Stalin prize of 100,000 rubles for his play and was made an Assistant Foreign Commissar. The boldness of the play's criticism can be explained only on the assumption that somebody exceptionally high in government authority considered it useful. It is no exaggeration to say that *Front* is a document of historical significance.

The play's characters, nearly all of them members of the army, can be divided into two groups—on the one hand, old Communists, veterans of the civil war, together with their circle of friends and subordinates; and on the other, the younger generation, more capable, better educated, and attracting to their ranks everything alive and healthy in the army. The first group is headed by General Gorlov, commander of a number of armies at the front. The second group is headed by General Ognyov, a young man in command of a single army.

Gorlov (as portrayed in the play) is of proletarian descent and a former worker himself. He has won many decorations and is well known both in and outside of Russia. He believes in physical force, in speed and dash, while viewing skeptically all modern innovations. The words "hero," "heroic," "heroism" are constantly on his lips and on the lips of his friends, including his admirers among members of the press. To this coterie belong Colonel Udivitelny, chief of the intelligence service, General Khripun, chief of the signal corps, and others.[22]

The head of the "young" party, General Ognyov, belongs to the intelligentsia: his father was a schoolmaster (just as the father of his supporter and another "positive type," General Blagonravov, was a deacon) ; he has had a good education, believes in the new technical developments of military science, is personally brave, considerate of his men, and a strict abstainer from alcohol. Siding with Ognyov is Miron Gorlov, director of an airplane plant, through whom Soviet industry voices its criticisms of the army (it is notable that not a workman but a director speaks in the name of industry). Miron happens to be General Gorlov's brother, which permits him to air bitter truths to the exalted commander.

The argument of the play concerns ways and means of recapturing a certain Russian station from the Germans. Gorlov prepares a military plan for the operation. But the plan is badly conceived because Gorlov is badly informed about the enemy and lacks any profound understanding of strategic problems. Nevertheless, he demands absolute and unquestioning obedience from his generals, among them the army commander General Ognyov.

---

22. The author draws a portrait of Gorlov which in many ways resembles Marshal Voroshilov. The deliberate nature of this take-off is seen from the fact that the town Gorlovka lies close to Voroshilovgrad (formerly Lugansk, and the home town of the redoubtable marshal). The resemblance was so striking that the commentaries on the play which appeared later had to refute the charge that the characters of the play were drawn from real people.

"I'll chop your head off for the least deviation," he says to Ognyov.

Preparations for the difficult military operation by Gorlov's general staff are intermixed with a party. An interesting character is the signal corps chief, General Khripun (a boon companion of Gorlov), who "has saved half a dozen bottles of old brandy." The signal contacts with other units are badly organized by Khripun, but he is highly indignant at a front newspaper which praises the signal corps work of the Germans and writes, with an eye on Khripun: "The stupidity of certain commanders and higher officers prevents our radio signaling from being brought up to its full efficiency. All other conditions for an improvement are present."

Gorlov, who still lives in the traditions of the civil war, also smarts under the criticism. "We'll defeat any enemy," he protests, "not by radio signaling but by heroism and valor."

The old officers regard the new ones not only as upstarts but as *defeatists* to boot. This term is much in use. Colonel Udivitelny speaks of General Blagonravov as being "dissatisfied with everybody and everything—it savors of defeatism." "These sentiments are well known—they're typically defeatist," he observes on another occasion.

Gorlov's strategic principles, which reflect the primitive military thought of the civil war, are stated with illuminating aptness.

"The main thing is the dashing attack—a staggering blow and then destruction. War is risk, not arithmetic," Gorlov proclaims. On another occasion he remarks: "One foreign critic recently observed about me: 'The Front Commander Gorlov cannot be fitted into the ordinary conception of a military leader.' These bourgeois experts are simply at a loss to understand how Gorlov, a man from the soil, with the soil in his blood, who is not a theorist and never went to military academies, licks the boasted generals, theorists, and academicians every time. The military leader's secret is in his soul. If his soul is brave, daring, dashing, he need fear nobody. . . . War is not an academy. . . . Don't reason—act! I have a few book strategists," Gorlov continues, *"who always prattle about military culture.* I'm obliged to press their brains into their proper places."

When Miron Gorlov, director of the airplane plant, arrives at the headquarters of his general brother the two engage in the following conversation:

GORLOV. Your airplanes are killing us. You supply too few of them, far too few.

MIRON. Never mind. You'll soon get a new present from us. It's so fast Goering will burst of envy.

GORLOV. I wish you thought less of speed and more of numbers.

MIRON. And I wish you'd stop this tune. We know it and are tired of hearing it from people like you. Enough! To hell with it!

GORLOV. Why so? I don't understand.

MIRON. For years and years we've heard some of our strategists shout: "Give us as many airplanes as you can make. Speed is a secondary consideration. The important thing is quantity."

GORLOV. They were perfectly right.

MIRON. If we had kept listening to those strategists we would have been done for now. The Germans would have shot us down like quail.

Through the mouth of the same Miron the author caustically criticizes the lavish handing out of awards and decorations to old generals who did little to earn them: *"The likes of you get too few black eyes. If I were the government I would be giving you more shiners, and such that everybody would see them—but fewer decorations."* Again on this theme, the author jests through the mouth of the soldier Ostapenko:

"Kalinin has got fairly sick of this decoration business. . . . Every day he has to decorate two hundred or even three hundred men, and everybody shows how happy he is with a hearty handshake. That's what's made him sick. It's regular hard labor, it is."

The author displays much courage in dealing with the subject of military commissars. It must be borne in mind that he wrote before these commissars were abolished and when officially they were still regarded as a notable success and were praised in newspaper editorials. But the spokesmen of the "younger generation" in the play speak of them with bitter scorn:

"I have a commissar," says Ognyov's supporter, General Kolos. "His name is Onufry Strategov—and no great shakes even in plain grammar. . . . I call him Onufry Hoof—this fits him better."

"Doesn't he take offense?" Ognyov inquires.

"No, he understands . . ." Kolos answers.

In this calm sarcasm perhaps better than in anything else one sees all the accumulated resentment of the army men against the party officials, of the fighters against the sleuths, and one realizes the inner ties that cement army elements together.

In one battalion, it is related in the play, "the political instructor and the commander have got themselves a cook and gorge themselves for all they are worth, while the soldiers' kitchen serves rotten food." When the soldiers beat up the cook, the political instructor exaggerates this into an important affair to the effect that "the enemy's agents have raised their heads."

In another passage Miron's nephew, Lieutenant Sergei, tells Miron about the men in his battery: "We live like one family. Do you know who the father in our family is?" "The political instructor?" Miron asks. "No, the battery commander," Sergei replies.

The daring of these remarks can be appreciated only when one recalls the oft-quoted words of Stalin that "the commissar is the father of the regiment."

The military operations have a successful ending in the play only because, disregarding Gorlov's strategic plan, and supported in this by the Kremlin, Ognyov carries through his own plan. He saves the situation and captures the station, the immediate objective of the operation. After this Gorlov is dismissed and is followed by his protégés, while Ognyov is given Gorlov's post.

So all ends well. The "purge" leads to victories. The sympathy of the audience is wholly on the side of "the younger generation," "the defeatists."

But if the "old-timers" are portrayed vividly and convincingly, the author has been far from successful in picturing the representatives of the younger generation. They are lifeless and artificial, endowed with ideal qualities. Korneichuk is perhaps not to be blamed for this. The movement of the young, non-Communist at bottom, carries with it so much that is oppositionist, so much accumulated, if latent, criticism, that under Soviet conditions it was impossible to give a realistic portrait of the young Red Army officer.

What the author omitted was supplied by the literary commentators. Sensational on the stage, *Front* also caused a flood of articles in the press and became the talk of the country. The Russian public sensed in the play a certain freedom of criticism of the Soviet system, even perhaps saw a dream of some reign of freedom. A prominent Soviet writer, Pavlenko, described the indignation which the play aroused in a friend, a chief of the Political Section ("This is scandalous!" his friend exclaimed), while recording his own opinion as follows:

The main thing is the right of criticism, of opposing the Gorlovs! The idea of the play is just this: Look how inactive, unenterprising, timid we are—how we permit a harmful man whom we have entrusted with the fortunes of our country to do whatever he wants under our very noses, instead of taking from him the power of deciding the nation's destinies. . . . The play generates courage to fight against everything that has survived its usefulness.[23]

Whether the critic realized the full meaning of this comment, it is impossible to say.

The struggle of different currents within the Red Army, as the foregoing pages have shown, was confined to the higher circles of the commanding personnel. It was carried on largely behind the scenes, but as it developed it expanded from the question of changes in commanding personnel to include the question of abolishing military commissars. The orthodox party elements who held to the traditions stressed the battle accomplishments of Communists in general and of army commissars in particular. An editorial in *Pravda* paid high tribute to "the political workers on the battlefield," and to those who demanded abolition of military commissars it answered: "It is now, in these days of stern trials, that the role of military commissars, of political instructors, and political workers have grown immensely." [24]

The editorial quoted examples of heroism on the part of commissars, such as the case of one who was blinded in battle but continued to "lead his brave men" for a whole day; or of another who, though wounded, kept on crawling with his men. The editorial wound up with an appeal to the military commissars to fight with determination. Then, as if in answer to criticisms of the commissars *Pravda* published an account

23. *Oktyabr*, 1942, No. 10.
24. *Pravda*, August 15, 1942.

of a regimental meeting of Communists quoting the commissar's report, an interesting part of which contrasted Communists and officers:

"The Communists, by their personal example," said the commissar, "inspire the soldiers to heroic deeds in the name of their fatherland. The machine-gunner and party candidate comrade Yaroshenko has covered himself with immortal glory. Communist Koshelenko fights bravely," and so it went on. "But," continued the commissar, "why do we have reverses?" "Some commanders," he explained, "don't know well enough how to direct the fighting and get confused at a critical moment."

In the discussion that followed some Communists complained that "the commanding officers in setting a task for the soldiers did not always do so with the utmost clearness." [25]

Thus, the struggle was entering a decisive stage. The party die-hards saw faults in the Red Army officers, the "young people" demanded abolition of military commissars. "In recent months at the front a strained situation has occurred," *Red Star* [26] stated. On October 6, 1942, it carried an editorial sharply criticizing the military commissars who showed little interest in military science. "The value of commissars," it wrote, "is not measured by the number of meetings and reports. Some commissars have no military knowledge and rely only on the reputation they acquired in the civil war." Three days later, on October 9, 1942, a decree abolishing military commissars was signed by Kalinin. "The commissar," the decree stated, "might have become an obstacle in the way of improved leadership and have placed the commanders in embarassing positions." The official commentaries said that the commissars had performed great services during the period of retreat, but that now, on the eve of an offensive, they were no longer needed. The principle of single command was thus restored. Some of the commissars were appointed to army posts, others were sent to military schools to be trained for officer duties. Many were discharged.

The abolition of military commissars was a great event in the inner life of the Red Army. Its importance was measured by the passions and the intense struggle which this question

25. *Idem*, September 4, 1942.
26. October 13, 1942.

had aroused before. This was a victory of "the young" over "the old" and over the strict party rule. Commenting on the reform, *Izvestiya* wrote that the Soviet High Command encouraged promotion of new officers to take the places of old ones, even while war was on. But this reform, gained as the result of heated discussion and struggle, could not fail to raise the confidence in their own powers of the officer personnel who had longed to free themselves of outside control.

The reform of October 9, 1942, which abolished the institution of military commissars, was not as radical, however, as may have appeared at first glance. Before the publication of the government decree the commissars enjoyed equal rights with the officers, as parts of the system of dual command in the army. The decree put an end, first, to the dual command, and second, to the interference of civil Communists in military affairs. It also abolished the title of military commissars.

But in another form political control was preserved in the system of political instructors in whose hands were placed the entire political work and the duties of observation of the loyalty of the officers and the army. These political instructors have been made subordinate to their superior officers, but even generals and colonels have, among their nearest subordinates, a "deputy commander in charge of political work" who is tied up with his special political police department.

Clause 3 of the decree of October 9 read as follows: "to introduce in the Red Army deputy commanders in charge of political work," who were now to wear military uniforms and receive military rank.

The order issued by Stalin simultaneously with the decree, on October 9, 1942, prescribed not only that "commissars be relieved of the posts they occupy" but also "that they be appointed as deputies in charge of political work to their respective military commanders." These deputies, although in military uniform, had, in the main, to do the same kind of work as formerly. "They have to concentrate all their attention," wrote *Pravda*, "on the political work among the troops. . . . Political work must be extended still further. . . . A political worker who permitted a slackening of political work would be committing a gross political error, even a crime." [27]

Appointed to the high post of Chief of the Political Ad-

---

27. *Pravda*, October 11, 1942.

ministration, Alexander Shcherbakov (of the Political Bureau and one of Stalin's closest assistants) expanded and intensified "the political work" in the army. He introduced the new office of "regimental agitator" and took strong measures to eliminate red tape in his vast organization. But his energy was often dissipated by bureaucratic inertia. Complaints poured in about the "meeting-holding mania" or that "many political workers continue to stay at headquarters and to write communications and reports." [28] "In military business chatterboxes are the most dangerous people." [29] "According to reports everything is satisfactory. In reality, the measures taken are bad." [30] "Dozens of speeches were delivered on the subject of Comrade Stalin's order, but on the eve of the attack it was revealed that in some units firearms were not in proper order. . . . Our 'agitation' does not always teach us to fight." [31]

In the fall of 1942 an important new rule was announced making the party Communists in the army responsible for the observance of certain rules by the non-Communists in their units. The rules covered keeping the firearms clean and performing similar routine duties, and the Communists failing to enforce their observance on the part of their comrades were liable to punishment. Naturally, along with this responsibility went special rights of control and supervision.[32]

On the other hand, new generals and high officials from among Stalin's party entourage were sent to various sections of the front to watch over the professional army generals. Every important section of the front had one of Stalin's old and loyal assistants. Zhdanov was in Leningrad, watching General Govorov; Kaganovich was in the Caucasus supervising General Tyulenev; in Moscow Shcherbakov exercised control over the military command of the central front. The names changed frequently but the system remained intact.

The methodical and deliberate measures taken to restore the distinctive attributes of the Czarist Army practically reached their goal. On January 6, 1943, shoulder straps, abol-

---

28. *Red Star*, editorial, November 22, 1942.
29. *Idem*, editorial, December 18, 1942.
30. *Idem*, September 10, 1942.
31. *Idem*, April 7, 1943.
32. *Idem*, September 10 and 19, 1942.

ished since the establishment of the Soviet regime, were restored in the army. Another step in this direction was the restoration of Guards Regiments, which, in the old army, were the picked troops inspired with a special loyalty to the throne. Beginning in 1941, but especially after the Stalingrad victory, the regiments that most distinguished themselves in battle were awarded the name of Guards Regiments, a status which carried with it such privileges as double pay for the soldiers and pay and a half for the officers.

Creation of a privileged section in the army was of course one of the principal objectives in domestic policy. Conferring of decorations, of which roughly half a million were awarded up to the middle of 1943, also created a privileged status and resulted in material benefits. In order to dilute the Red Army, hundreds of thousands of special N.K.V.D. troops were required to discard their green and blue hats and to don the ordinary Red Army uniforms.[33] Tens of thousands of "political workers," who performed nonmilitary duties, were also obliged to wear army uniform, while the same policy found its expression at the top of the party machine in the several members of the Political Bureau being made generals and Stalin himself marshal.

Thus, the relations between the two public bodies, the party-police organizations and the army, became, in 1943, relations inside the Red Army. The measures that were adopted, however, were unable to suppress the accumulating antagonism.

Such is the structure of the Red Army as it has been shaped by the progress of the war. Soldiers are kept under the incessant and watchful control of the party cells which, though they embrace but a small percentage of the rank and file, are extremely active at the same time and are themselves under the strict control of superior party organs. The middle officer stratum is kept under the constant observation of the reorganized military commissars, the Deputy Commanders in Charge of Political Work. Finally, the generals work under the surveillance of resident representatives of Moscow, the

---

33. These secret police troops of the N.K.V.D. (formerly G.P.U.) cause resentment in the army by the fact that they are seldom sent to the front, being kept in the rear to suppress popular disturbances should any break out.

new generals from the Central Committee. In this fashion the vast Russian Army lives and fights, held firmly in check by the elaborate party machine.

With the exception of Stalin, the Commander-in-Chief of the Red Army, Russian military leaders are given extremely little personal publicity in the Soviet press or on the Soviet radio, in striking contrast to the publicity showered upon military leaders of other countries such as Generals Mac-Arthur, Montgomery, Von Keitel, or Rommel. The daily bulletins of the Soviet Information Bureau mention in-numerable names of officers who distinguished themselves in this or that operation. They also contain long lists of officers awarded decorations. But this is as far as official limelight goes : many well-known names but no accepted celebrities.

Yet in Russia, too, the war has brought to the fore a whole cluster of brilliant military leaders, men of technical knowl-edge, daring, and talent. Soviet generals fully realize that they have earned a right to popular acclaim. Lately, they have been accorded a certain limited amount of recognition in the special orders of the day, which the Commander-in-Chief has been addressing to the leading victorious officers. Thus, there have been brought into fame a number of outstanding names : Vatutin, Rokosovsky, Popov, Konyev, Golikov, Vasilevsky (who has replaced Marshal Shaposhnikov, as Stalin's closest adviser), Govorov, Zhukov, Voronov, and a few others.

The position of the higher Red Army officers with a dis-tinguished war record is very peculiar. They are all, of course, members of the Communist party and loyal to their leader ; and being preoccupied with their military tasks, they stay aloof from internal politics, with which they make no attempt to interfere. But rule over millions of people, over their lives and deaths, direction of vast operations, great responsibilities and great risks are bound to produce men of strong will, of great initiative, and of courage. Their military successes, the gratitude of the nation, and their secure place in history elevate them in the eyes of their contemporaries, as well as in their own eyes. Thus names which only recently were unknown in Russia sweep forward to the front rank, eclipsing many old and prominent political leaders and as-suming the character not of party but of national heroes. It is unnecessary to explain what menace this implies for the existing political hierarchy, and how these dangers are viewed in a country which has so assiduously studied the history of the French and English revolutionary wars, of Napoleon, and of Cromwell.

The antagonisms have not been removed. After the previous record of relations between the army machine and the party-police machine, there can be little doubt that a stable equilibrium has not yet been achieved. No sooner has one set of problems been cleared up by the government than another, equally serious, confronts it. At the same time it is plain that the political sentiments prevailing in the multimillioned Red Army are far from being identical with those dominant in the ruling circles of the Communist party. Here, in the army, is centered the struggle between the two trends, the issue of which probably will predetermine Russia's policy of the near future.

II. BRITAIN AND GERMANY IN SOVIET POLICY

1. THE HEROIC ERA

OF ALL possible international combinations only one has always presented and will continue to present a grave, perhaps a fatal, danger to Soviet Russia. This combination is an Anglo-German alliance.

During its existence the Soviet Government has witnessed a great variety of power combinations directed against it. There was Germany in alliance with Austria-Hungary winning a short-lived success. This was followed by the Entente of the first World War with its abortive intervention in Russia. Then there were the Franco-Polish alliance, the Anglo-Japanese and Anglo-Chinese combinations, and the German-Japanese anti-Comintern alliance. The gravest danger of all was implicit in the Munich combination of Britain and Germany. But it was dissipated by Germany's ambition to rule the world.

The aims of Soviet Russia's foreign policy were to prevent or break up such a combination by cultivating the friendship of Germany, an open contrast to Soviet hostility to Britain. Russia could have achieved the same end by other means, such as coöperation with France and a rapprochement with Britain. Ideological considerations, however, barred her from taking this road.

The characteristic tendencies of Soviet policy were the product neither of fortuitous combinations nor of personal whims and ambitions. The direction of Soviet activity, as set by Lenin and faithfully continued by Stalin, was dictated by Bolshevism's world outlook and formed its natural and indispensable complement. The large world aims of Soviet policy and its specific peculiarities were as much its attributes as were expropriation of property, industrialization, collectivization of farming, and stern reprisals against inner enemies. All these features blend into a unified whole just as individual peculiarities of the human face form a characteristic physiognomy.

The basic elements of Bolshevism and the principles of its policy assumed their characteristic form in the early years of

Soviet rule. The place of Germany and Great Britain in the theory and practice of Russian Communism was fixed a long time ago. The practice has changed from time to time and there has been much zigzagging, but the principles of foreign policy remain the same. They are bound to remain unaltered to the end of this war, in so far as the main protagonist in the East of Europe remains the same.

In the prehistoric period of Bolshevism, i.e., before the revolution of 1917, Germany held a special place in the Bolshevist philosophy, being regarded as the classical country both of capitalism and of revolutionary socialism. Her industries were developing at a rapid pace; the centralization of industry and the numerical growth of the working class appeared to confirm prognostications and expectations. At the same time Germany, unlike Britain and America, had a large socialist party with a revolutionary program. It seemed as if everything in Germany was a brilliant confirmation of the orthodox theory, and Germany, more than any other country, held the interest of the founding fathers of Bolshevism. Her economic and statistical data were studied with close attention. Her socialist literature, especially her scientific publications, were read and debated in Russian circles at times more passionately than among the Germans.

If to the German intellectuals of the nineteenth century progressive "western Europe" lay west of the Rhine, to Russia at the turn of the century, the whole of Germany was seen as included within the great cultural realm of western Europe. The Bolsheviks went even further, and to them Germany appeared, though dimly, as the most valuable element of the European west.

To this another circumstance added its weight during the years of World War I. The Russian liberal groups and almost all of the democratic elements took their stand as *oborontzi* (defenders), that is, they favored an alliance with Britain and France—an "alliance with the democracies"—against "German militarism." The Bolsheviks, on the other hand, demanded "an immediate peace," a withdrawal from the war, and were severely critical of Russia's allies. The imperialism of Britain and France was bitterly denounced by the Bolsheviks of that time. The "equivalence" of both coalitions (the

German coalition and the Entente) was one of their tenets.
Lenin, of course, expressed no preference for the German
monarchy, but by directing all his criticism against a Russian alliance with Britain and France he opened the door for
an agreement with Germany.

In these facts lay the germ of future policies. The world
outside Russia knew little of the Russian policies and even
less of Bolshevism, but the seeds of the future were already
present in the political philosophy of early Bolshevism, such
as hostility to Britain; sympathy with anti-British movements all over the world; hostility to France and her allies
("vassals") in eastern Europe; willingness for peaceful coexistence with Germany; and hope for a German revolution.

"The German," wrote Lenin, "embodies the principle of
discipline, of organized effort, of harmonious coöperation
on the basis of the newest machine industry, the strictest
accounting and control." [1]

Later Germany figured in the philosophy and practice of
Communism, first, in the scheme of social revolution and,
second, on the plane of respectable cohabitation, of "coexistence of capitalist and socialist countries." The second aspect
gradually assumed more practical importance. The two,
though closely linked with each other, must be considered
separately.

Today, as we look back a quarter of a century, it is difficult to realize how firmly convinced Russian Bolshevism
was, during those early years, that events in Russia were
only the first act—merely a part, and not the most important part at that, of a vast world drama, and that the Soviet
state would not survive unless successful revolutions took
place in the rest of Europe. These were not mere conjec-
tures, the fruit of theorizing; they were an article of faith,
something as certain as that night follows day. When, a
year after the Bolshevik revolution, the empires of Central
Europe collapsed and the workers of Berlin and Vienna
elected soviets, Lenin's prognosis seemed to have been completely borne out and his claim to having a scientific policy
appeared confirmed. World revolution was on its way.

As he recalled those years later, Lenin, evaluating the
developments in Europe and seeing the ruin of his hopes,

---

1. *Izvestiya*, March 11, 1918.

showed that he realized the naïveté of those conceptions.
He wrote, with an apparently heavy heart:

When in the days gone by we were commencing the international revolution we thought: either the international revolution will come to
our aid, . . . or, in the case of (our) defeat, we shall have still served
the revolutionary cause. Actually, the movement proceeded along a
line not as straight as we had expected. The time for revolution in
other capitalist countries had not yet arrived.[2]

The first years of Bolshevism were the decisive years.
During those early years of the revolution the system of
ideas of a new era was taking shape. In those years young
men who later came to be leaders grew up and formed their
convictions which stayed with them all their lives. The
hoped-for and prayed-for world revolution needed a concrete protagonist.

At once, as the natural conclusion suggested by both
theory and practice, *staking everything on Germany* became
the first principle in the Russian Grand Strategy of world
revolution. Every capitalist country was expected to reach
a crisis shortly, but the fates willed it—so it appeared to
Moscow—that Germany should be the first of the "advanced
countries" to do so. "Backward Russia" and "advanced Germany," her favored complement, would together create the
first socialist structure capable of survival. "The principal
link in the chain of revolutions is the German link," Lenin
said, "and the success of world revolution depends more
upon Germany than upon any other country." [3]

Such was the Communist "Schlieffen plan," the strategy
of world revolution. Reduced to concrete terms it raised several problems. First was the problem of Poland, which
formed a barrier between the two countries. Next was the
problem of France, representing a possible threat to the
Russian-German bloc. Third was the question of the joint
foreign policy of the allied future Soviet-Germany and Russia in regard to such matters as peace or war with the
capitalist world, fulfillment or denunciation of the Treaty
of Versailles, and so forth.

The potentialities of Soviet activity, however, were narrow. The years which followed the German revolution

---

2. Lenin, "Report on Tactics, 1921," *Works*, XXVI, 452.
3. Lenin, "Report of October 22, 1918," *idem*, XXIII, 235.

were, for Soviet Russia, a period of civil war, blockade, and famine. The Red Army was barefoot and almost unarmed. Interference in the internal affairs of Germany in any military way was ruled out. Activity was of necessity restricted to the export of ideas and theories, to propaganda, and to instructing the Communist following. Meantime, the situation in Germany was taking an unfavorable turn. The German revolution, unlike the Russian, was on the downgrade, proceeding from extremely Red ideas to ideas of increasingly moderate color, so that within a short time power was in the hands of a government which was not only free of Communists but was actually a coalition with bourgeois elements included. In questions of foreign relations this government was primarily interested in Britain and France, not in Russia. At that very time it signed the Versailles Treaty and was preparing Germany to carry it out. It stood for a national restoration executed without new violent upheavals.

In the spring of 1920 the Polish Government began a war with Soviet Russia. Immediately the strategy of social revolution became flesh and blood. Poland was a natural ally of France, the latter's point of support in the east, a substitute for Imperial Russia in the anti-German bloc of powers. A Polish victory over Russia would also have been a French victory. On the other hand, a Polish defeat would have brought the revolution to the very heart of Europe.

After great initial successes the Polish armies were sent reeling back and a point was reached at which Britain was impelled to energetic efforts toward a restoration of peace. She proposed terms favorable to Soviet Russia, acceptance of which would have signified a readiness on the part of Soviet Russia to live peacefully side by side with capitalism. According to the ideas prevalent at the time, this would have been tantamount to a renunciation of immediate social revolution. It would have meant the liquidation for a long time of the main objective—contact with Germany. Reasoning thus, the government of Lenin rejected an immediate peace and ordered its armies to march on Warsaw, while Trotsky stated openly that "we will give decisive battle to the troops of the Entente on the Rhine."

On this occasion a method of Soviet foreign policy was applied which became obligatory under similar circumstances during all the subsequent years. *Conquest* of Poland was not and could not be the aim of the Soviet Government. Even a conquest with the objective of socialist reconstruction was rejected in principle. How could one advocate a policy of conquest when the Soviet Union itself grew up in the fight against all imperialisms! Every nation had the right of self-determination, and this principle applied equally to Poland. But self-determination was to be carried out by spontaneous mass action such as insurrection, by election of soviets, actual acceptance of new governmental authority, and so forth. Unlike the procedure in the usual type of conquest, in this case representatives of the Polish people themselves (Polish Communists) and not foreigners (Russian Communists) would occupy key posts in the government. A Polish Soviet Government, in fact, was formed in Bialystok and waited only for the progress of military events to move over to Warsaw.

War was already being waged on Polish territory, and the battle for Warsaw was drawing near. But in Lenin's eyes Warsaw and, for that matter, all Poland, held a secondary place. The center of his interest was Germany. If Warsaw fell, Soviet troops would have reached the German border; a German Soviet Government would have been formed and kept in readiness, and Communist and semi-Communist forces inside Germany would have been able, in view of the widespread dissatisfaction with the terms of the Versailles Treaty—so it was reasoned in Moscow—to overthrow the weak government in power. The first aim, which was dreamed of constantly for three years, would thus have been achieved. And so real, so close at hand did this achievement seem to be, that the next steps of the Russian-German bloc, especially on the question of its relations with France, were already being considered. In anticipation of a belligerent attitude on the part of the French Government, it was publicly stated in Soviet Russia that this bloc was not at all obliged to oppose the carrying out of the Versailles Treaty. On the contrary, it would act with all possible caution and wisdom and would maneuver so as to avoid immediate armed conflict with the war machine of France. This was the classical-Leninist policy.

The Soviet-Polish War ended unfavorably for Russia. The Red Army was driven back and Poland obtained a frontier which today would be called "strategic": extensive non-Polish territories placed under Polish rule pushed the Red specter far into the east—as far away as possible from Warsaw and also from Berlin. This was a serious defeat for the cause of world revolution. It provided one of the reasons for a partial return to capitalism—the N.E.P. initiated by Lenin.

2. GERMANY'S PLACE IN THE REVOLUTIONARY SCHEME

Moscow did not accept the defeat as final. It believed only that victory would be delayed for a short time. Political passions continued to rage in Germany and, in the spring of 1921, there were new uprisings in Central Germany. Germany's international position was also difficult—in the opinion of Moscow, even desperate. The habit of manufacturing new scientific theories as circumstances required led Moscow to the conclusion that, under the terms of the Treaty of Versailles, Germany would never be able to rise, recover economically, and restore more or less normal conditions of life. Russian Communism was convinced that Germany's "western orientation" was due to political blindness and that new conflicts between her and France would develop into a European cataclysm. As it foresaw events, successive and connected wars and revolutions would finally drive Germany to a Communist upheaval and an alliance with Moscow. Germany continued to play an important role in Moscow's strategy of social revolution.

In the first part of the year 1923 these hopes gave promise of being borne out. The Communist movement in Germany was spreading. Elections demonstrated its success and its numerical growth. To be sure, fighting spirit was waning, but this dangerous symptom attracted less attention. Moreover, a serious conflict with France was brewing. French troops, as an act of reprisal, occupied the Ruhr district, and Germany replied with "passive resistance." The economic life of Germany was thrown into complete disorder and inflation reached huge proportions. It seemed—in Moscow it was even considered certain—that the new international conflict would at any moment turn into a war. It seemed strange that no popular revolutionary outbreaks which would have rounded out the picture were anywhere in evidence. Finally, after hesitation and delay, under pressure from Moscow, an uprising was set to take place in Hamburg on October 23, 1923. It was later decided to call off the event, but the courier who was to bring the cancellation order to Hamburg missed his train.[4] The attempted uprising was crushed.

Meantime, contrary to expectations in Moscow, the Ger-

4. The courier was W. Krivitzky, who later broke off with the Soviet

man Government found a way out of its conflict with France. "Passive resistance" ceased. France promised to withdraw her troops gradually from the Ruhr, and soon began to do so. German currency was quickly stabilized and German economy suddenly entered upon a period of rapid activity and growth.

Taken together, all this was in violent contradiction to Moscow's scientific predictions. The disappointment in Moscow this time was even more painful than that which followed the defeat in the war with Poland. To break Polish bayonets did not seem impossible, but here was Germany moving away in an unexpected direction and opening for herself roads to progress without a military alliance with Soviet Russia; she was choosing agreement with rather than resistance to her adversaries. It was a double blow and a heavy one. In the first place it was clear that social revolution was making no headway; on the contrary, everything seemed to suggest that the capitalist world was growing in strength. In 1924-25 it was already openly admitted in Moscow that "the first period" of world revolution, the period of storm and stress, was over, and that "a temporary stabilization of capitalism" was taking place. This admission brought all the consequences that a great retreat has for an army. "Morale" began to decline, and the successors of Lenin, who died in 1924, waged bitter war against one another. During those years Russia also witnessed the gradual ousting of Leon Trotsky. Trotsky's deeply rooted internationalism made it particularly hard and painful to him to draw all the political conclusions from the defeat of the international revolution.

The great Master Plan of revolution—alliance with Germany—was of necessity reëxamined. To all appearance the revolutionary forces had to seek another channel. But it was not easy to give up the old majestic plan which had taken such deep roots in Bolshevist thought and which besides had the clarity and concreteness so necessary in dealing with elemental forces. Confusion was widespread.

Stalin held to the old viewpoint. As late as the end of 1924 he was still repeating that

---

Government, emigrated to America, and died here under mysterious circumstances in 1941.

of all European countries Germany is the one most pregnant with revolution; a revolutionary victory in Germany is a victory all over Europe. If the revolutionary shake-up of Europe is to begin anywhere, it will begin in Germany. Only Germany can take the initiative in this respect, and a victory of revolution in Germany is a full guarantee of victory of the international revolution.[5]

Meanwhile Zinovyev was in search of a new geography and was inclined to see a ray of hope in the East: "After the victory of Russian revolution," he said at approximately the time that Stalin spoke,

we all agreed that Germany's would be the next turn, after which revolution would make the rounds of all Europe. It is only now that the question is being persistently put whether this view of the further route of revolution as its only possible route is true.

Can it be that we are mistaken in appraising this route? We should consider other possibilities. . . . The East is moving forward far more resolutely than we expected. England proves to be much more shaken than appeared to us. . . . The East with its 900 million population is awakening.[6]

Stalin disagreed with this view. Even in 1925 he continued to insist: "The Dawes Plan is pregnant with an inevitable revolution in Germany. It has been created for the pacification of Germany, but it must inevitably lead to a revolution in Germany."[7]

From different sides various candidates for the vacant place formerly occupied by Germany were advanced. But what sorry candidates they were!

In 1926 a general strike in support of striking coal miners was declared in England. The general strike collapsed in a few days, but the coal miners continued their resistance for nearly six months and around them, for a time, Moscow hopes were centered. Subscriptions "for English coal miners" were collected from Russian workers; appeals, articles, reports were written. It would be no exaggeration to say that this strike played a more important role in Russia than in England. But it passed, leaving no trace as far as social revolution was concerned. England did not ascend to the vacant throne. She only produced one more disappointment.

A great revolution flared up in China. It looked as if

---

5. *Bolshevik*, 1924, No. 11, pp. 51–52.
6. Zinovyev, speech of March 25, 1925, *Pravda*, April 1, 1925.
7. Stalin, speech, December 18, 1925.

Zinovyev's expectations were to be justified. Simultaneously a national and a social revolution, the Chinese outbreak was also directed against all foreign privileges, against imperialisms. At that time the Kuomintang included both Communists and their opponents, and for the former the chief target was the British Empire. Would world revolution proceed through Shanghai and Nanking, now that it refused to come through Berlin? This time Moscow did not, as it did in the case of Germany, demand a Communist government in China as a condition of alliance; the strategy of world revolution ruled out this requirement for "colonial or semicolonial nations," and semicolonial China came in this category.

Hope and rejoicing continued from 1925 to 1927. Soviet representatives in China acquired great popularity, and an alliance with Moscow seemed almost an accomplished fact. But the alliance was never consummated. Chinese policy went its own way, and a cloud came over the relations between the former friends. From the Moscow point of view, the leaders of Kuomintang betrayed their revolution and were coming to terms with world imperialism. From the Chinese point of view, the country was following its own policy, guided by realistic considerations. The rift grew wider, and before long there was an armed clash on the northern border. That date marked the birth of the antagonism which has since developed between Chiang Kai-shek and Moscow.

The Russian hopes for China were blighted and once again the Communist movement, both in Russia and in other countries, had no clear perspective of further action. The confusion inevitably developed into a serious crisis.

The situation as it took shape by the end of the 'twenties, and as it persisted up to the present war, was as follows: while Soviet Russia grew stronger as a state and had a firmly established Communist government, the fighting power of Communism outside of Russia was constantly declining. At one pole the power of Communism was growing; at the other pole it was falling off. Despite the numerical growth of their supporters, the sister Communist parties abroad were deteriorating qualitatively—their revolutionary enthusiasm was vanishing. Out of the chaos of the first years

(1918–22) there emerged a single Communist "continent" surrounded by limitless capitalist oceans.

Toward the end of the 'twenties, in his struggle against his right-wing comrades, Stalin proclaimed the end of the "stabilization of capitalism"—the world, according to him, was growing unstable and a new era of international conflicts and revolutions was at hand. To be sure, no revolutions were in evidence, and Stalin's opponents had no difficulty in proving this fact. But a profound cleavage was unquestionably developing in world politics, first, in the Soviet-British relations, and second, as a result of the extraordinary growth of German National Socialism. The new Moscow formula said: it all depends on whether revolution forestalls war, or war forestalls revolution; which is to say, if revolution precedes war, then its victory will make war impossible; or, if war breaks out first, then revolution, by transforming the international war into a civil war, will cut it short. Thus new prospects and new hopes were being opened.

But where was it possible to expect a war-preventing revolution after 1930, i.e., during the years of the rapid growth of Nazism? Theoretically, all countries of Europe and Asia were declared to be fit places for such a revolution, but special attention was again centered on Germany. Outside of Russia, Germany had the largest Communist party in the world, a party which was backed by 4 to 5 million electors, had a huge press of its own, and was equipped with a fine and wide-reaching organization. Clashes with the Nazis, in which many young Communists lost their lives, appeared to be a symptom of the revolutionary spirit of the party.

Thus, as Stalin's campaign against capitalism in Russia grew in intensity (this was the time of the creation of collective farms) Germany was gradually slipping back to her old position in the scheme of world revolution, the first Communist ally-to-be. It was once again demonstrated that in the years when Russian Communism was overflowing with optimism (1918–23 and after 1929), Germany was accorded the leading place in the revolutionary picture.

Strange as it may seem today, neither the growth of Nazism before 1933 nor even its triumph in that year undermined this faith in the approaching victory of Communism in Germany. Moscow's reasoning followed these lines: In Germany a process of differentiation was taking place among the political groups (liberals, moderate socialists) situated midway between the two extreme camps, Communism and Nazism. A collision of the two forces was inevitable, with the chances of victory on the side of Communism. The rapid falling off in the strength of the German Social-Democrats, regarded by Communism as its hereditary enemy, seemed to be a highly positive factor, and all these circumstances, taken together, were regarded by Moscow as a symptom of the advancing social revolution.

In September, 1932, Moscow stated that the world was moving to "a new round of revolutions and wars; a sharpening of class contradictions is taking place in Germany: on the one hand there is the growth of fascism, on the other, of the revolutionary mass struggle which speeds up the creation of conditions necessary for a revolutionary *crisis*." [8]

Because of this German Communists remained inactive when, in 1932–33, the liberal government had to be defended against the Nazis. The road to revolution, which had been barricaded by the moderate parties, lay, it seemed, through "the temporary triumph of Hitlerism."

---

8. "There is a revolution in Spain; in China there is a revolutionary situation, and social revolution is victorious over a considerable territory of the country. . . . Certain other countries are moving toward a revolutionary crisis (Poland) or . . . may soon find themselves in a revolutionary crisis (Japan)." (Executive Committee of the Communist International.)

In the autumn of 1932, when the menace of Hitlerism assumed tangible form, the German Socialists made an attempt to come to terms with the German Communists. "We decided to negotiate, however, not with the German Communists but with their directing center, Moscow," Friedrich Stampfer, one of the leaders of German Social-Democrats, now in America, told the writer. "An acquaintance of mine, who was also close to Leo Khinchuk, the Soviet Ambassador in Berlin, asked him to give me an interview. After a long wait, due probably to the fact that the matter was first referred to Moscow, I was at last received by Khinchuk. He began by recalling the days when the German Social-Democrats gave support both to the Bolsheviks and to the Mensheviks (Khinchuk was a former Menshevik) in their struggle against the Czarist Government. Then, after describing the political situation in Germany, I put the question: Would it be possible to expect the coöperation of Communism in the struggle against National Socialism? Khinchuk promised to do his best and to remain in touch

The year 1933 is a period which, more than any other, Communism would like to see erased from the pages of its history. The new German Government constantly intensified its persecution of Communists, using the cruelest of measures against them. But on April 1, 1933, the Communist International stated: "The establishment of an open Fascist dictatorship . . . accelerates the rate of Germany's development toward proletarian revolution."

Eight months later a conference in Moscow again went on record to the effect that "a revolutionary crisis and the indignation of the masses against the domination of capital are growing in Germany." Finally, on December 31, 1933, the official review *Bolshevik* (No. 24) gave what may be regarded as a classic statement of the hope for a German revolution:

In Germany the proletarian revolution is nearer to realization than in any other country; and victory of the proletariat in Germany means victory of proletarian revolution throughout Europe, since capitalist Europe cannot exist if it loses its heart. . . . *He who does not understand the German question does not understand the path of the development of proletarian revolution in Europe.*

"There will never be a return to Weimar (i.e., to democracy)" [9] it was stated as late as November, 1933.

"We are fighting for a Soviet Germany. We will conclude a fraternal alliance with the U.S.S.R., arm all the toilers, and create a mighty revolutionary Red Army," proclaimed Wilhelm Pieck, the German Communist leader, in Moscow in December, 1933.

Even in 1934 Nazism was so little understood in Moscow that a spread of mass defeatism in Germany was expected. "The desire to see its government defeated in the coming war, defeatism, is growing in fascist countries. Growing too is the readiness of the masses to make any sacrifices in order

---

with me. Subsequently I received several visits from the Attaché of the Embassy, Vinogradov, and we discussed the details of a common fight against Nazism. However, in January, 1933, Vinogradov made his last visit in order to declare that, unfortunately, further negotiations were useless. 'Moscow,' he said, 'is convinced that the road to Soviet Germany leads through Hitler.'

"A few days later, on January 30, 1933, Hitler became Reichs-Chancellor."

9. Resolution of the Plenary Meeting, Moscow, November 28, 1933.

to overthrow the hated oppression of Nazism and the military." [10]

The absurdity of these views was bound to make itself apparent soon. The German Communist party was already defeated, was corroded within by *agents provocateurs,* thousands of its members were being tortured in concentration camps, while many had been killed. Who could be so blind as to believe seriously that this was the process of "formation of a revolutionary army for the decisive class battles"?

After 1934 a new orientation began and with it an inevitable disorientation. One more year went by, and the errors were admitted publicly. "An underestimation of the fascist menace" was acknowledged as a serious error of past years. Also admitted, if belatedly, was the error of the traditional Moscow view that "the Bruening government" (i.e., the liberal regime) "was a government of fascist dictatorship." An acknowledged error, too, was the hope that "the masses would soon turn their backs on Hitler," as well as the general view that "it is not fitting for the Communists to defend the remnants of bourgeois democracy." [11]

With the elimination of Germany from the scheme of revolution, the house of cards was about to collapse. An attempt was made to seek salvation in the so-called "people's fronts." But the new weapon was weak, half-hearted, insincere, and unconvincing. Everybody saw it only as a new maneuver, a tactical detour.

As a country of revolutionary hopes Germany was receding into the background. But she was coming more and more to the fore as a country of armed aggression. Again Soviet Russia's attention was centered on Germany, but this time for different reasons. About 1936 clear-cut plans were abandoned and discussion of the "geography" and routes of revolution came to an end.

For a time the attention of Russian Communism was drawn in another direction, Spain. From the summer of 1936 to the beginning of 1939 the Spanish Civil War, accompanied by a rapid growth of local Communism, seemed to open some prospects—the possibility, in the event of victory, of a Soviet

---

10. *Communist International,* 1934, No. 3, p. 9.
11. Report of the Executive Committee of the Communist International, July 26, 1935.

Government in a large country of the European West. But these hopes were weak and showed less of the enthusiasm which at one time burned so fiercely in Moscow when it was anticipating the German revolution. The importance to Soviet Russia of the Spanish Civil War lay not so much in the sphere of Communist revolution as in the field of actual foreign policy. It represented the first armed collision with Germany and so raised a multitude of questions regarding the concrete policy to be followed toward Germany.

Then came two years of European war marked by Soviet neutrality, followed by the war on the plains of Russia. New forces came into play, and what appeared impossible yesterday seemed real for tomorrow.

The question of a revolution in Germany again became a practical problem of the day, but this time it assumed a new form.

3. "WHEN THIEVES FALL OUT." BASIC CONCEPTS OF SOVIET FOREIGN POLICY

It has been shown how important a role was to be played by Germany in the world march of Communism, according to Soviet plans. Germany's place in the foreign policy of the Soviet state is the next subject to demand our attention. The distinction between world Communist aims and everyday Soviet policy is however wholly arbitrary, for the two are in fact united. The distinction has been made here merely for purposes of exposition.

In the very first year of the Soviet regime Germany had already assumed a distinct place of her own in the Soviet scheme. The Soviet Government's proposal of a general peace made to all the warring nations (November 21, 1917) was favorably received by Germany but unfavorably by the Allies. The separate peace negotiations between Soviet Russia and the German coalition which followed, and the actual termination of hostilities, were of tremendous help to Germany.

The situation at that stage was so paradoxical that it gave rise to talk about "the Russian riddle"—the first time this phrase was used. Since then the phrase has been constantly applied to Soviet foreign policy, culminating in Churchill's reference during the present war to "a riddle wrapped in a mystery." But for the first time this bewilderment was expressed by an anonymous German socialist, an admirer of Lenin and an enemy of his own Kaiser, who feared a German victory more than anything in the world. This German wrote, in January, 1918, "The behavior of the Bolsheviks, their readiness to make peace with Germany, is a psychological riddle." [12]

The peace negotiations in January, 1918, proved futile. Trotsky deliberately protracted the negotiations when it became clear that Germany's demands were of a sweeping nature. At that point Lenin reacted as the Soviet Government has reacted in similar circumstances ever since—having found himself in the power of Germany. As soon as Trotsky declined to sign the "annexationist peace treaty," Germany

---

12. Quoted by Lenin from *Novaya Zhizn*, January 24, 1918 (*Works*, **XX**, 201).

resumed, on February 18, 1918, its military offensive and occupied Dvinsk. Soviet troops were unable to offer serious resistance. Lenin insisted on acceptance of the German demands. However, no one knew how far Germany intended to advance. Meanwhile, Britain, France, and the United States, through their representatives, reluctantly offered help to Lenin and Trotsky on condition that Russia resume resistance against Germany. Lenin preferred peace with Germany, but if war could not be avoided, he was ready to accept the offers. Later, he himself described the agreement which he had made with the French representative, Count de Lubersac: "We shook each other's hand, I and the French monarchist, aware that each one of us would readily hang his partner. But our interests coincided." To this Lenin added words which have become the gospel of the entire Soviet period:

"Against the advance of the predatory Germans we utilized the equally predatory counterinterests of other imperialists. We resorted to maneuvering, dodging, falling back, which are obligatory in all wars, while waiting for the moment when the international revolution finally ripens." [13]

At about the same time Lenin despatched Lev Kamenev on a "secret mission" to London—to get English support against Germany, and also against the Japanese threat to the Russian Far East. Kamenev's trip proved a complete fiasco, the English having turned a deaf ear to all his proposals.

Thus did Soviet tactics shape themselves in the early months of the Soviet regime, expressing themselves, on the one hand, in negotiations with Germany and in concessions to her, and on the other in negotiations with Britain and France with the object of obtaining aid against Germany. This "maneuvering and dodging" Lenin regarded as the cleverest weapon of his international policy.

This policy was by no means generally accepted even among those who stood closest to Lenin at that time. It appeared to violate sacred principles: "We've broken off with the Entente because it wages a predatory war, and now we're again ready to make an alliance with it! The Entente stands for robbery and exploitation. After a hard struggle we managed to free ourselves from its iron embrace, and now we are

---

13. Lenin, *Works*, XXIII, 182.

again rushing into it!" One has to grasp this fanatical hatred of the Entente in order to realize the tremendous effect of Lenin's proposal to enter into military coöperation with it. It aroused not only the left Social Revolutionaries, who at the time had their members in the Soviet Government, and who refused to have anything to do with such a "treacherous and foul" act, but it brought forth a protest also from Lenin's most talented lieutenant, Nikolai Bukharin, who wrote in a formal statement: "I hereby announce my resignation from membership on the Central Committee and also as editor [of *Pravda*]." Of the eleven members of the Central Committee under Lenin, five went on record as opposed to negotiations with the Entente. Lenin, it appears, did not find it an easy task to train his disciples in his methods of realistic politics. He called them phrase-mongers and stigmatized their policy as "word-itch," citing the United States as an example to follow: "The North Americans, in their war of liberation against England at the end of the eighteenth century utilized the aid of her rivals, the Spanish and French states, colonial robbers as much as England herself." [14]

The separate peace with Germany was signed on March 3, 1918. The Allied governments recalled their embassies from Moscow and, early in May, British troops began to disembark in the port of Murmansk. This was the beginning of British intervention. Simultaneously, Germany opened her Embassy in Moscow, while continuing her occupation of the western provinces of Russia, the Ukraine, and the Baltic States. German troops were also in Finland, which had just seceded from Russia. In the eyes of the entire world, the great advantages gained by Germany were the objective consequences of Bolshevik policy.

Soon afterward, in the southern provinces, Cossacks under General Krasnov took up arms, and the "Volunteer Army" was started under Generals Alexeyev and Kornilov; they all had the support of the Entente. On the Volga, too, troops of the Entente (the Czechoslovak legions) were fighting the Red Army. The British continued to land troops in the north.

Faced with this situation, Lenin decided on action which contained the gist of the entire future policy of the Soviets, including their treaty with Hitler in 1939. Pressed by the

---

14. Lenin, "Concerning an Itch," *Pravda*, February 23, 1918.

White Armies and by popular uprisings, Lenin was able, with considerable difficulty, to restrain his adversaries. But the intervention of the Allies, with their armies, armaments, and navies, and their declared object of overthrowing his government, seemed too dangerous. In order to balance the forces of the Entente on Russian territory, Lenin turned to Germany. As will be shown later, the concept of balancing the forces of their opponents has been an *idée fixe* both with Lenin and with his successors, but never before or after did it find such clear expression as on this occasion.

On August 1, 1918, the People's Commissar Chicherin called on the German Ambassador in Moscow [15] and, speaking directly on behalf of Lenin, made him the following proposal: The Soviet Government, in view of the continuing British landings in the north, "would not object" to the contemplated German operations in that region. "An open military alliance with Germany," Chicherin stated, "was impossible in view of public opinion, but an actual working together is possible." The Soviet Government would withdraw its armies to the center of the country for the defense of Moscow, and the defense of Petrograd would be left to the Germans. The Germans would be allowed a corridor from the Karelian border to Murmansk for moving their troops, but they must agree not to enter the large cities. Regarding the hostilities in the south, Chicherin informed the German Ambassador that his government would drop its demand for a German withdrawal from Rostov and Taganrog if in consideration of this the Germans would "take action against the troops of General Alexeyev and would cease lending support to General Krasnov." "By this *démarche*," German Ambassador Helfferich concludes his story, "the Bolshevik Government asked for our military intervention on Russian territory." [16]

The agreement was embodied, in the form of an exchange of letters, in a secret rider to the Soviet-German Treaty

---

15. To avoid further attempts on the lives of German Ambassadors (Count Mirbach was assassinated in Moscow on July 6, 1918) the Soviet Government requested the new Ambassador not to leave his Embassy, and had its own Foreign Commissar call on him when necessary.

16. Karl Helfferich, *Der Weltkrieg*, III, 466–467. Louis Fischer was told of these negotiations by Chicherin (cf. Fischer, *Soviets in World Affairs*, I, 128–129).

signed on August 27, 1918. In this rider the German Government proposed to the Soviet Government that it would take action against uprisings and foreign intervention on Russian territory and promised its aid to that end. "The German Government expects that the Russian Government will take all possible measures in order to crush immediately the insurrection of General Alexeyev and of the Czechoslovaks. Germany, on her part, will adopt all measures at her disposal against General Alexeyev."

But the most important part of the secret rider concerned the operations against the British in the north of Russia. This part of the agreement was somewhat veiled. It stated:

The presence in the northern Russian regions of armed forces of the Allies represents a permanent and serious menace to the German troops stationed in Finland. Should the Russian action not reach the expected results Germany would find herself obliged to undertake this action. . . . The German Government expects that the Russian Government will not consider such action an unfriendly act and will not oppose it in any way whatever.

For its part, the Soviet Government, in a separate letter, confirmed its agreement on all points as well as its willingness to keep the entire treaty secret. This, probably, was the first secret agreement of Lenin, who a short time before had made public the secret agreements of the old Russian Government and who rejected in principle every form of secret diplomacy. Thus the matter was considered settled. German troops were expected to proceed to the north of Russia at any moment, when the whole project collapsed as Germany asked the Allies for an armistice and capitulated.

For a proper understanding of this policy of zigzagging and maneuvering, one must bear in mind that simultaneously with it the Lenin government was transforming its Berlin Embassy into a leading center of Communist activity in Germany, an effort directed against the very government whose military intervention in Russia Lenin was so anxious to secure.

Two days after the November armistice the Soviet Government denounced the "infamous" treaty that it had concluded with Germany in March. It might be thought that this greatly improved Russia's international position. But Lenin saw it differently. From his point of view, only a struggle between the two coalitions gave Russia a chance to survive. A victory for the Entente made the latter the master of the world and placed it in a position to throw all its forces against Russia. Nothing, in the opinion of Lenin, could be more dangerous than the unity and solidarity of the entire outside world.[17] Accordingly he was seriously alarmed at the sight of the German catastrophe.

By that time one of the most important principles of Soviet foreign policy, one which has remained fixed down to the present, had already reached its full development. It was similar to the British system of balance of power. Lenin regarded his Soviet state as a force external to the capitalist world and alien to the latter's internal conflicts—*tertius gaudens* when the imperialists are fighting each other and *tertius infelix* when they come to an agreement. Lenin, as did his successors, always saw himself, in matters of foreign politics, standing in front of a huge European scale. When the scales are more or less balanced, all is well. But when one scale begins to overbalance the other, the situation becomes tense. In that case, Russia must endeavor to increase the power of the weaker side.

This, of course, is precisely the theory of the balance of power. Great Britain held to it for several centuries—why should not Russia try it? In those days Lenin and his government were unable to see that Russia, in her geographical position, could not follow in Britain's footsteps.

A balance of power policy is of course a policy natural and common to all states. But only the insular and wealthy Britain was able to use it as the principal and strongest instrument in her European policy. Other countries, for whom isolation is fraught with greater dangers, supplement balance of power with other methods. Russia should be classed with these countries, since a system of alliances with other powers must be the most important part of her foreign policy. Nature had given the bear strength and weight; it gave the lion claws and the ability to spring. The failure that would result for Russia from the policy of a "third power" did not become apparent until many years later.

In one respect, however, Soviet policy deviated from the

---

17. "The Brest-Litovsk peace was a concession which strengthened us and broke up the forces of international imperialism." (Lenin, *Pravda*, August 28, 1921.)

classical system of balance of power. In cases when one country grows too powerful, Britain feels herself obliged to throw all of her own weight onto the scale of that country's opponents, since without such action the equilibrium cannot be restored. Situations in which the international scales achieve a state of equilibrium without outside help (as happened between France and Prussia in the second half of the nineteenth century) are exceptions and not the general rule. For the Soviet Government, "nonparticipation in coalitions of imperialist countries," and especially in coalition wars, was and still remains a firm principle which permits exceptions only in extreme emergencies. "Splendid isolation" as the basic idea of its entire foreign policy has become the rule, as will be shown more fully in subsequent pages.

After the defeat of Germany, Soviet Russia's only dangerous opponent was the victorious Entente. War against it was being waged both in Europe and in the Far East. In his search for a counterweight Lenin again turned to Germany. His revolutionary hopes were now interlaced with the prospect of reviving the German menace in Europe in order to compel France and England to abandon their military intervention against the Soviet state.

This was Lenin's plan and hope: A government with Communist orientation would be installed in Germany (this appeared possible at the beginning of 1919). This government would form an alliance with Soviet Russia, and the two allies would act jointly in foreign affairs without necessarily resorting to military action. It is important to note that Lenin regarded the existence of a Soviet government in Germany as an indispensable condition for a genuine German-Russian alliance.[18] But once such a government came into existence, "we Communists will facilitate and prepare such an alliance."

This question became so real and so serious that it was one of the subjects discussed at the Paris Peace Conference. Lloyd George, for instance, submitted a memorandum to the Peace Conference on March 25, 1919, in which he stated:

The greatest danger that I see in the present situation is that Germany may throw in her lot with Bolshevism and place her resources,

18. See, for example, Lenin's "Left-Wing Communism: An Infantile Disease," *Works*, XXV, 215–216.

her brains, her vast organizing power at the disposal of the revolutionary fanatics whose dream it is to conquer the world for Bolshevism by force of arms. This danger is no mere chimera. . . . If Germany goes over to the Spartacists it is inevitable that she should throw in her lot with the Russian Bolshevists. Once that happens all Eastern Europe will be swept into the orbit of the Bolshevik revolution, and within a year we may witness the spectacle of nearly three hundred million people organized into a vast red army under German instructors and German generals, equipped with German cannon and German machine guns and prepared for a renewal of the attack on Western Europe.[19]

At the same time, Lenin believed, further discord among the victors would drain their energy and distract their attention from Russia. He never ceased to examine the stars for evidence of a new series of wars. This gradually became another *idée fixe* which his successors inherited. "A war between England and France is inevitable," he prophesied with satisfaction on May 11, 1920; while in an outline of a pamphlet he was to write he listed (March, 1921) these potential conflicts:

The Entente versus Germany
America versus Japan (and England)
America versus Europe
The imperialist world versus Asia.[20]

Everywhere, at any moment, Lenin believed war could break out which would, of course, be to the advantage of the third power—Soviet Russia.

Hence, "our policy is to use disagreements among the imperialist powers to hinder their accord or, if possible, make it temporarily unattainable. This is the main line of our policy. . . . It made it necessary to sign an agreement with Bullitt,[21] for us a disadvantageous agreement, as to peace and an armistice." In this agreement America was offered tempting economic proposals the political object of which was later described by Lenin with complete candor:

---

19. Francesco S. Nitti, *Peaceless Europe*, pp. 95–96.
20. Lenin, *Works*, XXVI, 313.
21. William Bullitt was sent to Russia in February, 1919, to ascertain the terms on which the Soviet Government would be willing to conclude peace. He was handed Soviet proposals stating the readiness of the Soviet Government to conclude peace with the "White Governments" of Russia, as well as containing economic lures to the United States.

The interests of Japan are radically at variance with the interests of America. We naturally could not follow any other policy than one which aims at exploiting this difference between Japan and America in a manner that would set back the possibility of an agreement against us between Japan and America. We already have an instance of the fact that such an agreement is possible.

Because of this "we give America territory for economic utilization." [22] "At present we are unable to fight Japan," Lenin continued, ". . . We enlist the aid of American imperialism against Japanese imperialism."

At one of the meetings where Lenin expounded this view, he was asked: "Doesn't it follow that we are provoking a war between Japan and America?" "No," answered Lenin evasively ". . . but we have to hinder their coming to an agreement against us. . . . What saved us was that Japan did not wish to pull chestnuts out for America. . . . We would have been even safer if the imperialist powers had gone to war against each other. When two thieves fall out, honest people gain." [23]

"The basic rule," Lenin stated in the same speech, ". . . is to exploit the conflicting interests of the two capitalist states and systems. . . . We cannot live peacefully—either one side or the other will eventually win out. We have not forgotten that war will come back. . . . We cannot live in peace—memorial services will be sung either over the Soviet Republic or over world capitalism." But until this takes place, the principal rule is "to dodge and maneuver."

Stalin, who was beginning to gain prominence in those years, adopted the Lenin view of what the Soviet policy was to be, particularly in regard to Japan and Germany. Perhaps Stalin's main strength in the beginning was that he grasped the meaning of this policy better than his rivals. Thus, as early as 1921, he assailed Foreign Commissar Chicherin, when the latter failed to appreciate the importance of the internal conflicts of the capitalist world. "Chicherin," he said,

underestimates the internal conflicts of interests among the imperialist states (France, America, England, Japan, and so forth). Yet these conflicts exist and are the basis of the activity of the Foreign Com-

---

22. Lenin, *idem*, pp. 7–8.
23. Lenin, speech made on November 26, 1920. Made public for the first time in 1924. Cf. *Works*, XXV, 505.

missariat. . . . The meaning of the Foreign Commissariat's existence
consists in maneuvering among these conflicting interests.[24]

The idea took as strong a hold on Stalin as it did on Lenin.
Even in those early days Stalin never ceased to reiterate it.
"The object of the party," he wrote, for example, in *Pravda*,
August 28, 1921, "is to exploit all and any conflicting interests among the surrounding capitalist groups and governments with a view to the disintegration of capitalism."
Again in 1924 he said: "Contradictions, conflicts, and wars
among the bourgeois states hostile to the proletarian state
are the reserves of the revolution." [25]

But in the opinion of Lenin, as well as of the entire Communist party, the main conflict of interests was, even after
the defeat of the Central European Powers, between Britain
and France on one hand and Germany on the other. Germany
held the center of Moscow's attention.

From the point of view of immediate policy every step leading to a closer rapprochement between Germany and the victorious Allies was dangerous for Soviet Russia; conversely, a
deepening of disagreements and conflicts, a struggle between
them, removed the immediate menace. Since Germany was
weak and inclined to go far in yielding to France and Britain,
the Soviet Government, if it was to follow the principle described above, had to back Germany, encourage her, promise
her aid. On the other hand, to counteract the section of the
German press which saw Germany's salvation in a closer
agreement with the Entente, it had to picture the situation of
Germany under the Versailles Treaty in terms of complete
hopelessness. In this respect Soviet diplomacy successfully
complemented the revolutionary tenet, held also by German
Communists, which maintained that Germany's sole salvation was in an orientation toward Soviet Russia.

Germany moved closer to her "western orientation," collaboration with the Entente and the policy of *Erfüllung*
(fulfilment.). But the western orientation by no means

24. Stalin, speech at the Tenth Congress of the Russian Communist
Party, March 10, 1921.
25. Stalin, lecture delivered at Sverdlov University, April, 1924.
Cf. "Foundations of Leninism," 1939, p. 56.

involved a rupture with Moscow. On the contrary, German governments were invariably convinced that close ties with the eastern colossus added weight to any negotiations and bargaining by Germany with France and England. Coöperation with the Soviet Union became a fixed concept of German policy. The numerically strong Communist party of Germany, acting in accord with Moscow, maintained an implacably hostile attitude toward the various German Governments of the Weimar Republic, but in the sphere of international politics the situation was different.

All parties, from the Communists down to the Deutschnationale, favored the development of Soviet-German relations. Every step toward a settlement of disputes with France was instantly compensated by a demonstration in favor of Russia. Trade with Russia was encouraged, and large credits, with government guaranties, were granted the Soviets. During the period of industrial "concessions" inaugurated by Lenin, German capital, with the blessing of the Foreign Office, was ready to go to Russia with vast plans. Large numbers of German experts joined other foreigners in the rebuilding of Russian industries, while in the Russian war industries foreign aid was the monopoly of German officers and engineers. The first German military men to be used for this latter purpose arrived in Russia at the end of 1921, and the coöperation continued until the middle 'thirties. German plants supplied military aircraft, machinery, and so forth. Russia, in turn, gave Germany the right to use Russian territory for conducting military experiments and other operations which Germany could not, by the terms of the Versailles Treaty, conduct on her own territory.

Neither the German nor the Soviet Government considered their coöperation as a military alliance, since an alliance presumes, first, a far-reaching community of major aims in world policy, and second, a readiness for joint, coördinated military action. As seen by the Soviet Government, the object of its close coöperation with Germany was to create a strong counterweight to the French and British mastery on the continent.

For this very reason the Soviets kept a close watch on fluctuations in Berlin's policy. Every agreement that Germany made with Britain and France was received as a blow—evidence of the "united front of world capital" and of "an encirclement of the Soviet Union." Every dispute brought satisfaction in Moscow, where at such moments there was a feeling that the Foreign Offices in London and Paris, absorbed by the German problem, were not considering any aggression upon the Soviets.

Germany understood and appreciated this situation. Before international forums, such as the League of Nations, she urged that Russia be invited to coöperate. In a Balkan conflict she joined Russia in supporting Turkey against Greece. During the Soviet conflict with Chiang Kai-shek, Germany loyally assumed the role of a representative of the Soviets. For every important agreement she made with the West Germany made amends by a new agreement with Russia.

This Soviet-German policy matured in the early years of the Soviet regime. To the outside world, however, it was for the first time fully revealed in the Treaty of Rapallo, concluded on April 16, 1922. At that time a great international conference was being held in Genoa, where the main subject of discussion was the normalization of relations with Soviet Russia. After four and a half years of the new regime and a year after the inauguration of the N.E.P., there were many persons, particularly in England, who were inclined (as is the case today) to exaggerate to a high degree the "evolution" of Russian Communism and its willingness to come to terms with capitalism. They drew arguments to support this view from the general collapse of Russian economy, the terrible famine on the Volga, and similar facts, and they were convinced that the time had arrived when the Soviet Government would regularize its relations with the Great Powers and would, among other things, recognize the Treaty of Versailles. For their part, these powers were ready to grant Russia a large loan on specific guaranties. Finally, the prospect was held out that Russia would in that case be able to demand her share of German reparations (decreed by Article 116, Treaty of Versailles). Thus, while bringing Russia closer to the Entente, this settlement would have driven a wedge between her and Germany.

The Soviet Government, however, had no intention of following the course laid out for it. The evolution of Communism toward capitalism which was supposed to be taking place actually was proceeding on an insignificant scale. Recognition of Versailles was not to be thought of.

Five days after the conference opened, when it was adjourned for the Easter holiday, the Soviet delegation met the German delegation in neighboring Rapallo and signed an agreement in which Germany made highly important concessions to Russia. Among these were: renunciation of claims to compensation for losses suffered through nationalization of property in Russia (to the extent that Russia did not satisfy similar claims of other states); resumption of normal diplomatic relations; the most-favored-nation position in German-Soviet trade. For her part, Russia renounced her claims on Germany arising from former German occupation of Russian territories.

A stable system of relations was thus set up between the two countries. It suffered few changes in subsequent years during which the situation in Europe underwent important transformations.

After 1923 Germany found means for a rapprochement with Britain and France. A series of agreements eased the terms of the peace treaty for her and each such agreement gave rise to alarm in Moscow. This alarm was unwarranted. Germany had no intention of breaking the ties which bound her to Russia. She permitted herself action against the Soviet Union only on a few rare occasions, and each time this was quickly followed by action in the opposite direction.

On October 16, 1925, Germany, Britain, France, and Italy signed the Treaty of Locarno which was hailed as the final settlement of the tense postwar situation. But four days before that she signed a new trade agreement with Russia which the Soviet press christened the Anti-Locarno Treaty. Germany's entry into the League of Nations on September 10, 1926, was another step in her policy of reconciliation with the Entente. But on April 24, 1926, a treaty was signed between Soviet Russia and Germany committing the contracting parties to neutrality in the event of one of them being attacked by a third power: in this case the Soviet Government was assuring itself of German neutrality in event of a war with Poland or, more remotely, with Britain. The Communist International, in its thesis of May 29, 1927, noted with triumph that Germany would remain neutral in a war between Britain and Soviet Russia. "This neutrality is dictated by the position of German imperialism."

Similarly, upon entering the League of Nations, Germany, in a special communication, confirmed that she would "energetically oppose in the League of Nations the tendencies directed against the U.S.S.R." and, among other things, would not participate in the sanctions provided in Article 16. After joining the League, Germany insisted on the inclusion of Russia in the disarmament committee and, three years later, when Briand introduced his project for a European Federation composed of the members of the League of Nations (which would have ruled out Russia), Germany succeeded in inducing the League to invite Russia to participate in the preparatory work.

Reporting to the Central Executive Committee on December 10, 1928, Litvinov pointed out that, unlike some other countries, "Germany and Italy never complained about interference of the Soviet Union in their internal affairs." In his review of the international situation Litvinov noted unsatisfactory relations with Britain and France, satisfactory relations with the United States, and good relations with Germany and Italy:

Efforts to destroy these relations [i.e., with Germany] are directed by the states which have been unwilling or unable to establish similar relations with us. . . . But the forces directed at a severance of Germany from the Soviet Union can offer her as compensation only assurances and promises execution of which is incompatible either with their general policies or with the system of the Treaty of Versailles.

This pattern of Soviet-German relations remained unchanged even after 1929, when the forces of Hitlerism began to make rapid advances. Germany continued to hold her exceptional place in the foreign policy of Soviet Russia and vice versa. Speaking on December 4, 1929, Litvinov noted

the unchangeable and steady character of the foreign policy of the Soviet Union, its nonparticipation in the political groupings and combinations of some states against others. . . . We watch with sympathy the efforts of Germany to free herself from the fetters which bind her by dint of the Treaty of Versailles. We would warmly welcome the results of these efforts . . . but, of course, only in those cases where the adjustment of relations does not involve Germany in anti-

Soviet combinations. . . . Germany holds the first place in our economic relations with the west.

To be sure, the Soviet press, during that period, noted certain instances of deviation in German policy in a pro-British and anti-Soviet direction, as, for example, the action of a group of German banks in joining the international association of Russian creditors, and the creation of "the Russian committee of German industry," organized to eliminate competition in obtaining Russian orders. Despite these minor disturbances, "the agreements binding the U.S.S.R. and Germany have so solid a character that our economic and cultural ties with Germany continue to progress." [26]

Emil Ludwig's interview with Stalin on December 13, 1931, belongs to the same period. Ludwig remarked to Stalin that everywhere in Russia he observed "an extraordinary respect for everything American, even a worship of everything American." "Is this correct?" Ludwig asked. "You exaggerate," Stalin replied, "we have no special respect for everything American. . . . If one is to speak about our sympathies for any nation or, to be more correct, for the majority of any nation, one would, of course, speak of our sympathies for the Germans. There can be no comparison between these sympathies and our feelings for the Americans."

To conclude this survey reference should be made to the important declaration by Litvinov on July 25, 1930. He had just been appointed People's Commissar for Foreign Affairs and took the occasion to make a formal declaration concerning the principles of the foreign policy of the Soviet Union. His statement had no doubt been previously approved by Stalin and is, therefore, of especial interest. It contains the following points:

1. "Contradictions existing inside the capitalist world act as an obstacle to the formation of a uniform attitude toward the Soviet Union and hinder the working out of uniform methods of struggle against it."

This is the old Lenin thesis which was discussed above.

2. "The victor states conduct a most aggressive and hostile policy toward the Soviet Union, whereby there has been

---

26. E.G., *The Peace Policy of the Soviets:* Afterword to Litvinov's speech.

created a community of interests between the Soviet Union and the states which suffered in the war."

This point ensures collaboration with Germany.

3. "While not striving to participate in the groupings of some powers against others, we will yet sincerely strive to establish equal relations with all states which will desire them."

This point provides for the policy of a "third power."

4. "We will watch with special attention the policies of the near and neighbor countries in which the aggressive and chauvinist movement has lately noticeably grown."

This point refers to Nazism in Germany (and to its native counterpart in Japan) and as far as stated lacks concrete form. Its elaboration into a system of policy became the task of subsequent years.

4. BRITAIN IN SOVIET POLICY

On the whole, during the first fifteen or sixteen years of its existence, the Soviet Union's relations with Germany were maintained on a friendly level, only rarely disturbed by diplomatic complications. The opposite is true of Soviet relations with Britain. From 1918 down to 1934 these relations were almost uniformly unfriendly, the tension relaxing only on rare occasions to give place to brief attempts at friendliness. As will be shown later, Soviet-German relations between 1934 and 1938 assumed increasingly the character of a conflict, with Moscow constantly stressing its desire for peaceful coexistence. During the same years, Soviet relations with Britain, while improving, were still far from friendly, and not until 1939 was an attempt made to bring the two powers, together with France and Poland, into a single military bloc.

The causes which determined this course of Soviet-British relations lay both in the ideologies and in practical politics.

In the eyes of the ruling circles of Soviet Russia, the British Empire was the purest embodiment of capitalism and imperialism. It stood for centuries of industrial progress accompanied, until the second half of the nineteenth century, by extremely poor living conditions for the workers; for tremendous wealth amassed by fair means or foul; for a superrefined, hereditary aristocracy; for huge conquests and grabs in foreign policy; for oppression of Ireland and India; for the cynicism of the Boer War. All this made Britain not merely one of many capitalist states but the principal one— ideological enemy No. 1. France and America, frequently hostile to Soviet Russia held but second place. Supercapitalism and the British Empire were almost synonymous. Destruction of the Empire or injury to its system represented more than the halfway mark in the struggle for the overthrow of world capitalism. Any hint of a conflict between Britain and France, or between Britain and America, assumed magnified importance and was watched closely and carefully in Moscow. In the Soviet view Britain, with her unavoidable wars, was the center of world politics. Her downfall was regarded as inevitable.

The British attitude toward Soviet Russia and her policies

varied, depending on whether they were viewed from the European or from the world aspect (the two viewpoints which represented the basic difference between the two leading parties in England). During the period in question (1919–39) Britain's goal in Europe was to stabilize and consolidate existing relations, while in the world at large she sought to maintain and fortify the position held by the Empire. The Conservative party gave first place to the grandeur of the world empire; the Labor party (including the remnants of the Liberal party) gave first place in the international scene to European prospects. Russia figured in both aspects—for the Labor party predominantly as a European state, for the Conservatives also as an element in the Central Asiatic and Far Eastern system.

From the standpoint of European policy an early agreement with Soviet Russia that would terminate the old disputes and give a fillip to British trade appeared both necessary and possible. Unlike France, Britain had no alliance with Poland or Rumania. The deep-rooted territorial conflicts of eastern Europe were of comparatively minor interest to her. Moreover, the activities of the Communist International did not present a serious menace to Great Britain, where the Communist party was politically insignificant.

From the angle of the Empire, the viewpoint of the Conservative party, the situation was seen in quite a different light. All the old Anglo-Russian antagonisms of the Czarist era came suddenly to life as early as 1919 and to these were added new ones. As far as Europe was concerned, the Soviet Government refrained from territorial expansion, seldom raised the question of its lost territories, and appeared to be reconciled to its modest frontiers. Not so in Asia. In that continent Russia was exceedingly active, though her activities took new forms. She began to extend her influence in Turkey, showed marked friendliness to Persia and Afghanistan, fomented rebellion in India, supported the anti-British movement in China. In their activities in Asia the old Russian Governments set specific and limited aims for each particular juncture. The Soviet Government acted differently. It seemed to be determined to set fire to the whole of Asia. For this reason "propaganda" played an utterly disproportionate role in the Anglo-Soviet conflicts, a role far greater than in Soviet relations with other states. And, of course, "propaganda" was sometimes merely a euphemism for anti-British policy in the East.

Taken together ideological and realistic motives gradually solidified into a firm system of Anglo-Soviet relations, as Moscow envisaged them.

Stalin wrote about England:

English capitalism always was, is, and will be the most vicious strangler of popular revolutions. . . . The English bourgeoisie has always stood in the front ranks of those who crushed liberating movements of mankind.

The Soviet people will never forget the violations, robberies, and military invasion which were inflicted on our country a few years ago by the grace of English capitalists.[27]

The Executive Committee of the Communist International stated in a resolution that "Great Britain heads world reaction."[28]

Expounding his theory, Stalin said, at a Congress of the Communist party:

There are being created two principal but polar centers of attraction . . . in the world: the Anglo-American center for the bourgeois governments and the Soviet Union for the workers of the west and the revolutionary east. England and America attract by their riches, from them one can obtain credits; the Soviet Union attracts by its revolutionary experience.[29]

On the other hand, Winston Churchill told the House of Commons: "I will not pretend that, if I had to choose between Communism and Nazism, I would choose Communism. I hope not to be called upon to survive in the world under a government of either of those dispensations."[30] On another occasion Churchill spoke of "the dark power of Moscow" where "we have a band of cosmopolitan conspirators gathered from the underworlds of the great cities of Europe and America in despotic possession of still great resources."[31]

---

27. Stalin, "On the Menace of War," *Pravda*, July 27, 1927.
28. Resolution of the Executive Committee of the Communist International, May 29, 1927.
29. Stalin, speech at the Fourteenth Congress of the Communist Party.
30. Speech on April 14, 1937.
31. House of Commons, November 25, 1925.

"We must remember," Churchill told the House of Commons on May 13, 1932,

that the great mass of Russia, with its enormous armies and with its schools of ardent students of chemical warfare, its poison gas, its tanks and all its appliances, looms up all along the Eastern frontier of Europe, and that the whole row of small states, Finland, Estonia, Latvia, Lithuania, Poland—not a small state, but for this purpose in the line —and Rumania are under the continued preoccupation of this gigantic and to them in many ways unfriendly Russian power.

Lord Birkenhead, another member of the British Government, surpassed even Churchill in the vehemence of his anti-Soviet sentiments: "A junta of assassins and plunderers" [32] he called the Bolshevik leaders. The British press was equally outspoken. In Moscow no words were spared in answering "the notorious Mr. Churchill," "the man who was responsible for the intervention," "the greatest hater of Soviet Russia."

A further illustration of the Moscow attitude toward Britain was the predictions which were constantly made in Moscow concerning the British world. High expectations were held not only of great shocks within the Empire but of heavy blows from outside: England at war with other powers was predicted in Moscow every year, with the United States often seen as the military opponent. Disagreements between the United States and Britain were magnified to the proportions of a conflict—a conflict to the proportions of bitter strife. War between them was regarded as inevitable, and Britain's defeat as certain.

The wish was father to the thought. For example, in 1930, at a time when the diplomatic relations of Soviet Russia and Britain were more or less normalized, Stalin, explaining the international situation and the conflicts of interests among different countries, spoke as follows:

"The principal among these conflicts of interests is that between the United States and England. After the principal conflict comes the secondary . . . between America and Japan, between Germany and France, between England and France, and so forth." [33]

On another occasion Stalin made this statement:

---

32. Lord Birkenhead, speech, June 22, 1925. Cf. *New York Times,* June 23, 1925.
33. Stalin, *Problems of Leninism* (1931), pp. 494–495.

All these questions lead to one basic problem, the problem of the struggle for world hegemony between England and the United States. . . . The star of England is setting, the star of America is rising. What is this basic conflict fraught with? It is fraught with war. When two giants collide with each other, when this globe is too small for them, they try to measure their strength, they try to solve the vexing question of world hegemony by means of war.[34]

Manuïlsky, a loyal follower of Stalin and one of the leaders of the Communist International, told the conference of the Communist party:

Two forces will meet each other face to face in the future world war. They are, on the one hand, the strongly developed American imperialism; on the other, the declining British imperialism. We can foresee that in such a conflict Great Britain will suffer the same fate that Germany did. . . . In that war the Pacific Ocean will be the battleground.[35]

Anglo-Soviet relations during the period ending in 1934 were marked by three serious attempts at reconciliation: the first in 1921, under the British Coalition Government headed by the Liberal Lloyd George, and the second and third in 1924 and 1929, when the Labor government was at the helm. Each time the attempt terminated in failure. Each of these failures was followed by the advent to power of a Conservative government, the failure to normalize Anglo-Soviet relations being a contributing factor in the change of government. The Conservative governments stayed in power much longer than did their opponents, and on the whole theirs was the rule in Great Britain during the period between the two wars. For the outside world the anti-British tendency in Moscow was associated in the mind of the public mainly with the names of Chicherin and Litvinov. On the British side Lord Curzon and Sir Austen Chamberlain were the characteristic exponents of British policy toward the Soviets.

The temperature curve of Anglo-Soviet relations begins below the freezing point. The first two or three years of the Soviet era saw Russia's withdrawal from the European war, her peace with Germany, the civil war, and military intervention on Russian territory by Britain, France, the United States, and Japan. Siding with these latter powers were sev-

34. Stalin, speech of July 13, 1928, *ibid.*, p. 335.
35. Manuïlsky, speech at the Fifteenth Conference of the Communist Party, p. 52.

eral minor states. "The invasion of fourteen powers" was thus the opening page in the history of Anglo-Soviet relations.

Among the invaders France, which was closely tied to Poland and Rumania, was the most consistent and obstinate, while the Lloyd George government of England never ceased vacillating. In Moscow, however, Britain was considered to be the leading spirit in "capitalism's offensive against the land of socialism," particularly since she was the first to land her forces on Russian territory in Europe.

Britain's vacillations in the Russian question and her frequent shifts in orientation sometimes expressed themselves in quite violent forms. In 1918 Lloyd George and Churchill took an active part in organizing and equipping the White Armies. But as soon as the war came to an end Lloyd George proposed that the Soviet Government be invited to the Paris Peace Conference, which proposal was firmly turned down by France. Britain's next step was to propose a conference with Soviet Russia, to be held on the Prinkipo Islands. When this failed to materialize Britain and France lost faith in military operations on Russian territory and withdrew their troops soon afterward (in the summer and fall of 1919). A little later, in the early part of 1920, although the civil war in Russia was still going on, the blockade of Russia was officially brought to an end. Finally, not without Britain's consent, the first *"de jure* recognition of the Soviet Government" took place—it came from Estonia.

All these steps, however, were accompanied by zigzagging, meanderings, waverings, and threatening gestures at Moscow. While seeking the establishment of peace in Europe, the British Government was aware of the growing pressure of Russia in the Near East and Central Asia. This pressure was growing markedly in the Caucasus, which after the defeat of Germany and Turkey fell within the British sphere of influence. It also continued in Persia after the withdrawal of the Russian troops, when the British occupied the country. In Afghanistan, too, following upon the advent to power of the young king Amanullah, close relations were established between Moscow and Kabul, buttressed by the undertaking of the Soviet Government to pay King Amanullah the same annual subvention which had been formerly paid by the British.

In Turkey a new popular movement was developing under the leadership of Kemal Pasha, and Soviet Russia lent it support, in opposition to the policy of Britain, whose troops at the time were occupying Constantinople. The entire East was thus shaken by the postwar tempests. But whereas Britain played a conservative role in these developments, Soviet Russia's role was frankly revolutionary.

In April, 1920, despite Britain's efforts to prevent it, Soviet troops succeeded in occupying Baku, and a few months later this great center of the Russian-Moslem world became the scene of the memorable Congress of the Peoples of the East. The proclaimed purpose of the Congress was to unify the backward nations oppressed by capitalism in their struggle for independence. Actually, the activities of the Congress were aimed against Britain, for in that part of the world no other power, not even France, played as important a role as she did. The entire Near East, from Persia to Ceylon, lay within the British sphere of influence. Hence, the speeches, slogans, and battle cries of this interesting Congress, though formally aimed at imperialism and capitalism in general, were actually directed against London. "Brothers!" shouted Zinoviev, concluding his fiery speech on September 1, 1920. "We call you to a holy war, first of all against British imperialism! . . . In the East there will be no more domination by the English oppressors, no more capitalist oppression of the workers of the East!" This outburst was met by the two thousand delegates with rapturous acclaim. Jumping from their seats and waving their weapons, they cried, "We swear!" [36]

The year 1921 witnessed British *de facto* recognition of Soviet Russia, by the conclusion of the first trade agreement between London and Moscow. The relations of the two countries seemed to have entered upon the path of normalization. But simultaneously with this agreement, signed on March 16, 1921, Moscow signed other agreements pointed essentially against London. In the course of three weeks the Kremlin signed agreements with Iran (February 26, 1921), Afghanistan (February 28, 1921), and Turkey (March 16, 1921). This explains the demands made by the British Government simultaneously with its signature of the Anglo-Soviet trade

36. *Proceedings of the Congress of the Peoples of the East*, p. 48.

agreement. In a letter of the same date as the agreement Sir Robert Horne, President of the Board of Trade, listed the various anti-British acts, some of a military nature, committed by representatives of the Soviet Government in the East, and demanded that such activities be immediately discontinued. He openly mentioned India as the main point of contention, saying that, according to his information, the principal aim of Soviet policy was the overthrow of British rule in India, and that the British Government was long aware of the intrigues conducted to this end by various means and in various directions by the Soviet Government.[37] He went on to list numerous persons, especially natives of India and Afghanistan, who were enlisted by the Soviet Government for anti-British activities. The letter also noted the special anti-British function of the Soviet representative at Kabul, Jacob Suritz, the transport of arms to the Indian border, the opening of Soviet consulates along the frontiers of India, and similar anti-British acts. In his reply Chicherin pleaded with the British to let bygones be bygones and promised that such things would not happen again.

The two parties were no nearer to genuinely normal relations, however, and new conflicts developed. Hardly two months later, in June, 1921, British authorities in Constantinople arrested the Soviet representatives in that city. There followed a lengthy note from Lord Curzon, who accused the Soviet Government, its leading representatives, and the Third International of continuing systematic anti-British activities. The note cited numerous secret documents and statements (the Soviet Government declared them to be spurious), including a speech by Stalin in which the Soviet aim was defined as undermining the prestige of England and France in the East. "Propaganda in India," it was stated, "was the main object of the activity" of the Eastern Secretariat of the Third International, while "Turkey was the most realistic threat to the power of Europe in general and of the Entente in particular." Lord Curzon's note concluded with the highly threatening statement that "His Majesty's Government finds itself compelled to demand conclusive guaranties that the Soviet Government will put an end to this activity." In his

---

37. People's Commissariat of Foreign Affairs, *Anglo-Soviet Relations*, 1921-27.

reply Litvinov declared that "the Eastern Section of the Third International" had long since been dissolved, that Stalin had no connection with the Third International, and that several other facts listed by Lord Curzon were equally incorrect.

Thus, having shown some improvement, Anglo-Soviet relations after a few months again began to deteriorate. Moreover, the position of the Conservatives in England was growing stronger, and when, in October, 1922, Lloyd George resigned and was succeeded by Bonar Law and later by Baldwin, relations with the Soviet Government assumed a distinctly chilly character.

The Lausanne conference in the summer of 1923, at which a treaty was signed between the Allies and Turkey, struck a balance in the long succession of conflicts in the Near East. While Britain, differing in this respect from France, continued her anti-Turkish policy even after World War I, Soviet Russia sought an alliance with Turkey and backed her claims concerning the Dardanelles and the Bosporus. Britain strove to demilitarize the straits. Opposing this, Turkey, with the support of Moscow, demanded unrestricted control over the entrance to the Black Sea. The treaty, signed after a long struggle by the Allies and Turkey, was never ratified by the Soviet Union.

Preceding the conference by a few months was another diplomatic conflict that developed between the British and the Soviet Governments in connection with the sentencing to death in Russia of a Catholic priest, Mgr. Butkevich. "The execution of the sentence cannot fail to produce throughout the civilized world a feeling of horror and indignation," said the note of March 30, 1923, submitted by the British representative in Moscow to the Soviet Government, making "an earnest and final appeal for a stay of execution." The answering Soviet note voiced indignation at British interference in the internal affairs of Russia in language so sharp that the Foreign Office refused to accept it. Mgr. Butkevich was duly executed.

In connection with this conflict, the British Government delivered the famous "Curzon ultimatum," which has since become historic. In his long note, dated May 2, 1923, the British Foreign Secretary returned to the question of Persia,

Afghanistan, and India and the activities of the Third International; the treatment of British subjects in Russia; and,
lastly, the incident of the Soviet notes concerning the Butkevich case. Concluding his note, Lord Curzon made three categorical demands which were to be complied with within ten
days. They listed termination of anti-British propaganda,
payment of indemnities to certain British citizens for the
personal hardships and property losses they had suffered,
and withdrawal of the Soviet notes concerning the Butkevich
case. If the Soviet Government should fail to comply with
these demands within ten days, the note concluded, "His
Majesty's Government will consider themselves immediately
free of the obligations" of the Anglo-Soviet Trade Agreement. The threat amounted to a breach of diplomatic relations and probably involved even more dramatic consequences.

The note caused great alarm in Moscow, where it was interpreted as possibly the opening shot in new hostilities
which, despite the sharp tone of the Soviet press, the government was anxious to avoid. At that time a struggle was developing between the moderate Krassin and the radical
Litvinov backed by Stalin and the majority of the party.
Krassin, the forerunner of the future "rightist opposition,"
desired the establishment of normal relations with Britain,
regarded the activities of the Communist International as
harmful, and attached great importance to the development
of Soviet-British trade. His opponents regarded trade with
Britain and diplomatic activity in general only as a means to
the achievement of far-reaching political ends, beginning
with universal recognition of the Soviet Government. In the
eyes of this ruling group in Moscow it was out of the question
that the Soviet Government should cease to support "the
colonial and exploited peoples of the East." The granting of
Soviet concessions to foreign capitalists, among them English capitalists, was more in the nature of a maneuver in
foreign policy.[38] However, Lord Curzon's threat to break off
diplomatic relations had its effect. Moscow accepted in the
main the British demands, including the withdrawal of its

38. See, for instance, Lenin's reports on Concessions, November 20
and December 21, 1920; neither was published until after his death.
(Works, XV, XVI).

sharp notes in the Butkevich case, and the conflict was considered settled.

The Curzon ultimatum also had important consequences in London. The question of regularizing Anglo-Soviet relations again came to the forefront of political life in England, assuming one of the most prominent places in the campaign of the Labor party against the Baldwin government. By the end of 1923 the Ruhr conflict had been adjusted and a gradual normalization of Britain's relations with Germany had been achieved. There was a widespread feeling that the time had arrived when all international relations could be amicably settled and stabilized—a goal that had been eluding the politicians for the first five long years after the war. Everything could be straightened out, it was argued, if the pro-German policy were supplemented by a pro-Soviet policy. The British parliamentary elections of December, 1923, on the whole, underwrote this line of reasoning. The Conservatives lost their majority and their government resigned. A Labor government, entirely dependent on the support of the Liberals, came to power, and at once Premier MacDonald extended formal recognition to the Soviet Government.

This marked a great advance in Anglo-Soviet relations. Britain was turning her face toward Russia. She was making a second attempt to bring Russia within the comity of European nations.

For Moscow, too, this was a historical moment. It signified a durable peace with an empire which, in the Moscow view of world politics, had the power to make rain and fine weather and to prescribe either "encirclement of the Soviet Union" or a peaceful existence side by side with it. February 1, 1924, the day when R. M. Hodgson, the British representative in Moscow, informed the People's Commissar for Foreign Affairs, Chicherin, of the British recognition of the Soviet Government, was an important date in the history of Russian foreign policy.[39] On that occasion the Congress of Soviets adopted a solemn resolution breathing a spirit of friendship, in which it stated:

---

39. Its importance was not lessened by the action of Mussolini who, confident of the benefits it would bring him, extended Italian recognition of the Soviet government on February 7, one week after Britain had done so. Mussolini had vainly tried to anticipate Britain's action.

Coöperation of the peoples of Great Britain and the U.S.S.R. will unalterably remain one of the first concerns of the Union Soviet Government. . . . The Second Congress of Soviets of the U.S.S.R. extends its friendly brotherly hand to the English people and instructs the Soviet Government to take all the necessary steps with the English Government ensuing from the recognition of the Soviet Government.

In those days everybody in London was saying that the Soviet Government was no longer the orthodox Communist government of the period of the civil war; that it had already turned in the direction of capitalism; and that its policy followed definitely national and realistic lines. If the Soviet Government, it was said in London, did indeed adopt a national policy, then Anglo-Soviet friendship would endure for a long time, Moscow would not cultivate close coöperation with Berlin, nor aggravate the Near Eastern difficulties, and it would stop disturbing the peace of India. Moreover, the old troublesome questions regarding indemnification of British subjects for material losses in the Russian revolution would be certain to find a compromise solution.

These hopes were doomed to disappointment. Within a very short time new difficulties began to pile up, and the holiday mood of the first days of February was quickly dispelled.

The first Labor government in England was now being likened in Moscow to the Kerensky government in Russia, and was accordingly denounced for its "Menshevism." MacDonald became the embodiment of the hated Social-Democracy. At the same time he personified the same old British Empire and showed not the slightest intention of renouncing Britain's colonial possessions. A sharp charge was formulated against MacDonald in Moscow. The fight against the Labor government, Moscow said,

has become a fight for the preservation of mankind against mass extermination. Even in its relations with the Soviet Union it has demonstrated . . . the complete falsity of the assertion that it guards the interests of the working class. Our slogan is—liberation of the British workers rests on liberation of colonies.[40]

For his part, MacDonald was soon warning against "the monkey business of Russian diplomats," while English Conservatives were showing signs of growing opposition. Besides

---

40. Resolutions of the Fifth Congress of the Communist International, June–July, 1924.

political negotiations, economic ones, too, were initiated, involving such questions as settlement of British claims, the granting of a loan to Russia, and other controversial matters. The old claims, which played no part in Soviet-German relations, continued to poison the atmosphere in western Europe and America for a long time, with Soviet diplomacy displaying more obstinacy than flexibility in dealing with these matters.

Prolonged Anglo-Soviet negotiations were concluded on August 8, 1924, by the signing of an extensive preliminary agreement. The latter covered all spheres of Anglo-Soviet relations and claims but left open numerous points on which agreement had not been reached. It forbade each of the signatories to conduct political activities of any kind directed against the other contracting party.

By the time this agreement was signed disappointment in England was widespread. There was little doubt that the House of Commons would refuse to ratify the agreement, and the Russian question became a fatal one for the Labor government. Parliament was dissolved and a new election announced for October 29, 1924. Five days before the election the press published a sensational letter, allegedly written by Zinoviev to the English Communists, in which the head of the Communist International urged organization of Communist "cells" in the British Army and Navy. The Foreign Office, which communicated the letter to the press, made a strong protest in Moscow. The Soviet Government declared the letter a forgery, and MacDonald himself later admitted its spurious origin. But at the time of its publication it stunned the British public and had a powerful effect on the result of the parliamentary election. The Labor party was defeated and a Conservative government, in which Sir Austen Chamberlain was Foreign Secretary, came to power.

British relations with Soviet Russia returned to their former state. The agreements signed in August were not ratified or even laid before Parliament. The exchange of diplomatic notes regarding the Zinoviev letter yielded no results beyond contributing to the increased rancor of both sides.

On the continent the years 1924–29 were marked by rapid progress in economic reconstruction and political stabilization. Germany joined the League of Nations. Britain claimed a large measure of credit for salvaging and restoring German economy. Soviet-German relations during the same period, although fluctuating in degree of mutual warmth, nevertheless maintained a temperature considerably above the freezing point. In contrast to this progress, Anglo-Soviet relations deteriorated from year to year. As on previous occasions, the Conservative government showed more concern than did the Labor government over events affecting its farflung Empire—events in the non-European world—and in this field the period under review witnessed developments which were a source of increased friction between Britain and the Soviet Union.

For several years from 1925 on China and the anti-British activities in that country of Soviet Ambassador Karakhan held the center of interest.

On May 30, 1925, Shanghai was the scene of sanguinary clashes between the British police and crowds of demonstrating Chinese. Popular protests against police brutality soon developed into a great national movement which, in view of the dominant role of Britain in Chinese affairs, naturally assumed an anti-British character. Abolition of all capitulations and extraterritorial rights and withdrawal of British troops—no less—were among the demands. The material losses suffered by the British in China were very extensive, but their loss of political prestige was even greater.

Moscow was aflame with enthusiasm. The Soviet press was full of pro-Chinese and anti-imperialist, and especially anti-British, appeals. The movement in China was not of a Communist nature. Nevertheless Moscow decided (opposing the position taken by Trotsky) to give support to the bourgeois Kuomintang. The civil war in China, which dragged on for several years, led to a tense conflict between Britain and Soviet Russia in East Asia.

Another important event that gave rise to Anglo-Soviet clashes was the intervention of Russian Communism in the strike of the British coal miners. The lockout of the miners, declared on May 1, 1926, provoked a general strike which lasted a week. The lockout continued until November, when the miners gave up the struggle. During that period all Russia seethed with revolutionary appeals and contributed funds for strike relief of over a million dollars. This aid was represented to be the voluntary effort of Soviet workers on behalf of their British comrades. But since actions of this kind could not be taken in Russia without instructions from the Soviet authorities, the British Government protested. On June 10 Home Secretary Sir William Joynson-Hicks, speaking in the House of Commons, openly accused the Soviet Government of interfering in the internal affairs of Britain. The British Government published a *White Book* on Anglo-Soviet relations in which evidence was quoted in support of this charge. Meantime, a movement was gaining force among the members of the Conservative party for a complete rupture of relations with Soviet Russia. One of the leaders of this movement was Churchill, who said in one of his speeches: "We do not want the crocodile's egg from Moscow put upon our breakfast table." [41] "If the Russian Bolsheviks," he stated in another speech, "can pull down Great Britain and obliterate the British Empire as a force in the world, they are convinced the road will be clear for a general butchery followed by an universal tyranny. . . . What folly Lloyd George committed when he brought these Russian intriguers into our midst." [42]

This movement in England was growing rapidly, so that Litvinov was able to report to the Central Executive Committee on February 21, 1927, that "the anti-Soviet campaign in England, which never ceased, flared up once more." Indeed, two days later Sir Austen Chamberlain handed the Soviet representative a stern note which began: "The relations existing between His Majesty's Government and the Government of the U.S.S.R. continue notoriously to be of an unsatisfactory nature." It went on to say that the chief organ of the Communist party, the Politburo, "which is the real dominating authority in the Union," was particularly aggressive in its hostility toward the British Empire. Chamberlain cited Bukharin's promise to extend revolution from China to India, quoted from articles in the Soviet press, and concluded with the threat to break off diplomatic relations if changes were not made in Soviet policy. After police raided and searched the offices of "Arcos," the Soviet trade organization in London, Chamberlain, on May 27, 1927, notified the Soviet

41. *New York Times*, January 22, 1926.
42. *Idem*, June 20, 1926.

Government that Britain was breaking off diplomatic relations. In those years of European pacification, pacifist optimism, and world trade boom, this step of the British Government appeared extremely stern and perhaps more threatening than it was.

Moscow interpreted it as the beginning of the great international campaign against the Soviet Union. Speaking before the Moscow Soviet, Premier Rykov said that the British Government would now seek "allies who would be willing to attack our Union," and the Moscow Soviet passed a resolution in which it stated its conviction that "the toiling masses of the entire world were facing the menace of a new and still more terrible war." Governing circles were greatly alarmed. Those months saw the inception of the principle that the alarming international situation demanded the elimination of internal enemies. This time, the first occasion of the kind, there were no executions, but the deposed Trotsky was banished from Moscow to Turkestan, and Zinoviev expelled from the party.

The conflict, of course, never reached the stage of military hostilities, but its dark shadow extended over the whole of Europe. The French Government, though continuing diplomatic relations, on the whole followed in the footsteps of Britain, and its relations with Moscow became very strained. Poland followed suit. The United States ruled out all thought of a rapproachement with Russia. Everybody appeared to assume a menacing attitude. The sole exception among the bigger powers was Germany, whose Foreign Minister, Gustav Stresemann, declared to Chicherin that Germany would in any event remain neutral and would refuse to follow British counsels and wishes. It is possible that the position taken by Germany made common action against Moscow impossible at the time; in the eyes of Soviet leaders the situation in 1927–28 was conclusive proof of the correctness of their traditional policy: conflicts and disagreements in the capitalist camp safeguarded the Soviet Union.

This situation continued for nearly three years. Trade between Britain and Soviet Russia was steadily falling off. The Soviet Government pursued an active anti-British policy in Central Asia and as far as possible in the Far East. The agreements between the Soviet Union and Persia, and be-

tween Persia and Afghanistan, were concluded soon after the
Anglo-Soviet rupture (October–November, 1927), while the
visit of King Amanullah of Afghanistan to Moscow, which
caused a sensation at the time, served as a demonstration and
emphasis of a program, both directed against Britain: a traditional enemy of Britain who had attempted to wage a war
"for the liberation of India," King Amanullah arrived in
Moscow at the climax of the Anglo-Soviet conflict, having
traveled from India, where he referred to Mahatma Gandhi
as his "best friend." At the same time King Amanullah regarded himself as the leader of the Pan-Islamic movement.

British diplomacy also worked hard in Central Asia, gradually succeeding in strengthening its positions. Amanullah
suffered a crushing defeat in his own Afghanistan. In China
the Soviet influence so declined that from 1927 on relations
between the two governments grew rapidly more and more
hostile. In 1929 a military conflict arose in Manchuria, a conflict in which the British Government backed the Soviet opponents.

As in 1924, the period under discussion of British hostility
to Soviet Russia was terminated by the coming to power of the
Labor party. In June, 1929, Ramsay MacDonald again became
Prime Minister. This time, however, neither he nor his party
entertained the high hopes which had been placed on coöperation with the Soviet Union five years earlier. MacDonald
acted slowly, and not until four months later, in October,
1929, was a new agreement for resumption of normal diplomatic relations concluded. Everything now was very matter-
of-fact. Even Soviet orders, which had been expected to show
increases as the result of the new relations, failed to stir much
excitement. Nor did the Conservatives adopt a less negative
attitude. The House of Lords, where they predominated, reacted to MacDonald's step by a vote of 43 to 21 against resumption of diplomatic relations with the Soviet Union.

Moscow likewise indulged in no illusions, since the international tension showed no signs of abating. The Soviet press
continued to speak of "the ever-growing danger of war." "It
is no longer possible to say merely that the imperialists are
preparing a new attack on the U.S.S.R. They are about to
complete these preparations." [43] "We would be naïve and

---

43. *Communist International* (editorial), 1930, No. 9.

featherbrained," Litvinov stated, "if we believed that we have assured for ourselves external security."

The Labor government in Britain remained in power for about two years. It was succeeded by a coalition government under the premiership of MacDonald. During the four years of MacDonald's premiership (1929–33) the prevalent condition of Anglo-Soviet relations was a state of unstable equilibrium, of non-friendly, cold, diplomatic neutrality. It turned out that even the advent to power of the Labor party failed to effect a radical change in the situation.

It was during these years that a violent and threatening controversy broke out between London and Moscow on the question of religious freedom in Soviet Russia. Other governments as well as the Vatican joined in the controversy. The British Government even devoted a *White Book* to this question (August, 1930). Moscow's response was to declare the representations by other governments intervention in Russia's internal affairs, and to establish a war chest under the slogan "Our Reply to the Pope of Rome." At the end of 1930 a serious conflict developed in connection with Communist propaganda in India, and Foreign Secretary Arthur Henderson declared in the House of Commons (October 20, 1930) that the Soviet Government did not carry out the pledges exchanged in 1929. The Soviet Government naturally protested. The campaign against Soviet exports to Britain, on charges of "dumping" and "forced labor" (the latter charge regarding exports of timber) assumed considerable proportions. In the United States, Canada, France, Belgium, Holland, and Rumania, measures were taken, or were being considered, to check the flow of Soviet imports. The British Government publicly reminded Russia of unsettled British claims, which were estimated at more than 4 billion dollars.

The obverse side of the military alarm felt in Moscow was the political trials, at which the defendants admitted all charges and confessed their ties with foreign governments. Those years witnessed the sensational public trials of the Industrial party, the Group of Economists and Experts, the Social-Democratic party, and the Labor-Peasant party. In the first named of these trials, held in November, 1930, the prosecution, i.e., the Soviet Government, "placed on record," on the basis of preliminary investigation, the fact that France

and Britain set the year 1930 as the date for war on Russia
but for certain reasons were obliged to postpone it until 1931.
Statements accusing the British Government of taking part
in plots of this kind, which were put in the mouths of the
defendants, moved the British Foreign Secretary to utter a
protest both in the House of Commons and through the diplomatic representative in Moscow. Moscow's explanations
were declared to be unsatisfactory.[43a]

These trials as well as the press campaign against Britain
and other powers served as a preparatory step to the extensive building up of the Russian Army. Stalin stated in early
February, 1931, that "we cannot afford to slacken our pace or
relax; if we do so, we shall be beaten." Two weeks later an
appeal on behalf of the Red Army proclaimed: "War is inevitable with the capitalist powers which are feverishly preparing for an invasion of the U.S.S.R." By "capitalist
powers" was meant Britain, first and foremost.

At the Congress of Soviets in March, 1931, Molotov stated
that the return to power of the British Conservatives would
constitute the greatest danger to the U.S.S.R., and that
France was also extremely hostile. The following day the
Soviet press reported that a delegation of German industrial-
ists had arrived at Moscow to conduct negotiations for an
improvement of economic relations between Russia and Germany.

The May Day appeal in 1931 reiterated the accusation that
Britain and France were preparing to make war against the
Soviet Union, and on May 6 a protocol was signed with Germany extending the Russo-German treaty of neutrality for
another five years. At this time, too, the failure of the Anglo-
Soviet negotiations dealing with settlement of old claims was
announced in London, and a little later the work of the Anglo-
Soviet commission engaged in the study of this question was
suspended. Improvement could be found only in trade relations. To counteract the competition of Germany, which in
those years of acute world economic crisis continued to extend

---

43a. The chief defendant in the trial of the Industrial party was
Professor Leonid Ramzin, who was found guilty and sentenced to death.
The sentence was commuted to ten years' imprisonment. Thirteen
years later, on July 8, 1943, the "confessed traitor" was awarded for his
inventions a "Joseph Stalin Prize" of 150,000 rubles and the Order of
Lenin.

new credits to Moscow for purchase of German manufactures, the Board of Trade also began to guarantee export credits to British firms. On the other hand, the Imperial Conference at Ottawa adopted anti-Soviet decisions, and in carrying them out the British Government gave notice to Soviet Russia, in October, 1932, terminating the existing trade agreement. However, a new trade agreement was concluded soon afterward.

On the continent, tension in Soviet relations with France, Poland, and Rumania began to slacken in the middle of 1931. Negotiations were initiated for the conclusion of nonaggression pacts, and after protracted arguments treaties were signed between Soviet Russia and France and Poland. The Soviet press, which in 1929–30 saw the French Government as a great menace, ceased talking about France in the old belligerent tone. Equally changed was its tone now in speaking of Poland. But the treaties of 1932 (with France, Poland, Finland, Latvia, and Estonia) were not in any way directed against Germany, and in general their significance was not very great. Soviet relations with Germany remained satisfactory, and new agreements and credits came thick and fast. Even when a Moscow student, Stern, fired upon the Counsellor of the German Embassy in Moscow, the official Soviet explanation accused Poland of trying to embitter Soviet-German relations by such means.

No marked improvement could be noted in Soviet relations with Britain in those years (1930–33). In the autumn of 1931 the Conservatives with Stanley Baldwin at their head entered the government of Ramsay MacDonald. A year later a serious diplomatic conflict broke out between London and Moscow. *Izvestiya* of November 13, 1932, published a report to the effect that the British Foreign Office had instructed its agents to furnish documents, real or forged, in order to implicate Stalin in the unemployment disturbances in England and in the unrest in India, and to establish a connection between the Soviet Government and the Communist International. The same issue of *Izvestiya* carried an editorial which, in connection with the British oil field concessions in Persia, accused Britain of striving to obstruct a rapprochement between Soviet Russia and the United States. Foreign Secretary Sir John Simon declared in the House of Commons that in addition to the inflammatory statements printed in *Izvestiya*, he had received information from the British Ambassador in Moscow that "instructions were recently issued to the British Communist Party to form nuclei in military units and similar organizations." In view of all this, he told the Soviet Ambassador that he demanded an apology from the Soviet Government for the language used in the *Izvestiya* report. The Soviet Government refused to apologize. Instead it declared that it accepted responsibility only for officially printed and circulated orders of the government, not for articles.

This terminated the conflict. But the incident showed how strained Anglo-Soviet relations were even at the very moment when the Japanese invasion of the Far East created an entirely new situation in the Orient as well as a new combination of powers; when the economic crisis drove Europe into bankruptcy and payments on foreign loans were stopped; and when Hitler was already donning his silk hat to make his first call on Hindenburg to receive the power of ruling Germany.

5. THE OLD IN THE NEW

The advent to power of the Nazis in 1933 at first changed nothing in Moscow's policy. Nazism was regarded as a phenomenon of German internal politics, similar to Fascism in Italy. It was pointed out in Moscow that relations with Italy remained normal despite Mussolini's repressive measures against his own Communists; that Italy had been one of the first countries to recognize the Soviet Government; and, finally, that Mussolini's Italy and Soviet Russia were linked by several treaties and by foreign trade. Why should not the same be possible with respect to Hitler's Germany, it was asked in Moscow. This view of Nazism as confining the Nazi revolution to inside Germany and as, on the whole, leaving intact existing international relations was widespread in those years and prevalent far beyond the confines of Russia.

In the beginning, Hitler's preoccupation with German home politics, dealt with in a methodical and thorough fashion, seemed to give reason for hope that Germany would follow "the Italian way." Hitler suppressed Communism and democracy in Germany, and waged war against the Jews, but, speaking in the Reichstag on March 22, 1933, he said, obviously for Russian ears: "The battle with Communism in Germany is our internal affair. . . . Our diplomatic connections with other powers are not affected thereby."

This was the very formula that Moscow desired. Subsequently, on May 5 of that year, Germany and the Soviet Union exchanged documents ratifying the agreement to extend the life of the Soviet-German treaties of 1926 and 1929, on which their collaboration had rested for many years. Everything, therefore, seemed to remain as before and to require no change. As for the persecution of German Communists, this was regarded not only as following the Italian pattern but even as a favorable symptom of the intensification of the class struggle—the last spasm of rage of the wounded beast of capitalism. It in no way affected diplomatic relations.

How far from reality Moscow was in its estimate of the Nazi regime is shown by the fact that it chose that particular moment to stage the sensational "trial of British engineers," employees of the British firm of Vickers, who were accused of sabotage and similar criminal activities. It was obvious from the start that the trial would damage Anglo-Soviet relations. But the Soviet Government did not believe that a new era had dawned in foreign relations and that a new policy was required.

The Vickers employees were arrested in March, 1933, and others having been arrested soon afterward, forty persons, both British and Soviet citizens, faced indictment. Prime Minister Baldwin spoke of the arrests in the House of Commons, while the British Ambassador in Moscow lodged a protest and departed from Russia. The guilt of the accused was not proved to the outside world, and the entire proceedings were in the nature of a stage trial. Anglo-Soviet trade negotiations then in progress were interrupted. The conclusion of the trial on April 19, with a verdict of guilty against the majority of the defendants, was followed by a Royal proclamation prohibiting importation of certain Russian goods, affecting about 80 per cent of normal Soviet imports into Britain. The Soviet Government retaliated in kind. Negotiations for the liberation and evacuation from Russia of the sentenced British engineers dragged on for two months, and only on July 1 were the British prisoners released, whereupon the embargoes were removed and the two governments resumed trade negotiations. During those two months, however, an international economic conference was held in London, and at that conference Germany came out, openly and cynically, against the Soviet Government. Reckoning on the growing rift in Anglo-Soviet relations, Hitler's representative, Hugenberg, submitted a sensational memorandum in which, reviving Hitler's old idea of a German-British alliance against Russia, he proposed a solution of the world economic crisis at the expense of Soviet territories.

The Soviet Government protested against the memorandum in Berlin, but it manifested no desire to change its attitude toward Germany and Britain. Such a change would have been tantamount to an overthrow of established policy—to acknowledging a confusion of orientation. This was naturally put off as long as possible.

Thus the old line of policy continued. When Moscow spoke of war danger, it pointed its finger first of all at Japan and next at "Japan's ally," Britain. Of Germany as the main source of war danger it did not venture to speak for a long time. In a long public report made on November 6, 1933, Litvinov singled out Japan as the principal menace to peace. Speaking in New York on November 24, 1933, he referred to the League of Nations, from which Germany had just withdrawn, saying that "Geneva is a dead body, and if no death certificate has been signed it is only because the doctors fear the knowledge that the heart has stopped beating." A month later (December 28, 1933) Molotov was saying that "the U.S.S.R. had no grounds for a change of policy toward Germany. . . . We want to have the best relations with Germany, as with other countries. Both the Soviet Union and Germany will derive nothing but good from such relations."

As to Britain, however, Molotov stated that "our efforts to maintain and develop relations with all big countries . . . have not yet, to our regret, been realized, or not fully realized in regard to one big power—Great Britain."

To the same period belong the resolutions of the Executive Committee of the Communist International, pointing to the enemies who menaced Soviet Russia on all sides—"the Japanese militarists, the German fascists, the English imperialists, the intrigues of Italian and Polish imperialism," but chief among the enemies were "the English imperialists in the role of *principal* organizers of war."

This was wholly in accord with the traditions and policies of the Soviet Government. In an anonymous editorial the official review *Bolshevik* wrote: "Our principal enemy in Europe during the intervention and ever since, has been English imperialism." [44]

During that period the star of Lazar Kaganovich was rising high. Kaganovich rated next to Stalin. A year after Hitler's advent to power, in a report at the Moscow Conference of the Communist party, on January 17, 1934, Kaganovich restated the principle of foreign policy formulated by Lenin and Stalin, in these words: "Our object is to exploit all con-

---

44. *Bolshevik*, 1933, No. 11. The editorial was written by Karl Radek. Its faith in the old predictions unshaken, as if nothing had happened to disprove them, Moscow continued to expect a war between Britain and the United States. "The basic fact in the imperialist camp is the Anglo-American conflict of interests," a resolution of the Communist International declared in 1935.

flicts of interests among capitalist countries." He went on to list these conflicts of interests: Britain versus the United States, Germany versus France, France versus Italy, Britain versus France, Italy versus Germany. His analysis concluded, he addressed himself to Germany:

"If the German Government wishes to establish relations with us similar to those which prevailed before the fascist regime, our government is ready to reciprocate."

At the same time Kaganovich said of England:

"Our relations with England continue to be constantly strained. The die-hards are striving to become the principal organizers of all intrigues, down to a war against us."

This speech by one of the most prominent Soviet leaders is significant for the precise reason that it left everything as it was before—in the matter both of relations with Germany and of relations with Britain.

A week after Kaganovich's report Stalin made a report at the Congress of the Communist party. He was cautious in discussing Germany's anti-Soviet policy. Was fascism to be blamed for that policy? No, he answered.

Fascism is not the cause of it, if only because, in Italy, for example, Fascism did not stand in the way of establishing the best relations between the U.S.S.R. and that country. Nor is the cause in the alleged change in our attitude to the Treaty of Versailles. The cause lies in the changed policy of Germany . . . resembling the policy of the German ex-Kaiser who at one time occupied the Ukraine and sent his troops marching on Leningrad, in the process turning the Baltic countries into a training ground for this campaign.

Meanwhile German policy was growing more and more hostile. The leaders of Nazi Germany attacked Soviet Russia with increasing frequency. Their tone, too, grew more vicious, their denunciations more vehement, their demands more sweeping. Germany was brandishing her sword.

In January, 1934, Hitler concluded his pact with Pilsudski and in April, 1934, Germany turned down Litvinov's proposal for a joint guarantee of the frontiers of the Baltic States. This was the opening shot in Germany's diplomatic offensive in which Hitler's argument asserting the existence of a menace to Germany from the east played the dominant role in subsequent years. To reassure Germany, Britain proposed an "eastern Locarno," a system of continental treaties, with the participation of Russia and Germany, which would also guarantee the borders of these two countries. This proposal, though accepted by Moscow, was rejected by Berlin, after negotiations lasting many months, on the alleged ground that Germany could not permit Soviet troops on her territory even if they were there to defend her.

In March, 1935, citing the militant speeches made at the Congress of Soviets, Hitler announced the resumption of German rearmament.

As a reaction to this, the Soviet Union concluded an alliance with France, and Soviet policy entered upon the path of "collective security," to prepare for which there had been several months of preliminary spade work. For the next three years, down to the Munich crisis, collective security was the official policy of the Soviet Government. The new policy stood for closer ties with the democracies against Germany; membership in the League of Nations; opposition to Italy in her aggressive attack on Abyssinia; struggle against Germany and Italy in Spain. At its basis lay the treaty with France signed May 2, 1935, later supplemented by a Soviet-Czecho-slovak treaty. At the same time, the Soviet Government advertised its adherence to democratic principles in its home policies and began the task of drawing up a new constitution, this again being largely for the benefit of the outside world. A coalition of anti-Nazi forces was thus in the process of formation, creating widespread confidence that the slightest attempt at aggression on the part of Germany would instantly set in motion the perfectly adjusted mechanism of international guarantees.

Many people to this day entertain serious misconceptions of the Soviet policy of that period (1935–38), and that policy is frequently completely misunderstood. It is represented as a radical break with the Soviet past, with the fifteen years of obsession over its role as the "third power," with the policy of collaboration with Germany and of antagonism toward the western powers. It is sometimes pictured even as a belated admission of past errors. Actually, the Kremlin policy of those years continued without the slightest break with its old principles, although outwardly it was dressed in a different style.

To be sure, it was a policy of an anti-German coalition in

which the voice of Moscow at times was even louder than the other voices. Moscow never tired of criticizing England and Russia's ally, France, for their tolerance toward Germany, their lenient attitude to her acts of aggression. For its part, after every such act, the Soviet Government proposed far-reaching measures of resistance, measures which at the time were too radical for Russia's partners. When German troops occupied the Rhineland, the Soviet Government notified the Foreign Office of its view of the situation: action must be taken immediately or it would be too late. When Germany intervened in Spain, the Soviet Government insisted on more active opposition instead of a policy of "nonintervention." When Hitler launched his Sudeten campaign, the Soviet Government demanded armed resistance on the part of France and Czechoslovakia, and promised its aid. The Soviet press never ceased accusing the great and the little powers of criminal tolerance of Fascism and Nazism. It seemed there was no power in the world more antagonistic to Hitlerism than Soviet Russia.

At the same time Moscow openly pursued a policy of a different kind. For example, on January 28, 1935, at the high tide of "collective security," and at the very moment when the Soviet Government was preparing the treaty of alliance with France, Molotov spoke as follows at the Seventh Congress of Soviets:

For our part we can say that we have never wished for anything other than the continuance of good relations with Germany. . . . Not racism, nor fascism is the obstacle—normal relations with Italy are objective proof of the possibility of developing collaboration between countries with completely opposed social systems.

As another year went by, filled with reports of German rearmament, Molotov appeared before a session of the Central Executive Committee on January 10, 1936, submitting his regular report in which, among other things, he said:

"I'll say frankly, the Soviet Government would like to establish better relations with Germany than those existing at present. . . . But realization of this policy rests not [only] with us but also with the Government of Germany. . . ."

Some two months later Molotov gave an interview to the editor of *Le Temps* (March 19, 1936):

The main trend among our people, the trend which determines the policy of the Soviet Government, considers an improvement in relations between Germany and the Soviet Union possible. . . . The participation of Germany in the League of Nations would be in the interest of peace and would be favorably regarded by us.

"Even of Hitler Germany?" asked the editor.

"Yes," replied Molotov, "even of Hitler Germany."

Alongside these open and public offers of conciliation, there was much sounding by the quiet means of diplomacy, of which only muffled reports reached the avid newspaper correspondents and the equally avid diplomats of other powers. In the beginning of 1937, for example, the *New York Times* noted that "there has been a diminution in editorial attacks against Germany in the Soviet press" [45]; simultaneously with this the Soviet Government replaced its Ambassador in Berlin, Jacob Suritz, a Jew, by Constantine Yurenev, an "Aryan." Diplomats of other countries in Moscow gave the alarm. The United States Ambassador to Berlin, William E. Dodd, wrote in his diary on April 10, 1937, that he had heard from Walter Duranty that secret negotiations were in progress.[46] According to other reports, the Soviet trade representative in Berlin, Kandelaki, played a role in these overtures. It is most probable that the stage of real negotiations was never reached and that the Moscow hints and advances produced no results. The German press declared that real negotiations were confined to economic matters.[47]

During the prewar period, therefore, there were two facets to Soviet policy: it stood for a coalition against Germany and urged active operations against her, and at the same time it was poised for an accord with Germany. It would be a mistake to assume that the two attitudes contradicted each other, or that they reflected a clever maneuver, a deception. They

---

45. *New York Times*, April 9, 1937.

46. "When I told him [the British Ambassador] of the three stories I had heard about German-Russian negotiations, he showed a good deal of concern. I told him I was not convinced, but that it seemed that something was on. I had the feeling he wanted to telegraph what I had said to Downing Street at once." *Ambassador Dodd's Diary, 1933–1938*, p. 398.

47. On occasions, however, when Berlin required that Moscow remain neutral, it found a different language. At the time of the German-Czech tension, in August, 1938, for instance, the German Ambassador deemed it necessary to remind Litvinov that Germany had preserved neutrality during the Soviet-Japanese conflict in the summer of that year.

merely represented two policies intended for different occasions.

One such occasion would have been possible German aggression in western or Central Europe against such countries as Czechoslovakia or France. The military forces that
would have opposed Germany from the west appeared then,
in the middle 'thirties, huge and invincible, particularly as
they were expected to include Britain as well. In those days,
Moscow, like the rest of the world, was convinced that the
forces of an Anglo-French bloc were superior to the forces
of Germany. It was accordingly believed that should Germany strike in the west, the invaded nations would be able to
resist without any great effort on the part of the Soviets.
The Soviet Government would either stay neutral or perform
its duties as an ally in more or less formal fashion. Indeed, at
the time of the Sudeten crisis, the Soviet Government was
ready to give some support to Czechoslovakia. But not for a
moment did it conceive of the possibility of a large-scale war
with Germany, which was not possible under the geographical conditions then in existence, and for which it believed
there was no special need. Soviet participation was to be
confined to such support of Czechoslovakia and France as
was then being given to Loyalist Spain, i.e., armaments, a
certain number of volunteers, and the powerful mechanism
of the secret police. The situation would provide a classic application of the old conception—a war waged largely between
groups of "imperialist powers," with the Soviet keeping its
powder dry.[48]

The other occasion for which the Soviet Government was
preparing itself was a possible German attack on Russia.
Only in the event of such an attack would it be necessary to

---

48. John T. Whitaker in *We Cannot Escape History* (p. 269) reports a conversation with Maxim Litvinov of December, 1937: "I
pointed out that Russia was the ally of Czechoslovakia and would be
obliged in that event [in case of a German invasion of Czechoslovakia]
to make a war against Germany. 'How do you square this obligation
with a policy of isolation by Russia, as you have just outlined it to me?'
I asked. Litvinov chuckled. 'Don't tell me about our treaty with Czechoslovakia,' he said. 'I drafted that treaty. Read the text again more
carefully and you will see that you are wrong. We are obliged to come
to the aid of the Czechs under the League of Nations' machinery and
then only if France has assumed her obligations.' I shrugged my shoul-
ders.—'Well?' I queried. 'Well, France won't fight. France is through,'
said Litvinov."

adhere to the system of collective security. The need of allies and of a second front would only on such an occasion become urgent, and the greater the number of allies and of fighting fronts the better off Soviet Russia would be. Hence the necessity of treaties specifying with utmost precision the obligations of the allies. The treaty with France fell far short of guaranteeing the Soviet the unconditional assistance desired by Moscow. The reservation in the treaty calling for assistance only to victims of aggression was especially dangerous. In order not to leave a legalistiç loophole for its allies, the Soviet Government made strenuous diplomatic efforts to broaden the definition of "an aggressor nation." Entry into the League of Nations, the complicated mechanics of treaty-making—everything was to serve the main purpose, the securing of allies for Soviet Russia. As far as Moscow was concerned, collective security was another name for the second front in the event of a German attack on Russia.

It would be futile to criticize Soviet policy from the point of view of morality. The only valid criticism that can be applied to it, as to all international policy, is whether it is purposeful, rational, useful for its country, and capable of realizing the political aims of its government. Such criticism the designs and actions of the Soviet Government in 1934–39 fail to withstand. The notion that it was possible to build a system of conductors which would draw German lightning to other countries—that it was possible for Russia to weather the storm under an umbrella of treaties—that it was improper to make hard-and-fast alliances with some Great Powers, especially with Britain, against others—all these false notions followed fatally from Moscow's basic concepts of foreign policy. France, which in relation to the German menace stood, by and large, in the same position as Russia, was ready to take up arms and did so when further delay promised a general defeat. The Soviet Government chose other ways. In historical perspective, even the Franco-Russian alliance of 1914 proved a more rational policy than the dual policy of isolation and lightning rods of 1935–1939.

In the matter of Soviet relations with Britain the old antagonism, though somewhat abated between 1935 and 1939, by no means disappeared entirely to give place to true collaboration. Britain actually directed her efforts to preserving the European status quo, while continuing to hope that once Hitler achieved equality in arming Germany and enhanced his prestige, Germany would rest satisfied. Britain refrained from a policy of pacts and obligations, playing, as formerly, on the balance of power. She would have been most satisfied with a world situation in which France and her allies (Poland, Czechoslovakia, and the Balkan States) would have balanced Germany, while Germany and Japan would have balanced Communist Russia. In this system of balances, Britain, while collaborating with France, would still have played the role of the third power which does not let itself be drawn too actively either to one side or the other. Soviet anti-British isolationism and British anti-Soviet policy of balance of power were thus supplementing each other.

During those years, while Moscow's relations with Paris and Prague took on an increasingly friendly character, Soviet sentiment toward Britain was decidedly cold. Evidence of this was the attacks in the Soviet press which frequently accused the British of "defending the interests of fascism." *Pravda*, for example, wrote: ". . . the line of British imperialism in the defense of interests of fascist Germany to the detriment of the cause of peace is being followed with unparalleled zeal." [49] In those years Moscow regarded it as certain that if Germany attacked Russia, Britain would remain neutral. The Congress of the Communist International which after repeated postponements met in Moscow in the summer of 1935, charged "capitalist governments" with encouraging Nazism. During the visit of Anthony Eden to Moscow Litvinov criticized, in the presence of his guest, the British policy of encouraging German rearmament. "No weapon has yet been invented," he said, "which could shoot in only one direction and which, turned in the other direction, would unavoidably miss fire." [50]

Nor were those years free of international conflicts, which broke out as if nothing had changed in Berlin. The holding of the Congress of the Communist International in Moscow gave rise to a British note protesting against the violation

49. *Pravda*, March 20, 1935.
50. Litvinov, speech at the reception to Eden on March 26, 1935.

of the Anglo-Soviet treaty which bound both countries to refrain from propaganda against the other party. Moscow left the protest unanswered. The most militant action was the diplomatic note of August 23, 1935, by the United States, which recorded the violation of the Litvinov agreements.

The most serious crisis in Soviet relations with Germany occurred in the second half of 1936. In July of that year General Franco's rebellion against the Spanish Government broke out in Spanish Morocco and developed into a civil war. Italy's participation in preparations for the rebellion was publicly established, and Germany's part was also considered open to no doubt. Moscow was convinced that war could not be localized in Spain, and that Europe and probably the whole world were on the brink of a great catastrophe. It believed that war with Germany might break out any day.

The most important consequence was Moscow's decision to exterminate all internal opposition. The opening of the series of famous Moscow trials, which began three weeks after Franco started his rebellion, was one of the symptoms of the near panic which swept Soviet ruling circles.

As week followed week relations with Germany grew more and more taut. The German press wrote about Russia in hysterical tones, and *Völkischer Beobachter* predicted a march into Europe "of the 12 million best-armed soldiers in the world." [51] Voroshilov made numerous militant speeches against the Nazis and Stalin telegraphed the Spanish Communists (October 17, 1936) promising help. Soon afterward Germany and Japan signed the Anti-Comintern Pact, and the Soviet Government began mass arrests of German citizens of whom one was sentenced to death. (He was reprieved when the German Government threatened to break off diplomatic relations). Hitler's speeches during the years of the Spanish Civil War rejected all possibility of coöperation with Soviet Russia and demanded her complete isolation by other powers. "Ever since I assumed power in the Reich," he stated on one occasion, "I have striven to establish the best possible relations with most states; only with one state we have not sought relations: Soviet Russia." [52]

---

51. *Völkischer Beobachter*, August 22, 1936.
52. Hitler, speech, February 20, 1938.

The high-water mark of Hitler's success in this policy was the Munich Conference (September, 1938), from which Soviet Russia was excluded and which German diplomacy later interpreted as granting Germany a free hand in eastern Europe. Isolation of Soviet Russia was a fact. Britain held to her old policy, which Moscow interpreted as a potential Anglo-German alliance against Russia. As a result, anti-British sentiments began to be voiced with increased force. In Munich, Molotov stated, "the Government of England and the Government of Germany won a victory in getting France to renounce support of Czechoslovakia." [53] At the same time George Dimitrov wrote: "In Britain the partners of German fascism are seeking ways to crush the voice of the opposition press and criticism . . . they calmly permit the sinking of British ships by the fascist interventionists [in Spain], they are encouraging the reactionary forces in other countries in every possible way." [54]

The relations of Britain and Russia showed no improvement down to the spring of 1939 when, after a new German blow at Czechoslovakia, Britain began negotiations with the Soviet Union with a view to formation of a wide "peace front," including also France and Poland.

By that time it had become increasingly clear that the British scheme of an equilibrium had run on the rocks, and that the furious aggressiveness of Germany could not be balanced by an opposing combination of powers. Changing her policy, Britain began to play a highly active part in the anti-German combination.

For Moscow, too, the policy of collective security reached an impasse in 1939. Like London, Moscow strove to play on the balance of other forces. It wished to see Hitler's forces balanced or even outweighed by the forces of France, Britain, and their allies, and the forces of Japan balanced by the forces of America, Britain, and China. London wanted to use Moscow as one of the weights on its scale. Moscow wanted to throw the British weight on its own scale. London would have preferred the position of the third power as an ideal one for itself. Moscow rated just as highly, if not higher, its own noninvolvement in conflicts. These were two schemes of for-

53. Molotov, speech, November 6, 1938.
54. G. Dimitrov, *After Munich*, 1938.

eign relations which could not be combined into one, as the Anglo-Soviet negotiations of 1939 actually proved. The British scheme triumphed with the conclusion of the Munich Pact (September, 1938), and Chamberlain seriously believed that he had achieved an equilibrium of forces, "peace in our time." The Soviet scheme triumphed with the conclusion of the Moscow pact with Hitler (August, 1939) and Stalin hoped that he had achieved his goal, "noninvolvement in imperialist rows." There was a difference, however, between Britain and Soviet Russia. When Hitler started the great war in 1939, Britain discarded her old system of isolation. The Soviet Union, whose isolationism was bound up with a whole political philosophy, continued to cling to it.

With the outbreak of the European war the situation seemed to have assumed the familiar old pattern: Soviet Russia returned to collaboration with Germany—the relationship she had maintained from 1918 to 1934 and which she had striven to restore afterward; while her relations with Britain once again became antagonistic, a condition characteristic of the entire Soviet era. "A strong Germany," Molotov stated, "is the necessary condition of a lasting peace in Europe." [55] At that moment armies of two countries were already poised for an exchange of blows on the French border. The stronger Germany was, the longer she would be able to resist the superior forces of Britain and France, and the greater would be the hope that the war would not terminate in the dangerous hegemony of the new Entente in Europe.

The old concept of two thieves falling out and so helping the honest man to win seemed to be in actual operation. To be sure, the defeat of France brought many schemes, plans, and combinations crashing to the ground. Beneath the surface a tense struggle between Germany and Russia was already going on in Finland, in the Balkans, and in Turkey, and it all reached a climax in the explosion of June 22, 1941. But later in Russia, while thousands of buildings were bombed and shelled to rubble and while millions of men lost their lives on all fronts, Moscow schemes, theories, and principles of foreign policy were not among the things buried

---

55. Molotov, report before the Supreme Council on October 31, 1939.

under the debris. History has demonstrated once again that erroneous theories and false ideas are stronger than steel and concrete. They have been able to survive even this huge catastrophe.

III. THE STARS IN THEIR COURSES

1. BRITAIN, AMERICA, AND EASTERN EUROPE

THE Great Powers, in their world policies, now draw close together, run almost parallel for a certain time, now diverge one from the other, then come together again only to separate once more. Ten years ago, when British engineers were tried in Soviet Russia on charges of economic espionage and fists were being shaken in London and in Washington, he would indeed have been a bold man who would have prophesied that a few years later the foreign policies of Soviet Russia, Great Britain, and the United States would be brought into line by a close military alliance. At that time London regarded Moscow as the source of all evil, and nobody in Moscow dared to question the view that the heart of that mortal enemy, international capitalism, lay on the banks of the Thames.

Today, the situation is reversed. Today a suggestion that the political orbits of the present allies may once more diverge is apt to be received with incredulity and protest. Yet Great Britain, the United States, and the Soviet Union each has its own European and world policy—evolved not from arbitrary notions but from existing circumstances and established principles. Frequently this national policy is not reduced to a system, or even formulated in precise terms. Nevertheless, it is a real policy, so real that in the case of each of these countries it has determined the pace and form of its participation in the present war. That it will also determine its postwar policy is hardly open to doubt.

The principal components of traditional British policy with regard to the continent of Europe can be listed as follows: opposition to domination of any power over all other powers; support of the second strongest power against the strongest; creation and support of coalitions against powers having designs for dominating Europe; renunciation of territorial ambitions there. This system of foreign policy has, of course, become known to history as the policy of *balance of power*. Other countries besides Great Britain have followed the balance-of-power policy but they have supplemented it by other methods. In the case of Great Britain, however, this system has predominated for many centuries. It can, therefore, be regarded as British policy par excellence.

After 1918 the policy of balance of power often was dismissed by public opinion as obsolete. It was regarded as something crude and barbarous, incompatible with the new spirit in international relations as expressed in the high moral principles of the League of Nations and the concept of universal disarmament. From that time on a community of nations was to replace military alliances, and a high supernational authority was to solve all international controversies in accordance with principles and not by sheer physical force. Countless books and articles were written and innumerable speeches were made during the first decade after World War I, in which this subject was discussed.

There was a time, a few centuries ago, when the political world was inclined to idealize the balance of power. Every condition of balance was believed to reveal something divine, some preordained harmony, whether in the balance of stars and planets, the functioning of the human organism, or in international relations. A stable international balance of power was regarded as a guarantee against war. At the beginning of this century, the contrary became true. Balance of power was denounced as a child of evil. It was held to be a satanic device of aggressors and conquerors for bringing other countries into submission. Imperialistic designs and machinations were now seen to be rooted in the balance of power.

Needless to say, nothing in the balance of power came from either God or the devil. A means of self-defense of some countries against others, it was forced upon them by external conditions and was a natural outgrowth of those conditions. On occasions, of course, it also served purely aggressive aims. There is not much reason in denouncing this system; no country has ever existed that did not make use of this weapon at some time or other. The Soviet Union, too, from Lenin to the present, has made extensive use of it.

Despite the severe criticism heaped on the concept of balance of power after 1918, the old play of political developments continued on its uninterrupted course. France made alliances in the Balkans and in eastern Europe in order to counterbalance a possible German resurgence. Germany's tentacles reached out to Hungary, Austria, and, later, Poland, in order to counterbalance French strength. Great Britain, traditional champion of balance of power, was vigilant in efforts to prevent any European nation from acquiring mastery over the continent which might serve to create a united Europe, a Europe politically opposed to Great Britain.

In recent centuries, having reached the peak of their powers, Spain had ruled over the Netherlands, France had extended her influence as far as Egypt, the German Empire had spread to the Adriatic, Poland had stretched down to the Black Sea, and Turkey had touched Austria and Galicia. For geographic reasons, such roads of expansion were closed to Britain. No less active and warlike, and even better endowed with wealth and perhaps even with ability than other nations, Britain directed her expansion beyond Europe, achieving considerable success in acquiring overseas territories. Her territorial acquisitions on the continent of Europe were finally lost in the fifteenth century, after which time, so far as Europe was concerned, Britain's policy could aim only at preserving her influence and at preventing Europe from uniting into a single military camp. A military and economic blockade has always been the greatest menace to England, and so her foreign policy has always been shaped to counteract this danger.

England's principal adversary, therefore, has always been the nation which for the moment was the strongest in Europe, i.e., the nation most capable of creating a united continent. Neither the form of government nor the domestic policy of the various countries was of concern to her. Originally, Spain was her greatest enemy; later, with the rise of France, Paris became the main adversary—first the Bourbon kingdom, then the Republic, and finally the Empire. Then, as Russia emerged victorious from the Napoleonic Wars and came to the forefront, British policy was directed toward promoting anti-Russian coalitions. Later England watched with satisfaction the rise of Prussia in her struggle against a powerful France, and up to 1904 she outwardly maintained a neutral attitude toward the rivalry between the Russian-French and the German-Austrian coalitions. This attitude changed only when Germany's dominance became an actual menace.

The policy of balance of power was the natural and inevitable consequence of Britain's particular position in Europe, a typically English weapon of self-defense. When the use of this weapon was a point at issue, differences between Tories and Whigs ceased to exist, just as at present there are no differences between Conservatives and Laborites.[1]

This trend of British policy has had peculiar consequences.

First, although land-hungry outside, Britain had no territorial claims within Europe. Even in lands across the Channel, where her own safety was at stake, she helped to create two small independent states, Belgium and Holland, rather than set up vassal countries. As a result, Britain acquired a reputation for territorial disinterestedness for herself (although not for her allies where their territorial ambitions were concerned).

Second, Britain's attitude toward the strongest European power had an important bearing upon relations with small and weak nations. Britain naturally became the protector of the independence and sovereignty of various small nations on the continent. It often happened that territories and peoples were sacrificed for the sake of important European combinations, yet, in times of European crisis, many small nations relied upon the supporting strength of the British Empire.

During the interim between the two world wars, Britain's

---

1. It is sometimes stated that England has lately abandoned, or is being forced to abandon, the system of balance of power. In a brilliant if paradoxical form this view is expressed by Professor E. H. Carr in his *Problems of Peace* (pp. 191–204). Professor Carr holds that as Britain's superiority of sea power and her economic domination recede into the past, she is compelled to renounce the policy of balance of power. This thesis is far from being thoroughly proved. To be sure, Britain has been obliged to relinquish the attitude of "splendid isolation." But the latter was only a chapter (covering the second half of the nineteenth century) in the long history of balance of power policy. Splendid isolation is ended, but Britain cannot abandon the policy of balances and counter-balances unless she is reduced to the status of a second- or third-rank power. If the present war ends in the defeat of Germany, Britain will retain her position in Europe (even if not throughout the world) and, consequently, the essential lines of her foreign policy.

policy followed the same course. Between 1919 and 1939 the strongest power in Europe was, or appeared to be, France. In her opposition to French mastery, Britain was ready to grant great concessions to Germany, and the Anglo-French discord regarding the German question was chronic down to 1936. Because of this opposition to France the British took exception to the Polish expansion into Soviet Russia in 1920; they were the first among the Great Powers to make an agreement with Moscow. The thorn of anti-French policy pricked continuously.

Britain did not discard her old traditions when she joined the League of Nations in 1919. The League was not conceived as a European but as a world organization, and the British Empire, spreading over the five continents, had no misgivings in joining it. Besides, the League of Nations had no means for limiting the independence of England's foreign policy, nor her military strength. Thus England was in a position to continue *inside* the League the same policy of balance of power that she had followed before the League had come into existence.

One of the most difficult problems facing the policy of balance of power has always been the territory which separates Russia from the great nations of Europe and Asia.

West of Russia a long belt of land, 100 to 300 miles wide, stretches from the Arctic Ocean to the Black Sea, on to the Caspian, and from there to the deserts of Central Asia. It is populated by a great number of small nations and forms a wall between Russia and the world. Here live Finns, Estonians, Latvians, Lithuanians, Poles, Slovaks, Czechs, Hungarians, Bulgarians, Rumanians, Serbians, Slovenes, Croatians, and Turks—to list only those in the European section of the belt and omitting the minor nationalities. Even so, these fourteen nations have a combined population of over 100 million people. Their territories, often used as theaters of war, frequently formed strategical frontiers of Russia or of her adversaries. The problem of stabilizing political relations in eastern Europe is concerned primarily with this long and narrow belt of territory with its multitude of small and medium-sized nationalities.

In its last phase, between 1870 and 1914, the stability of

international relations in Europe rested, from the British point of view, on the fact that Germany and France balanced each other in the west, while Russia balanced the two German monarchies in the east. The mechanism of balance of power functioned so well that Britain had no need to abandon her state of isolation.

Of the two German monarchies, Germany faced the west, as did her guns, but at the same time preserved friendly relations with Russia. Facing east was Austria-Hungary, a state organism of a strange nature, consisting mostly of Slavs, with a minority of Hungarians (19 per cent) and Germans (23 per cent). Austria-Hungary managed to keep going and even to expand at a period when the principle of the national state was achieving ever-greater triumphs in European politics. She was a kind of remnant of the Middle Ages surviving in the modern world.

But she was not merely a relic of the past. In a political sense, particularly from the point of view of Great Britain, she was the principal counterweight which balanced the Russian colossus and barred Russian expansion. The 50 million inhabitants of Austria-Hungary provided a pool for a formidable army, and besides, if necessary, the Dual Monarchy could draw on allied Germany as a reserve. The stability of the east European frontiers corresponded to the ratio of military strength between Russia and both her western neighbors.

In 1917 Russia ceased to play the role of a great military power, and in 1918 her opposite power, Austria-Hungary, collapsed. Both balance and counterbalance vanished from the scene, and in 1919 Britain raised no objections to the splitting up of the Dual Monarchy into a number of independent states. Russian expansionism and Russian military power having disappeared, there was no need for Austria-Hungary.

In the 'thirties the situation changed. A new Russian Army was being created, and the Russian problem, although in a new form, assumed a fresh significance. But in place of two German monarchies there emerged, on the other side of the great barrier, a new Germany. Germany now strove to assume the functions of both monarchies and became the Third Reich, bringing Czechoslovakia and Austria under her rule.

A synthesis of Germany and Austria, the Third Reich thus faced both the west and the east.

The war for the destruction of the Third Reich and its reconversion into Germany raises for the whole world, and first of all for Britain, the problem of guaranteed stability of east European relations. Unlike the Russia of the 'twenties, Russia after this war will remain a formidable military force. But this time again her counterweight, Austria-Hungary, will be missing. All the principles of British policy come in conflict with one another. The alliance with Russia and the need of this alliance after the war demand that Russia be allowed to decide the fate of her neighbor nations and their territories. The traditional policy of the independence of small nations requires that the latter be protected against the Great Powers. The principle of European balance of power also requires new state organisms, acting as substitutes for Austria-Hungary.

It is perfectly natural that while the war continues a deep confusion on these questions reigns in Britain, and that all trends are represented in her public opinion—from the pro-Russian "sphere of influence" down to an independent federation of states of the "Middle Zone." [2] The latter project, tacitly aimed against Soviet aspirations, advocates a superstate federation of all the small and medium-sized nations between the Baltic and the Adriatic. All nations and states, from Poland in the north to Rumania and Yugoslavia in the south, in short all that lies between Russia and Germany-Italy, would come within this federation.

Fundamentally, this proposal resembles the restoration of Austria-Hungary, but with these two differences: first, it could not be monarchic in form, and second, its territorial scope, both in the north and in the south, would be much larger. This federation of states would have a population of about 100 million (the population of Germany, exclusive of the population of the annexed territories, is less than 70 million), and a territory of 1,100,000 square kilometers (as against Germany's 470,000 square kilometers).

From the purely statistical point of view this project may

2. The program of such a federation and the implications of the "Middle Zone" are the subject of particularly careful study carried on by the British review, *The Nineteenth Century and After*.

appear to give the most rational answer to Britain's quest
for a new east European power. This Middle Zone has a considerably larger population than Germany. If it is smaller
than Russia, it nevertheless presents a serious counterweight, particularly in the light of the potential safeguarding
alliances which it would have with the western nations in
the event of a conflict with Russia or Germany. The strength
of this federation, however, is highly problematical. The
new superstate would have two extremely weak spots—its
variegated national composition and the inevitably voluntary
nature of its membership. It would be made up of seven
former states and of not less than ten nationalities, all of
whom follow different lines of orientation. The Czechs and
the Serbians would operate within the federation as an anti-
German but pro-Russian element; the Poles and the Hungarians would be anti-Russian. There would be other conflicting elements. It would be extremely difficult to give the
foreign policy of this federation a uniform direction, and in
the event of a serious international conflict the military
power of this state would be of questionable value. The core
of such a federation would be Poland, Czechoslovakia, and
Yugoslavia, while its largest component part would be Poland, with a population of from 20 to 35 million, depending
on the final boundaries, east and west, to be established.

Another solution of the problem could have been, for instance, a Polish-Czech federation, almost achieved in 1940–42
but dissolved again in 1943; or a Polish-Czech-Hungarian
federation advocated by certain Polish circles. There is also
the idea of a Yugoslav-Greek federation, as well as the pro-
jected coöperation between the two federations and the
eventual inclusion of Hungary and Rumania therein.

While the war is on, Britain, Russia's ally, is naturally
constrained in discussing the subject. As soon, however, as
Germany shows definite signs of weakening, this problem
will assume a central place in Britain's east European policy.

In the years preceding the present war the foreign policy
of the United States and England frequently diverged. But
there are certain aspects of American policy which corre-
spond to those of Britain in so far as European problems are
concerned.

Britain regards any nation seeking mastery of Europe—by conquest or otherwise—as her most dangerous enemy. To America such a nation would be an equally serious menace. A European nation that succeeded in welding together 300 to 400 million people as well as in commanding the joint industries and the joint navies of France, Italy, Germany, and perhaps Britain, would indeed threaten the vital interests and the independent existence of the United States.

Hence the analogous policies of Britain and the United States in 1914–18, and since 1940. The war aim of both is the stabilization of intra-European relations, the creation of a system of mutually balanced forces. Only such a balance would permit the Anglo-Saxon Powers to stand aside from many of the problems of the Old World. American isolationism and American interventionism in European affairs are the obverse and reverse of the American medal, the two forms of the same basic attitude toward Europe, a continent that looms as rich, restless, occasionally impotent, and potentially dangerous. Having no territorial aspirations in Europe, America is not interested in European frontiers, especially not in those of eastern Europe. The only thing she may be interested in is the adjustment of interstate relations in a manner that will ensure stability for a long period and will not create, as a result of the war, a new preponderance of one power capable of turning the plains of Europe into a breeding ground of a new war.

Stabilization of intra-European relations is the main aim of American policy in the Old World, and this is doubly true of her attitude toward east European problems. America is not greatly interested in either Poland or Yugoslavia or Finland, taken as individual countries, nor in their frontiers, their disputes with other countries, and particularly in their relations with their great eastern neighbor. But these countries acquire importance in her eyes as bricks of the future edifice, which shall be stable and fireproof.

In America's relations with Russia this is one of the motives which determine her wartime policy. To be sure, the problems of the Far East, as well as future economic relations with Russia, play an important role. But an expansion of Russia on a great scale, as well as Russia's possible revolutionary influence upon the rest of Europe would in American eyes cancel all schemes for stabilization. Expansion of Russia as a state and her possible role as a hotbed of revolution are incompatible with American interests.

In this respect America shows greater independence than Britain. While London is struggling in a network of political contradictions and often is inclined to yield for the sake of a compromise, Washington can permit itself the luxury of an appeal to principles.

Nevertheless, there exists a great affinity of the British and the American policies in Europe. The closeness of views has also found expression in the relations within the war coalition and, first of all, in the programmatic declaration of the war aims of America and Britain.

2. RUSSIAN POLICY IN EUROPE

The foreign policies of Soviet Russia have followed an independent course.

Domination of the entire European continent by a single power has been as greatly opposed to the interests of Russia as to those of Britain, and even more so than to those of America. It has made no difference whether the mastery was threatened by a monarchy or a republic, a democratic or a fascist state, a revolution or reaction, the revolutionary dictatorship of a Napoleon or the racial dictatorship of a Hitler. Nor has it made any difference whether the threat was directed against a Czarist, a Communist, or a democratic Russia. Opposition to any overlordship in Europe by any single nation has been the natural reaction, one might say the law, of the foreign policy of Russia.

This fact has served to align the policies of Russia with those of Britain and the United States. But the unity resulting from this stems rather from the negative than from the positive interests of these powers; it connotes an agreement relating to a common attitude toward an aggressor rather than to plans for permanent peace.

Unlike her two principal allies, Russia is not an island or a sea power, but a European continental power; her goal cannot be merely the maintenance of an equilibrium of European forces, since she is herself one of the factors in this equilibrium; and her natural opponent is not the strongest European power but rather the one that plays the leading role in *the east*. The sovereignty of small nations has been far from inviolate for Russia. Neither the status quo nor equilibrium of forces has been the essential goal of Russian policy. Russia's principal adversaries were Turkey, Poland, Sweden, and Austria, whereas Britain's opponents were mainly Spain and France. Russia and Britain fought the same adversary only when he bore the threat of domination over the entire continent: Napoleon, William II, Hitler.

Sovereignty of small nations found little favor with Russian policy. As late as the nineteenth century, when the idea of national liberty prevailed all over Europe, in practical politics as well as in theory, it had but a negligible influence in

Russia where its application would have led to the secession of several national territories. None of the Russian political parties, including the revolutionary parties of this and the last century, supported national separatism. The Bolsheviks were no exception. The principle of national independence was employed during the last century only as Russia's weapon outside her borders as, for instance, in her struggle with Turkey, in her designs in the Balkans, and in similar instances. In this respect Russian policy has always differed from British policy, which regarded the independence of small nations as an important factor in the safety of Britain. For Russia, there was no necessary connection between the ethnographic concept of a nation and the state.

The democratic parties which supplanted the old regime early in 1917 held power for eight months and therefore were not able to establish a coherent system of foreign policy of their own. They were willing, however, to recognize the formation of an independent Poland and the cession to it of Polish territory held by Russia. They might have agreed, though reluctantly, to the independence of Finland. But this was the limit of their concessions.

The foreign policy of this short democratic period, so entirely new to Russia, was the product not so much of experience as of revolutionary idealism. Whatever its source, however, it came close to the ideas held by Britain and America at that time. These views represented a "western orientation" in international relations, and opposed to the old imperialism they reflected a repetition within the Russian leftist camp of the struggle of ideas which raged during the nineteenth century within the Russian moderate camp; the former "Westerners" and "Slavophiles" were now known, in revolutionary parlance, as democrats and Bolsheviks.

The Soviet state which succeeded the democratic republic, struggling to emerge from chaos, broke sharply with the "western orientation" in its foreign policy. The attitude of Soviet Russia on self-determination of nations and the right of secession underwent an important evolution in the early years of the Soviet state.

Before 1917, during the "preparatory period" of the Bolshevik party, self-determination of nations was a principle with which the party grew up. Yet, although recognizing the right, the Bolsheviks regarded national secession from Russia as undesirable. It is interesting to note that socialist groups within the national minorities of Russia which followed Bolshevik policies (the Polish Social-Democratic party, the Latvian Social-Democratic party, and so on) refused to include separatist demands in their programs.

Lenin himself conceded unrestricted national self-determination to the component nationalities of Russia from the very beginning of Soviet rule. In 1917, so long as he remained in opposition, he stirred national separatism in order to "wreck the state machinery of the bourgeoisie." When he came to power, he found the machinery wrecked, and for the next three years (1917–20) every nationality and every territory within the boundaries of the former Empire "self-determined" itself. Among those who made use of the proclaimed self-determination were Finns, Poles, Georgians, Tartars, Lithuanians, Latvians, Estonians, even Cossacks, and numerous Russian provinces. On the other hand, Communist elements within each small nation supported the Moscow centralism and were bitter opponents of the independence of their own nation.

The Moscow government relied not only on the strength of its own army but also on the support of its followers within the former territories of Russia. It had no intention of accepting the dismemberment of the Russian state, nor was it willing to wait for a return to the fold of the seceders by means of gradual consolidation. At the same time it did not wish, under any circumstances, to renounce the doctrine of self-determination of nations. In this paradoxical situation the timely aid of the local Communist parties played the decisive role. A practice was developed which grew to be the rule throughout the subsequent period, and without a proper understanding of it no true appreciation of the postwar situation is possible.

According to the non-Communist interpretation, self-determination is an act of the will of the people expressed either by means of direct ballot (plebiscite) or in an act of parliament. Eight plebiscites have been held since the last World War, and the popular ballot has to this day remained the principal instrument of self-determination of peoples.

The Soviet Government, however, has been unable to make use of this system.

A plebiscite in the Baltic States, the Caucasian republics, and other areas which seceded in 1918–19 would have at that time undoubtedly resulted in repudiation of Soviet Russia. In all instances the problem confronting the local population was not principally one of state affiliation, i.e., whether its territory should stay in or out of Russia, but rather one of the choice of a social system. Not even Moscow doubted that the results of a plebiscite would be a blow to the Soviets.

Expression of the will of the people through the ballot as a necessary part of self-determination has ceased to be a decisive tenet with the Soviet Government. Ideologically this attitude fitted in easily with the general Bolshevik criticism of democracy. If the "will of the majority" as a basis of democracy may be ignored until the new dictatorship has re-formed the entire social system, certainly it may be ignored in deciding the subordinate question of self-determination. Since freedom of speech and of the press only perverts the will of the people to make it serve the interests of small groups, nations naturally must resort to other means to effect their self-determination. And, finally, if the minority of a people have the right and the duty to force their will upon the majority in the name of the true interests of the entire people, the same minority within smaller nations must also decide the question of state affiliation.

Strictly speaking, this was abandonment of the idea of "self-determination of nations." Henceforth the true expression of popular will was seen not in ballots but in direct action, spontaneous elections of soviets, and manifestations of revolutionary sentiment in general.

The principle of self-determination, however, continued to be regarded as inviolable, and Soviet policy appeared sometimes to be clothed in peculiar raiment. The Soviets took pains to avoid creating the impression that they laid claims to any non-Russian territories. When in 1920 Soviet troops, after driving the Poles from Kiev, set out on the march to Warsaw, a new Polish Government consisting of five Polish Communists was set up at Bialystok to prevent any impression that the military campaign was in the nature of a Russian conquest. Nineteen years later the march on Finland was accompanied by the formation of the Finnish Government of Kuusinen at Terioki (December, 1939). In Lithuania, Latvia, and Estonia the local parliaments, under pressure from Moscow, "requested of the Central Executive Committee of the U.S.S.R." in July, 1940, that their countries be admitted to membership in the Soviet Union. Once again it was sought to avoid the outward appearance of conquest.

These methods have taken deep root in the Soviet Government's system of foreign policy and will have to be reckoned with in the final stages of the current war. Independence of small nations and their self-determination by the will of the majority is not a fundamental object with the Soviet Government. There is a difference in this respect between the attitude of Soviet Russia and that of her allies.

The same considerations apply to the general question of territorial aggrandizement as the goal of foreign policy. The major program for Soviet policy sets forth, officially and unalterably, the goal of extending the Union to include other nations. This goal, as officially proclaimed, is expansion without aggression, i.e., expansion through voluntary adhesion. But the idea of the Soviet Union is that it is a federation of all countries "which have fallen or are falling away from capitalism." [3] The Soviet Union is viewed as a large magnet built to fulfill this object.

The history of the public law of the Soviet Union is the story of an ever-expanding federation. The Constitution of the first Soviet Federation was written in 1918. In 1919–21 five more Soviet republics were formed. In 1922 these six formerly sovereign states were proclaimed the Soviet Union, and in 1923 the first Constitution of the Union of Soviet Socialist Republics was promulgated, incorporating six member states. In 1936, when the Constitution was amended, the Union embraced eleven members. In 1940 five new republics were brought in, raising the membership to sixteen. "Admission to the Union is open to all socialist Soviet republics,

---

3. Stalin: "For the slogan: the United States of Europe, we'll substitute the slogan: the federation of soviet republics of advanced countries and colonies which have fallen or are falling away from the imperialist system of economy." (*Problems of Leninism*, pp. 337–338).

whether already existing or that may come into existence in the future." [4] The Constitution even provides rules for admitting new republics to membership in the Union.

Of course, this is mere legalism which carries little weight in Soviet Russia. But it is symptomatic of the mode of thinking which controls policies as well. Expansion of the Soviet state is nowhere frowned upon. On the contrary, it is one of the state's highest goals, and is regarded as one of the greatest achievements to be realized by mankind. On this question the old prerevolutionary imperialism and the new revolutionary Communist messianism meet. The Great Empire of the Czars as the ideal of nineteenth-century Slavophilism, Russia's "unique stature," her great mission in the world: *Ex oriente lux!* Juxtaposed to this: the Great Republic of Socialism, the world revolution of the poor, the abolition of economic slavery, the torch of equality borne from the east to the oppressed peoples of the west: *Ex oriente lux!* These two streams of thought, so alien to each other, draw close and almost merge in the idea of the expansion of the state.

In fact, the official Communist ideology sees the expansion of the Soviet Union, aside from everything else, as the only means of preventing future wars. What the peoples and politicians of the entire world are vainly seeking—to make the present war the last war—is implicit in the concept of expansion and extension of the Soviet Union; for the admission of new territories and states into the Union transforms them into component parts of a vast socialist association within which wars are regarded as impossible. According to this view, the fullest realization of this goal, with the whole of Europe and, in time, the whole world, brought into the Union, will raise life to its highest plane, to eternal peace in a community of nations.

This blend of sociology and faith emphasizes the tremendous importance attached to state expansion in Communist ideology. It is easy to understand why, set beside these great aims, the worn-out principles which bar the road to Communist progress—the principles of independence and sovereignty of small nations—must appear utterly insignificant.

Apart from these aims of Communism, however, other

4. Cf. Official Declaration made upon the formation of the U.S.S.R.

wholly concrete and practical considerations have impelled the Soviet Government in the same direction. From the needs of the security of the state the old idea of "strategic frontiers" was reborn in the Soviet Union. By its very nature, by the character of its power, by its history and ideology, the Soviet Government sought security of its state not so much in alliances and treaties, not in the League of Nations, in short, not so much in measures of "collective security" (in which it had little faith) as primarily in the strengthening of its own position, particularly in territories where it faced the most danger. Apart from its world-socialist aims, the Soviet Government performed its everyday tasks, as it understood them, by extending the Soviet system to large new territories.

It was a fundamental principle of the Bolshevik doctrine that no reliable, faithful, and lasting ally could be found in the capitalist world. This conviction was more than a theoretical conjecture. It was actually the cornerstone of the foreign policy of Moscow. It was responsible for the exclusiveness, the self-limitation, and the political autarchy of the Soviets, which found their expression in distrust of alliances, a tendency to rely exclusively upon Russia's own forces, and the consequent exaltation of the might of the Soviet state, its military strength, and its vast territorial expanse.

The pushing back of frontiers as a measure of military defense was a fitting complement to the great world aims of the Moscow ideology. The years 1939–40 witnessed extension of strategic frontiers over the entire western border, from Finland to the Black Sea. But the 23 million persons who were brought into the Union were instantly incorporated also within the system of Soviet socialism. During those years problems of defense were paramount, but the result was also the extension of Sovietism to new large regions.

It is extremely important to bear in mind the dualism inherent in this policy. The Soviet Government sees itself and its country isolated in a hostile ocean of capitalism. It professes to see all the dangers that threaten it, down to "encirclement" of the Soviet Union. It will not regard itself as secure by virtue of treaties of friendship with neighboring countries or with Great Powers or of economic ties. The only thing in which it is prepared to believe is adherence to the Soviet Union.

In January, 1938, Ivan Filippovich Ivanov, a minor official in a district Communist organization, had some very unpleasant experiences. He held the post of propagandist in the Communist Youth League (*Komsomol*) in the out-of-the-way Manzurov district of the Kursk region. While attending political classes at Kursk, Ivanov had an argument with two other active Communists, Urozhenko and Kozelkov, about the future of socialism in Russia. The two latter Communists maintained that socialism had won a complete victory in the Soviet Union and that there was, therefore, "a full insurance against intervention and the restoration of capitalism." Ivanov argued against this idea, maintaining that the full insurance could be provided only by "the final victory of socialism" in the other countries of the world, in other words, that the true defense of Russia lay in the extension of the socialist revolution to the outside world. It was along these lines that this central problem of Russian policy was heatedly discussed in a Russian backwater almost on the eve of the war.

The argument had bad consequences for Ivanov. His views, which linked Soviet defense and security with an anti-capitalist revolution in the world outside, were branded as Trotskyism. He was "removed from his job," marked for expulsion from the Komsomol, and threatened with all the consequences attendant on being purged from the Communist organization. In despair, Ivanov wrote a letter to Stalin asking him to pass on the merits of the argument and on "whether the members of the Regional Committee were right in declaring me a Trotskyist—which I consider an injury and an insult."

Stalin replied to Ivanov on February 12, 1938. "You are right, Comrade Ivanov, and your opponents are wrong," Stalin wrote. Inside Russia, he went on to explain, socialism won its victory and thus demonstrated the fallacy of Trotskyism. But the case was different when the bearing of the situation on matters abroad was considered. "Can socialism victorious in one country regard itself as fully secure against the danger of a military invasion [intervention] and therefore against attempts at restoring capitalism?" Stalin answered that it cannot.

In the event of any success the invaders will try to destroy the Soviet system and restore the bourgeois system in the occupied regions.

We would be in a position to say that the victory [of socialism in the Soviet Union] is complete, if our country were situated on an island and if it had not many other [capitalist] countries around it. But since we live not on an island but in "a system of states," a considerable number of which are hostile to the land of socialism, thus creating the danger of intervention and restoration, we say openly and honestly that the victory of socialism in our country is not yet complete.

This problem remains to be solved. . . . It can be solved only by uniting the serious efforts of the international proletariat with the still more serious efforts of the entire Soviet people.

These "serious efforts of the international proletariat," i.e., the policy of the sovietization of other countries, are thus represented as promising Russia the only guarantee against war. Stalin's reply, which formulates the basic idea of Soviet foreign policy, springs from considerations of defense, and not of a Communist offensive against the capitalist world. In this letter Stalin does not set as his policy the object of liberating the workers of all countries from economic oppression. He takes his stand as one concerned primarily with the defense of Soviet Russia. But the conclusion at which he arrives is a reversion to the old position: Soviet Russia can never feel herself secure so long as other countries are ruled by capitalist governments no matter whether they be liberal or conservative, democratic or fascist. Only when a system of government similar to the Soviet Government is established in other countries, and, first, in the small and large countries along the Soviet border, will the Soviet land be truly secure.

The requirements of self-defense and the purely national policy of state security have thus revived the old question of the political regime in the neighbor countries. Foreign policy is here interlaced with internal policy: the social system of Soviet Russia (internal policy) demands similar systems in neighboring countries (foreign policy), and Russian socialism will continue to be endangered until this condition is established.

3. POLITICAL ORBITS OF THE GREAT POWERS

The common objects which unite American and British policies in regard to the European war were expressed in the Atlantic Charter of August 14, 1941. This document, which was drawn up while peace still prevailed in the Pacific, remains to this day the principal statement of British and American war aims in Europe. The Atlantic Charter is neither an enumeration of concrete conditions of peace of both countries, nor a piece of hypocritical political declaration, as was sometimes claimed. It is a document which gives an ideological and idealistic expression to the very real interests of America and Britain, and as such must be regarded as a first-rate historical document of its era.

Originally signed by the leaders of these two nations, the Charter has since been accepted by all anti-Axis powers. At a meeting of the Inter-Allied Council in London six weeks after the signing of the Atlantic Charter, the governments of the Allied nations, Soviet Russia included, expressed their adherence to it. There were, however, some important reservations. The Soviet Government, through its Ambassador, Ivan Maisky, made a long and cautiously formulated Declaration, which may be regarded as the Soviet's own charter. In certain points this Declaration coincided with the terms of the Atlantic Charter; in others it differed, sometimes very materially. After reading the Soviet Declaration, Ambassador Maisky made a careful announcement to the effect that his government subscribed to "the basic propositions" of the Charter and would sign it.

The widespread opinion that the Soviet Government is bound by a joint Allied program of peace is, therefore, only partially correct and hence misleading. The Soviet Government from the very beginning has emphasized the special character of its aims. The following point-by-point comparison of the two documents will make clear the extent of the differences:

The Atlantic Charter	The Soviet Declaration
14 AUGUST, 1941	24 SEPTEMBER, 1941

Statements in brackets are the author's commentary.

1. "Their countries seek no aggrandizement, territorial or other." [This is the basic idea of the British and American policy on the European continent, both in time of war and in time of peace. It also denies any desire on the part of these two countries to acquire any rights disguised as "mandates" in European territories, the denial being implicit in the words "territorial or *other*."]

1. [This article, in the form stated, does not and cannot exist in the Soviet program. The idea underlying the structure of the Soviet Union is that it is a Union of republics which expands gradually through inclusion of new territories.]

2. "They desire no territorial changes that do not accord with the freely expressed wishes of the peoples concerned." [This article is again one of the basic principles of the European policy of America and Britain. Its weak points are: (a) vagueness regarding the method by which the population is to express its will—whether it is to be through parliament, plebiscite, soviets, insurrection, or the general mood (these questions may assume real importance by the end of the war); (b) vagueness regarding the identity of "the peoples concerned." The Charter avoids stating clearly that the people concerned

2. [The question whether territorial changes after the war will be permitted and in what form, is not considered in the Soviet Declaration. This is partly connected with what was said in Paragraph 1. Furthermore, "wishes of the people," as commonly understood, are wishes of the majority of the people; while "freely expressed" presumes a political rivalry of different programs for the support of the people. The Soviet Government subscribes to neither requirement. In all cases which have so far occurred in Soviet practice, the voters were offered only one program and the voting took place only after military oc-

is the population of the disputed territory, that, for example, the fate of Danzig is to be decided by the population of Danzig. While rejecting this formalistic view, the Charter refrains from giving a clear answer to the question: Will the decision rest, as regards Danzig, for example, with the population of Poland and Germany, or with that of the neighboring regions, and how will the opposing interests be reconciled? The same consideration applies to a multitude of other territorial problems of eastern Europe.]

cupation. In general, the Soviet Government is prone to subordinate the territorial question to other and, in its opinion, higher aims. For example, the addition of East Prussia to Poland, which is considered desirable by both Poland and Russia, could be accomplished only in violation of the will of the local population.]

3. (A) "They respect the right of all peoples to choose the form of government under which they will live . . ." [In this article the word "choose" may be misleading. It does not refer to the active right of a new self-determination in regard to the internal political system, i.e., it does not stipulate the extension of democracy to all peoples, but only to the negative right of the state of not being interfered with in its internal political system. The only exception to this rule is the signatories' attitude toward the Nazi Government; another article of the Atlantic Charter rules out a peace

3. (A) "The Soviet Union has put and is putting into practice the high principles of respect for the sovereign rights of peoples. It has been and is being guided by the principle of self-determination, sovereignty, and equality of nations. The Soviet Union asserts the right of every people to: (a) state independence; (b) inviolability of its territory; (c) its right to establish a social system and select a form of government which it deems expedient and necessary." [The difference between the Atlantic Charter and the Soviet Declaration is revealed in the emphasis which the Soviet treaty with that government.]

Declaration lays on the right of establishing not only a form of government but also a new "social system." Thus provision is made, for instance, for Hungary's return to the Soviet system and also, of course, for nonintervention in Germany or in Austria in the event of revolutions in these countries toward the end of the war.]

(B) "They wish to see sovereign rights and self-government restored to those who have been forcibly deprived of them." [This principle, next to Article One, is one of the principal British and American war aims. It also covers the three Baltic countries brought within the Soviet Union in 1939–40, the Soviet sovereignty over which has not been recognized by the United States and Britain.]

(B) In a more general form, this provision is partly included in the above "right of every people to state independence." But the Soviet Declaration avoids the precise terms of the Atlantic Charter, since restoration of self-government, as an aim of the war, might provide an excuse for raising the question of the Baltic countries and other territories formally brought into the Soviet Union. Some considerable time after the announcement of the Atlantic Charter, when the Soviet Government had already stated its view regarding those territories in no uncertain terms, Stalin found it possible to formulate the Soviet war aims in a new way.[5] "Equality of nations and inviolability of their territories; liberation of enslaved nations and restora-

---

5. Stalin, speech, November 6, 1942.

tion of their sovereign rights; the right of every nation to arrange its life in accordance with its own wishes; rendering of economic aid to the nations that suffered losses; restoration of democratic liberties; destruction of the Hitler regime." At the time this statement was made (November, 1942) a Soviet demand for "liberation of enslaved nations" could no longer cause misunderstanding. As for the meaning of democratic liberties in Stalin's declaration, the matter will be discussed further in another chapter.]

4. "They will endeavor, with due respect for their existing obligations, to further the enjoyment by all states, great or small, victor or vanquished, of access, on equal terms, to the trade and to the raw materials of the world which are needed for their economic prosperity."

4. [This problem, which mainly concerns the colonial demands of Germany and Italy, is not dealt with in the Soviet Declaration.]

5. "They desire to bring about the fullest collaboration between all nations in the economic field with the object of security for all, improved labor standards, economic advancement, and social security."

5. [This provision, aimed against economic autarchy, could not be included in the Soviet program (1) because the Soviet Government, in practice, if not in theory, frequently followed the principles of far-reaching economic isolation; (2) because the Soviet Government does not believe that "improved labor

standards, economic advancement and social security" can be achieved under the present system.]

6. "After the final destruction of the Nazi tyranny, they hope to see established a peace which will afford to all nations the means of dwelling in safety within their own boundaries, and which will afford assurance that all men in all lands may live out their lives in freedom from fear and want. . . ." [This article sets up three objectives: (a) destruction of Nazism; (b) peaceful neighborly relations after the destruction of Nazism; (c) social improvement.]

6. "Deliverance of our peoples and our future generations from the criminal and sanguinary Nazism which is incompatible with human culture." [The Soviet Declaration confines itself to the first of the three objects set up in the Charter. Although having little faith in the possibility of a lasting peace after the destruction of Nazism, it nevertheless speaks of "collaboration and friendship." It does not believe, either, in the possibility of achieving "freedom from want" under a capitalist economy.]

7. "Such a peace should enable all men to traverse the high seas and oceans without hindrance."

7. [The Soviet Declaration does not touch upon this question.]

8. (A) "They believe that all of the nations of the world, for realistic as well as spiritual reasons, must come to abandonment of the use of force." [Universal and everlasting peace figures in the Atlantic Charter only as a dim goal. Universal disarmament is treated separately from disarmament of the vanquished and is postulated

8. (A) "The Soviet Union has asserted the necessity of collective action against the aggressors . . . Striving to reach a radical solution of the problem of making freedom-loving peoples secure from all danger from aggressors, the Soviet Union has simultaneously carried on a struggle for complete universal disarmament." [The Soviet

in a general, noncompulsory form, the result, no doubt, of the experience in negotiations for universal disarmament in the 'twenties and 'thirties. But this article serves as an introduction to the demand for the disarmament of Germany.]

Declaration thus contains also the "radical solution of the problem"—universal disarmament, although it does not believe it possible under present social conditions.]

(B) "Since no future peace can be maintained so long as land, sea or air armaments continue to be employed by nations which threaten, or may threaten, aggression outside of their frontiers, they believe that, pending the establishment of a wider and permanent system of general security, the disarmament of such nations is essential. They will likewise aid and encourage all practicable measures to lighten for peace-loving peoples the crushing burden of armaments." [This is one of the most important articles of the Atlantic Charter—the program of disarmament of Germany and her allies.]

(B) [The Soviet Declaration completely passes by the question of disarming Germany and her allies. Confining itself to the demand for universal disarmament, it makes it embrace also the disarmament of Germany. This is a very important point in considering the postwar settlement, and will be discussed further in a subsequent chapter.]

The Atlantic Charter was drawn up soon after the Soviet Union entered the war. Its authors were anxious to formulate it so that it would not alienate the new ally. For this reason a number of items were either toned down or omitted altogether.[6] For her part, Soviet Russia is interested mainly

6. Returning to Washington after the conference, President Roosevelt, in answer to criticism voiced in the press, was obliged to include in his message to Congress relating to the Atlantic Conference the two items left out of the Charter—freedom of religion and freedom of the

in the East of Europe: the Balkan problems with all their complications; Poland and Czechoslovakia; the Baltic countries, and Finland. The Soviet Government sees the guarantee of its security in the widening of its influence over the multinational territory along its western borders. To Britain the importance of this territory lies, as formerly, in its being an independent force between Germany and Russia. To the Soviet Government this territory is a source of danger so long as it remains completely outside its sphere of influence, and it views these problems as being of the utmost urgency, since the conclusion of the war is the only suitable moment for their solution.

Thus, the welding of the war programs of the big three Allies under the formula of "a war for democracy" is both superficial and misleading. Democracy is certainly a great cause but the war cannot be described as a "war for democracy." Even for America this definition is too narrow. America is fighting for something far bigger than preservation of any particular system of political institutions. Britain is fighting for her self-preservation, her Empire, her standard of life. With differences, the latter description applies also to France, Holland, Norway, Poland, and all the other occupied countries. And, finally, this also applies to Russia. Russia is not fighting for democracy. As the Communists see it, she is fighting for the preservation and expansion of the Soviet system, while to the Russian people as a whole this war means something much more fundamental than this or that political or economic system.

The present war is not a war "for" but a war "against." Only Germany and Japan have a positive goal; for their adversaries the war has a negative meaning: against militant nationalism and against world hegemonies. It is a defensive, not an offensive, war. It is for this reason that all efforts have been in vain to give a unity of ideals and not merely of military operations to this war, in which the Chinese and Soviet dictatorships—representing over a half a billion people—are united with the democratic republic of

---

press. "It is unnecessary for me to point out," he wrote, "that the declaration of principles includes of necessity the world need for freedom of religion and freedom of information."

the United States and the monarchist democracy of the British Commonwealth—representing about 200 million people—as well as with a number of European countries ranging from democratic Czechoslovakia to the formerly fascist Greece.

A greater unity of ideas and war aims of the United Nations would be possible only when the major goals of their policies coincided. So far this condition has not been met.

IV. WAR AIMS OF SOVIET RUSSIA

1. WARTIME POLICY

THE policy that Soviet Russia was to follow in the event of an international war was formulated and worked out in detail over a period of many years. The whole period since 1914 was considered by Moscow an era of wars which generate revolutions and of revolutions which generate wars. For, said Lenin, "the world never knew an important revolution which was not bound up with war." To this Lenin returned again and again: "The experience of the history of revolutions, of great conflicts, teaches that wars—series of wars—are inevitable." [1] This view, incidentally, determined Lenin's wholly hostile attitude toward all disarmament programs. He regarded them as material for propaganda and not as matters of realistic policy. For his own country he considered a maximum degree of military strength to be a first necessity.

At various congresses in Moscow and in the press problems of future wars were analyzed and studied with thoroughness. As the fruit of such studies the programmatic theses of 1927 [2] present a most interesting classification of future wars. These fall into three groups:

(1) "Wars of imperialist states among themselves." This refers to wars of Great Powers exclusive of Soviet Russia. The first World War as well as the present one from September 1, 1939, to June 22, 1941, also come under this definition. In wars of this kind Soviet Russia stands aloof from military operations, while her friends in all the belligerent countries are obliged to follow the traditional rule, i.e., to convert the war into revolution.

(2) "National-revolutionary wars against imperialism, including colonial war." This refers to China, Central Asia, and similar territories, where the imperialist side may be represented by France or Holland, or, most commonly, by Britain. In wars of this kind the national and colonial movements are entitled to Communist sympathy and help as

---

1. Lenin, *Works*, XXIV, 122, and XXVI, 12.
2. The Eighth Plenary Session of the Executive Committee of the Communist International, May 29, 1927.

against the parent states and Great Powers. Only in the latter states should war be converted into "civil war," i.e., revolution.

(3) "Wars of capitalist counterrevolution against proletarian revolution and countries of socialist reconstruction." By these are meant wars against Soviet Russia. The policy to be followed here assumes clear outlines. The Soviet Union would defend itself, while the Communist parties within the countries of its opponents (Britain and France were held to be the principal opponents) were to hamper the military operations of their governments and as far as possible convert their antiwar activities into a pro-Soviet revolution. Thus a war against Soviet Russia (a war "on vertical lines") was to be converted into internal wars in the countries of her opponents (wars "on horizontal lines").

An interesting fact about this classification is its failure to include the type of war of which an actual example appeared after June, 1941—a war involving a coalition of Soviet Russia with Britain and the United States. It cannot be said that a combination of this kind was completely ruled out by Bolshevik theory. Its possibility under certain situations had to be admitted. But the admission was made reluctantly and in terms that were too general, while in the official theory any possible alliance of Russia with the principal democratic countries of world capitalism was not even mentioned.

There was a time, at the very beginning of the Soviet regime, when many Bolshevik leaders regarded the suggestion of such a possible coalition as an outrage against the basic principles of their doctrine. Lenin's efforts to teach these leaders realistic politics have already been mentioned in this connection. But, as the years passed, this irreconcilable attitude changed, and the same Bukharin who at one time was so perturbed at the thought of such a coalition later stated in a speech on the Communist program:

"We have grown up so much that we can conclude a military alliance with the bourgeoisie of any one country and use its help in order to crush the bourgeoisie of another country. This is a question solely of strategical and technical expediency." He could not help foreseeing revolution even in the countries of Soviet Russia's allies, however: "If as time goes on the bourgeoisie of such an allied country happens to suffer a defeat, other tasks will arise, which you will easily visualize yourselves." (Here the minutes record: "Laughter in the audience.") [3]

Echoing Bukharin, the draft program spoke of this combination vaguely and tentatively: "Since formation of coalitions between proletarian states and certain capitalist states against other bourgeois states is quite permissible, the question of policy in war depends on each individual case." But there was complete clarity in the declaration that in all circumstances "the proletariat of all countries" was obliged not only to defend the Soviet Union but also "to expand it in order to expand the base of revolution."

Despite the Bolshevik dislike for it, the Soviet-English-French coalition began to loom increasingly as a possibility, as the anti-Soviet trend in German policy grew more and more pronounced after 1933. At the same time it was emphasized with increasing frequency that should such a coalition materialize, Soviet Russia, by virtue of her special position, would wage her own, separate, war. "An answer to every attack on the territory of the U.S.S.R.," wrote Radek on December 16, 1933, "would be military action of the Soviet Union. . . . But a situation might then arise in which the Soviet Union would be engaged in actions parallel to those of the enemy of its enemy, or would therefore be interested in joint action with him." These cautiously formulated phrases of *Izvestiya*, which were no doubt checked in the Kremlin, were a program of an eventual coalition with Britain and France:

First, such a coalition could come into being only in the event of an attack (by Germany) on Soviet Russia—this was regarded as an indispensable condition.

Second, in such a war the course of action of the Soviet Government would be "parallel" to that of Britain and France, considered to be "enemies of our enemies" and not allies, the term ally being studiously avoided. This is none other than the idea of a separate war within the framework of a military coalition.[4]

---

3. Bukharin, speech on the program of the Communist International, November, 1922.
4. Fifteen years earlier these same principles were set forth in the

The problem, strictly speaking, received no further study, although it constantly grew in importance. Clarity was deliberately avoided—the theme was an awkward one. A war coalition of Soviet Russia with Britain and France demanded from the Communist parties of those capitalist countries that they support their national governments so long as Soviet Russia was fighting on their side. This was obviously a delicate subject. At the Congress of the Communist International in 1935, after stating that the main task of the Communists of the world was "to help bring about a victory of the Red Army by any means and at any cost," Mr. Ercoli, presenting the official report, evaded the concrete problem:

"If anybody asks us what this position means and how we are going to act . . . we can give but one answer—in each given case we shall act as Marxists. . . . We have a leader, Comrade Stalin, who has always found the line that led to victory. . . ." [5]

This was all the report offered. At first glance it may appear to be very little—"act as Marxists," "we have Stalin." After fifteen years of theoretical studies and of practice based on these studies—after volumes of resolutions—the statement sounded like an admission of confusion, a loss of orientation. Actually, there was hidden in it something of great significance. It was the admission that henceforth Communism would not always be able to conduct its foreign policy in the open, with its strategy publicly announced; that its policy could not be the product of collective discussion by all Communist parties; that certain inevitable actions would have to be taken, which to many would be unexpected and incomprehensible; that complete power and authority would be placed in the hands of the leader; and that obedience, even

resolution of the Central Committee of the Bolshevik party, which was written by Trotsky and had the approval of Lenin. The resolution said: "In a war with Germany we adopt all means in order to arm and equip our revolutionary army in the best way with all its needs, and to obtain this wherever we can, consequently from the capitalist governments as well. At the same time the party preserves complete independence of its foreign policy, undertakes no political obligations toward the capitalist governments, and considers their proposals in each individual case from the standpoint of expediency." In terms of today, the first part of this resolution might be described as dealing with lend-lease aid and the second part with a separate war.

5. *Communist International*, 1935, Nos. 23–24.

to sometimes incomprehensible directives, was the chief duty of all the component elements of world Communism. The argument ran something like this: When there is a storm at sea, the prime duty of everyone aboard the ship is to obey the captain. Discussion connot be tolerated. Not freedom of action but order and military discipline are what is needed. And only the captain knows what course to follow and what is to be done at every moment.

This position represents the antithesis of the vivacious political movement, the lively exchange of views, the struggle of ideas, of the early 'twenties when the Communist International was being built. Properly speaking, the old organization of the Communist International became superfluous if the only standard was "we have the Leader." It was not without reason that many years later, on May 15, 1943, the Executive Committee of the Communist International, in deciding to dissolve its organization, cited the proceedings of the Congress of 1935, which thus became its last Congress. If strategy is the business of the Commander in Chief, congresses are useless.

During those years Europe was being given an object lesson in foreign policy by Berlin, a lesson which dimmed the reputation of traditional international diplomacy. It was demonstrated that the most towering aims could be achieved by the crudest of methods. The Fuehrer was arming Germany, but swore that his only object was "equality of rights" for Germany, not war—and people were much impressed. He was building a mighty air fleet, but only as a defense against the Soviet air fleet, he asserted, and many accepted the statement at its face value. He annexed territories, but each time swore that he would never do it again—and there were sighs of relief in the chancelleries. He never tired of "guaranteeing the frontiers" and of making repetitious speeches about peace—and he was almost believed. The crudest form of deception proved to be a first-class weapon in world politics, while wise international diplomacy, gray with age, proved itself a farmer's daughter, inexperienced, stupid, and repeatedly deceived.

All this helped intensify the Moscow tendency toward authoritarianism. Let the Leader make history. This was no time for schemes, systems, and principles. Abstractions yielded place to vigorous action, to "realistic policy." Communism entered the war with this mental attitude, an attitude which in turn determined Soviet war policy. There was no renunciation of Communism—only a new strategy.

Communist thought now proceeded from the premise that, in their scope and intensity, the new series of wars and internal upheavals would be unprecedented in history and therefore require a special domestic and foreign policy. The Soviet state which expected to be involved in the war must, even before the war broke out and especially during the course of the war, turn itself into a military camp based upon rigid discipline and absolute obedience. In anticipation of the reverses and retreats inevitable in all conflicts, of maneuvering among dangerous political reefs, of concluding new alliances and breaking off old ones, the Leader was to be invested with absolute authority and be given the right to lead without being compelled to explain his military plans and his diplomacy when it was important that these be kept secret. To this end the Leader had to be lifted so high above the masses that nobody would dare to criticize him.

Opposition was not to be tolerated either on the eve of the war or during its progress. Doubts cause criticism, criticisms bring opposition, opposition internal strife, and strife may mean defeat. Doubters must be destroyed. It is better to destroy, even at home, a thousand innocent people than to have the common cause destroyed. Not relaxation but tightening of the reins of the regime is necessary. It might be a good thing, perhaps, in order to prevent some serious reversals, to let the generals, officers, and strategists have more independence. But what was to be done if they should carry that independence into the major strategy of the war? No, it was safer to risk a retreat than to relax the checks on the officers. It might be a good thing, perhaps, to make some concessions to the peasants and raise their morale, if only by promises of future reforms. But was it possible, in embarking upon campaigns for a new social order, to make concessions at the same time to the old order at home? It would have been better, perhaps, to release hundreds of thousands of people from prisons and concentration camps and to enlist them in the work of defense. But so much resentment had accumulated in the breasts of these people that it would have been necessary either to continue on the path of concessions or to return them to their distant places of confinement. No, better no concessions to anybody—no compacts with any movements—no amnesty, no democratic laxity, no political liberties.

Applied to foreign policy, this trend of thought was bound to lead to an independent, separate war. Of course, at each stage of it one would have had to look for allies, and to reckon with them when they were found. But friends and allies might change—inevitably they would change. And time was when the friendship with Germany was declared to have been "cemented by blood." Later, the Moscow radio would repeat, "Long live democracy!" at intervals. Later still, drinking a toast to President Roosevelt, Moscow notables would exclaim: "God help him in his efforts!" Later, again, promises would be given to Japan that strict neutrality would be observed. Then the Communist International would be dissolved. Diplomatic maneuvering would be more frequently used than ever. It was important not to merge with the allies, not to become dissolved in the democratic sea. A common war—that was possible, but postwar aims remained different. One had to follow one's own road.

Another problem related to the coming war occupied the minds of the Communist leaders: the problem of the revolutionary consequences of the war. The axioms and basic theses were still found in Lenin's idea that every profound revolution was bound up with war, and that in our epoch great wars engendered revolutions.

In the case of a purely imperialist war (i.e., one in which Russia did not participate) revolutionary events could occur in the countries of either coalition or of both; while in a war against the Soviet Union, revolutionary upheavals, it was expected, would shake the countries attacking Russia. Hence, from 1934 on, threat of revolution was one of the arguments used against Germany and Japan. Stalin, for example, spoke in January, 1934, in these words:

The situation is developing toward a new imperialist war. . . . But where is the guarantee that the second imperialist war will give better results than the first? On the contrary, it is bound to tangle up the situation still more. Moreover, it will be certain to unleash the revolution and will challenge the very existence of capitalism in many countries, as occurred in the course of the first imperialistic war.

Regarding the countries that would venture to attack the Soviet Union, Stalin said, on the same occasion:

It is scarcely possible to doubt that the second war against the Soviet Union will lead to a complete defeat of the attackers, a revolution in several countries of Europe and Asia, and a rout of the bourgeois-landowner governments.

Let not the gentlemen of the bourgeoisie blame us if on the morrow of such a war there are missing from the scene some favored governments now, by the grace of God, reigning safely. If the bourgeoisie chooses the path of war, the working class chooses the path of revolution.[6]

These categorical statements about wars and revolutions and the extensive literature popularizing these ideas marked the middle 'thirties, the period when Moscow witnessed a growing interest in the glorification of ancient national heroes, especially military ones, and when the new national notes in Soviet expressions of patriotism began to attract the attention of the outside world. This embryonic nationalism was readily interpreted as Moscow's renunciation of all aims other than those related to national defense. "Evolution of Bolshevism" was again the favorite topic in all languages. Side by side with these trends, however, the unimpaired soundness of the traditional Communist ideas was constantly stressed by the Communist leaders. In this there was no real contradiction. As formerly, "turning an imperialist war into a civil war" was held to be one of the chief aims of policy during a war.[7]

In 1938, almost on the eve of the war, an old article of Stalin's on "Three Characteristics of the Red Army" was reprinted in the Soviet press and multiplied in hundreds of thousands of pamphlets. In this article Stalin saw as the first characteristic of the Red Army its function as "an instrument of the workers' and peasants' rule," and as the second its being an army "of the brotherhood of peoples of our country," of all the nations comprising the Soviet Union. But the third characteristic was this:

6. Stalin, speech at the Seventeenth Congress of the Communist Party.

7. See, for example, Resolution of the Congress of the Communist International of 1935.

"Our army," wrote Stalin, "is an army of the world revolution, an army of the workers of all countries," for, as he went on to explain, it was trained and educated in the spirit of internationalism. A blend of old internationalism with Soviet nationalism has been the basic line of Communist ideology of the last decade. Revolution was not repudiated, nor was Communism, but the supreme consideration was the safeguarding of the Soviet Union. Nucleus of world Communism, the Soviet Union was the only fatherland, and its defense, a national task for the Russians, was an international task for all Communists. Hence, expansion of Soviet territory also became a goal of world Communism—a peculiar substitute for revolution.

For among the many prophecies and prognostications of Lenin, Trotsky, and Stalin which eventually came true, a very important one failed to materialize. The prediction of "a series of terrible wars" after the peace treaties of 1918–19 came true. The diagnosis of the world situation as one of unstable equilibrium, and the appraisal of the role of Soviet Russia in contributing to that instability were correct. The conviction, offered as counsel to others, that it is impossible to appease Hitler and the assertion in 1938 that "war is already on" were also correct. But over a period of twenty-five years these evaluations of facts of international relations were invariably accompanied by predictions of internal revolutionary upheavals resulting from international crises. The shocks, the decisive political battles, however, never materialized; internal crises of a revolutionary nature grew ever fewer; at the same time, where internal crises did occur, they bore an antirevolutionary rather than a revolutionary character. In no country did "war against war" assume anything like the proportions of a strong popular movement. In no country was there anything remotely suggesting "conversion of an international war into a civil war." In particular, the expectation of an antiwar movement in Germany also remained unrealized. But how many sincere hopes were attached in Moscow to this scientific prediction!

The invariable failure, over a period of a quarter of a century, of all promises and expectations of victorious revolutions has had its effect on Russian Communism. Today it is no longer confident that the new war will yield different results. The war in Europe is already more than half through, perhaps drawing to a close, but no important revolutionary movements have been observed anywhere. The old tenet that the world is "in a helpless situation" until revolution opens a new road is no longer unreservedly accepted. More and more frequently this statement of Lenin's is quoted:

"There are no absolutely helpless situations. . . . To try to prove in advance a case of absolute helplessness would be mere pedantry, playing with ideas and catchwords. In this and similar questions the true 'proof' can be supplied only by practice."

If a war could end without revolutions, it was all the more important that the sphere of the only Soviet state be expanded. This form of expansion of the sphere of Communism implied a division of the task of Communism in the war into a number of individual tasks:

(1) In Soviet Russia, a victory over the German coalition and the expansion of the Soviet sphere.

(2) In countries adjacent to Soviet Russia, creation of pro-Soviet or pro-Russian movements acting in opposition to their former governments.

(3) In countries allied with Soviet Russia, support of their war effort, and especially support of future Soviet claims to an extended sphere of influence.

(4) In countries of the German coalition and in occupied Europe—the only countries in which the old revolutionary scheme remained intact—creation of revolutionary movements.

This last group was also the only one which fitted into the framework of the old Communist International.

Experience has shown that the outside world, and the great allies of Soviet Russia in particular, are reconciled to possible territorial changes in favor of Russia but are painfully sensitive to so-called "sovietization" of new territories, i.e., to the expansion of Communism. In other words, to these friends of Russia nationalism and its aims are more acceptable than Communism. As a counterpart to this, past experience, especially that of the Soviet-Finnish War of 1939–40, demonstrated to the Soviet Government how great a mistake it is to conduct a war which has the Communist International for its sponsor.

When at the end of November, 1939, the Soviet Government decided on a war with Finland there was immediately formed in Moscow a new Finnish Government composed of prominent members of the Communist International with Otto Kuusinen at their head. The outside world saw in this the confirmation of the view that the Communist International was an organ of Communist imperialism. At the time this impression caused considerable damage to the efforts of Soviet diplomacy. Opponents of the Soviets gained new adherents in those who otherwise would have been ready to recognize Russia's right to new "strategic frontiers" in Finland. Dissolution of the Kuusinen government in March, 1940, was a notable defeat for the Soviets.

The fact was noted in Moscow. When the new war broke out it was decided not to repeat the error. Both Communism and the Communist International were pushed into the background. *Communist International,* the old official journal of the organization bearing its name, no longer appeared in a number of foreign language editions—English, French, German, and Spanish—and even its Russian edition was forbidden for mailing to other countries. Communist organizations in many countries were also made less conspicuous; they now preferred to appear under non-Communist denominations, such as Anti-Fascists, Patriots, and so on.

National slogans replaced Communist slogans. "Slav conferences," a nonparty Union of Polish Patriots, a nonparty movement of Yugoslav guerrillas, nonparty newspapers, nonparty broadcasts in all languages from Moscow, appeals to the religious elements in neighboring countries—these and similar activities took the place of the work of the Communist International. The more insistent the discussions of war aims between Moscow, London, and Washington, the clearer the claims of Moscow to dominating eastern Europe, the more dangerous, even harmful, the Communist International became. "You say you do not aim at extending your frontiers?" the press of the world asked Moscow. "Very well. But you have another firm, the Communist International, and under the name of this firm you will be sovietizing other countries."

From the point of view of Communist policy the Communist International had to be "liquidated." The actual disbanding came, if anything, too late. But at the moment of the Soviet-Polish rupture (April–May, 1943) when the world, looking to the precedents of 1920 and 1939, expected the setting up of a new Polish Government by Moscow, Stalin, overcoming his previous hesitation, dissolved the International and thus disarmed the critics of its anti-Polish action. Though delayed, the dissolution of the International justified Moscow hopes: it was appraised by many as an abandonment of the program of international Communism, which was precisely what Moscow desired.

With all that, it would be a great mistake to overlook the fact that Communist leaders in Russia continue to be loyal to the banner of the Communist International and that they rolled up that banner with the same feelings and the same hopes with which the American soldiers rolled up their banner on Bataan. As late as 1938, in his *History of the Communist Party of the U.S.S.R.*," Stalin deemed it necessary to repeat the oath he uttered over the grave of Lenin:

"On leaving us Lenin bade us be loyal to the principles of the Communist International. We swear to you, Comrade Lenin, that we will not spare our lives in fortifying and expanding the union of the toilers of the whole world, the Communist International!"

The thing that mattered to Stalin was not the form, the outer garb, but the inner content. He made no attempt to conceal it in his comments on the dissolution of the International. He saw the advantage of the act in making it impossible to suspect Moscow of the intention of interfering in the life of other peoples and of bolshevizing them. At the same time, in his opinion, the dissolution would facilitate the unification of popular, i.e., pro-Soviet, movements, "regardless of party affiliation or religious faith, into a single camp of national liberation." [8]

Similarly, the Executive Committee of the Communist International in its resolution of May 15, 1943, proposing to dissolve the organization, referred to the precedent of the American Communist party, which had been out of the International since 1940. Henceforth all the national parties

---

8. Stalin, letter to Reuter's correspondent King, May 29, 1943.

were to have the same status as that of the American party.

Plainly, nothing was further from Moscow's thoughts than to deprive itself of such a forceful weapon of world policy as the power to direct the activities of numerous parties in other countries. Coördination and management of those activities were more necessary to the Soviet Government now than at any time before. Never in the history of Soviet Russia was there a moment when aid from inside Britain and America and from the neighboring European countries was more important than it is now when the end of the war may be in sight.[9]

The mortality rate among international political organizations is very high, and nearly always the cause of death is internal strife. The Communist International was spared this fate. Its existence was not threatened at the moment of its dissolution by the internal struggle of the national parties which composed it, and there is today no reason to expect any disagreements or antagonisms which would set the Communists of one country against those of another— the Communists of America or of Britain, for example, against those of France or Russia. The single leadership, the guiding iron hand, the instructions and material help continue from Moscow without the official Communist International.

An independent policy in the countries of occupied Europe, acting as a counterpoise to the policies of the London governments-in-exile, has played a prominent role in the activities of the Soviet Government both before and since the dissolution of the Communist International.

As a military factor guerrilla warfare has played an important part in this war for all governments. During the long period of the German occupation each government-in-exile has worked out its own system of relations with the fighting groups of its country, and at the same time the strategy and tactics in the struggle against the forces of the invaders gradually assumed a definite form in each of these

---

9. One important motive for dissolving the Communist International had its source in considerations of internal politics. But this aspect of the matter lies outside the problems of foreign policy which are the subject of this chapter.

countries. Secret printing presses, counterfeit documents, arms, acts of sabotage, as well as military activity—these are the weapons of guerrilla warfare, of which the outside world has known next to nothing. Every military act of the guerrillas produced inevitable countermeasures on the part of the occupying forces and inevitable victims from among the innocent population. The more intense the fighting, the greater the number of victims; while an attempt at a popular uprising, even of local scope, was doomed to be drowned in rivers of blood and to lead to wholesale razing of towns and villages. The strategy and tactics of guerrilla warfare, therefore, presented problems of exceptional difficulty. These were solved in different ways, according to the circumstances of each case. By and large, however, the dominant tendency in this warfare has been not to stake everything on a single operation, but to spare the population, and to wait for the approach of the Allied armies of liberation before setting in motion a general uprising.

The governments-in-exile tried to time strong popular uprisings to the moment when the Allied armies approached their particular lands, and they could be transformed into military operations in line with those of the liberating armies. In the interim these governments confined themselves to paving the way for the future and, through their agents, to organizing single acts of resistance. Revolts of disarmed populations having no chance of success without help from outside would only serve the Germans as a pretext to bathe whole nations in blood. Great devastation, deep despondency, and a breakdown of morale among the tormented nations would be the result of such tactics.

In the ideology and practice of Moscow, however, guerrilla warfare has occupied quite a different place. In Moscow it is viewed as a peculiar synthesis of a military, anti-German organization and a popular revolutionary movement. The largely voluntary character of the guerrilla bands, their self-imposed discipline, their highly secret and dangerous operations, brought them close to the type of traditional underground revolutionary organizations.

This view of guerrilla warfare has been taken over directly from the Russian civil war of 1918–20, in which guerrillas played a highly important role. Since those days the associa-

tion of guerrilla warfare with revolutionary fighting has
taken deep root, whence the great importance of guerrilla
movements in Soviet international policy. In eastern Europe
guerrilla organizations have become the points of support
for building the future sphere of Soviet influence, and in
western Europe they have become the nuclei of revolution.
At first their activities were directed only against the Axis
Powers. Their banners carried only patriotic, national slogans. They promised full liberty at home, and accused Hitler
of suppressing religion, particularly the Catholic religion.
But what differentiated them from other national movements
was their method of attacks and uprisings, at any moment,
whatever the price. These popular uprisings of revolutionary
character were intended to spread wider, rise higher in their
aims, and to assume new aims under changed political conditions. They were to be transformed into precursors of that
revolutionary movement which has been awaited by Communism throughout the past quarter century.

Since the second half of 1942 this policy has developed on
a growing scale in Yugoslavia, Poland, Czechoslovakia,
France, and other countries. Everywhere its progress has
followed a more or less uniform pattern, for it has been
guided from a single center. The question around which
everything revolved was this: Was the resistance to be active
or passive? Was the attitude to be one of watchful waiting
or of aggressive action? Moscow broadcasts in all Slav languages and Moscow representatives in all occupied countries
were calling for action which, growing from day to day
was designed to lead spontaneously to great popular uprisings against German and Italian rule. Demands for such
action have been addressed from Moscow to all the London
governments-in-exile, although everybody was aware that
they would be refused.

The question of guerrilla warfare has provoked and intensified conflicts between Moscow and London. The first
such conflict, although not the most serious, related to the
Yugoslav question and the struggle between the opponents
and supporters of the War Minister, General Draha Mihailovich.

The radio station "Free Yugoslavia" sponsored by Moscow
accused the Yugoslav Government and its supporters of

"proclaiming the slogan of inaction, of patient waiting for better times"; because of this, "the Yugoslav guerrillas had to engage in a struggle not only against the occupation troops but also against the traitors, the Chetniks of Mihailovich." This internal struggle which at times became sanguinary was directed against some very influential and by no means inactive military organizations of Mihailovich. The London radio, speaking in the name of the Yugoslav Government, demanded subordination of all fighting forces to Mihailovich. But "Free Yugoslavia" (broadcasting from Russia) replied:

How can the National Army of Liberation and the guerrilla groups be required to submit to Mihailovich who, together with his Chetniks, as has been proved by documents, is taking part in the offensive of the armies of occupation against our resisting people? . . . The struggling Yugoslav people is being stabbed in the back by the so-called Mihailovich Chetniks, who are everywhere fighting on the side of the invaders helping them to suppress Yugoslav guerrillas.

Guerrilla bands entrenched themselves in some Yugoslav districts (mainly in Bosnia), set up a local administration, and established communication with Moscow. The Yugoslav Government accused these groups of having set up "small Soviet republics." The guerrillas, for their part, conducted their propaganda on a national, not a class, basis and tried to enlist the support of the clergy, while one of the planks in their program was freedom of religion in opposition to the German war on Christianity. "Are these the soviet republics we are building?" "Free Yugoslavia" asked. "Isn't it ridiculous to assert that Father Karamarkevich and dozens of other priests are building soviet republics in Yugoslavia?"

A nationalist note intermingled with the social one. The Mihailovich movement was often expressive of all-Serbian nationalism, whereas the guerrilla movement was a protest against the Serbian mastery over Yugoslavia. In general the Partisan movement bore considerable resemblance to the Spanish Loyalist movement of the Civil War period, the two movements having in common a tremendous enthusiasm, a readiness to sacrifice, and a strong democratic sentiment. But, as in Spain, the crystallizing centers were provided by the Communist party machine and the guidance came from abroad.

Actually, this movement received its support from Moscow

and, with its goal looming in the future, it was the "People's," if not officially the "Soviet," Yugoslavia for which the government, the army, and the patronage of a Great Power were ready and waiting.

Somewhat later than in Yugoslavia, the situation in Poland followed a similar development, except for the fact that neither the Polish Government in London nor the revolutionists in Poland had large military forces to back them. The inner struggle, however, was over the same question: passivity or action?

"Can the people be mobilized under the banner of passivity?" the Polish *Wolna Polska* (Moscow) asked.

Can the people be mobilized under the banner of waiting? . . . They will be wrong who hope by means of insinuations to dig a gulf between the fighting guerrillas, the people's vanguard, and the nation as a whole. Who, giving orders from abroad, can forbid the people to engage in active struggle? . . . We regard propaganda of the policy of passivity, of waiting, as treason to the interests of Poland. . . . The lying arguments about avoiding the sacrifice of unnecessary victims cannot withstand criticism.[10]

To these appeals from Moscow and to certain guerrilla acts in Poland, Premier Sikorski replied from London: "I cannot give orders for a revolt because I should risk drowning my nation in a sea of blood."

At that time the Soviets were landing parachutists in Poland for the purpose of organizing "cells of resistance" and a series of uprisings. Sikorski protested this "interference with Poland's internal affairs." When some of the parachutists perished, Moscow put the blame on the Polish Government, but in London it was declared that "the Polish Government had given no such orders," i.e., to kill these agents. Thus in Poland, too, civil war was assuming a sanguinary form.

Sikorski's protest brought on himself and his government, "the apostles of passivity," a sharp attack from the "Polish Patriots" in Moscow:

The Premier has no need to offer excuses for not raising the slogan of uprising. But an uprising is not a Chinese dragon which leaps out of a box when one presses the button. . . . The Premier cannot summon to an uprising, but he does proclaim the slogan of waiting with clear conscience. . . . Now those who set out to battle the enemy must

10. *Wolna Polska*, March 1, 1943.

fear not only the German bayonet but also a shot from behind a corner, a treacherous stab in the back.[11]

Similar events have taken place even in Czechoslovakia in spite of her repeated protestations of loyal coöperation and of friendliest relations with Moscow. Directives beamed in the Czech language by Moscow broadcasts have been of a much more radical nature than those from London. Premier Beneš recommended "watchful waiting," but the Communist organs accused him of spreading "sentimental slush." Far-reaching plans have been devised also in regard to Czechoslovak units formed in Russia under Colonel Svoboda, whose military successes had been stressed in *Pravda*.

On guerrilla warfare in Czechoslovakia the *Communist International* had this to say:

> The weakness of the Czech national struggle lies in the fact that in Czechoslovakia they still wait for liberation from outside, to come as a result of the defeat of the Hitlerite armies on the war fronts. It is no longer possible to wait patiently for the development of military events at the front—it is necessary to organize fighting activity in Czechia and Slovakia. But among the members of the popular front [i.e., between the Czech Communist party, on one side, and the Beneš and socialist parties on the other] there are differences of opinion as regards the possibility and expediency of armed Partisan warfare against the occupants.[12]

Moreover, these tactics were not confined to the Slav nations. The same problems have arisen in western Europe. On May 13, 1943, commenting on leaflets which had been circulated in Holland and which called for a general uprising, the Dutch radio in London said: "Do not let yourself be provoked." This was accompanied by the statement that appeals to direct action were actually playing into the hands of the Germans who were waiting to pounce on Holland with heavy reprisals.

As in other occupied countries, the French Communists have built their own guerrilla movement, the semi-Communist organization of Free Riflemen. The Free Riflemen argued bitterly against those who denied the possibility of forming guerrilla armies in France because of the regular terrain and few mountains in most parts of the country. Maurice Thorez, the leader of the French Communists, who has

---

11. *Idem*, No. 2.
12. *Communist International*, 1943, No. 1.

remained in Moscow throughout the war years (a French military tribunal condemned him as a deserter during the period of the Soviet-German Pact), came out in the autumn of 1942 with bitter denunciations of "believers in waiting who, it is said, are waiting for the second front," "the irresolute people doubting the necessity of immediate energetic action," and the people who criticize "Partisan activity and all forms of fighting action." "Passivity is dangerous," Thorez exclaimed.[13]

On May 9, 1943, General Giraud considered it necessary to address the French people in the following words:

"Above all, do not grow impatient. Do not give any pretext for savage and sanguinary repression. Wait until we are ready to strike together, from the north as well as from the south, and from the east as well as from the west."

General DeGaulle was undoubtedly personally of the same opinion, but the participation and influence of Communists in his organization probably prevented him from making a similar declaration.

Russian guerrillas operating in the rear of the German Army are one thing. Their purpose is that of guerrillas of every army in every war: they are disrupting the front and the supply lines of the enemy. Guerrilla activity under Communist leadership in occupied countries is something else. Here the leaders have tried to direct the burning hatred of the populace into another channel.

As we have seen, in the Communist conception the Partisan movement has many of the features of a revolutionary civil struggle: complete secrecy, mutual responsibility, centralized leadership, methods of armed fighting, and strict discipline. This is precisely the idea of a revolution as entertained by Russian Bolshevism until 1917. The history of the Comintern records a number of rebellions and general strikes which were paid for with large numbers of victims, although the futility of these rebellions and strikes could easily have been foreseen. Rebellions of this kind weakened the resistance of various nations to foreign occupation.

The chief aim of the new Partisan organizations, bearing different names but similar in essence, has been to create a

---

13. *Communist International*, 1942, Nos. 8–9.

basis for postwar movements in which the present anti-German motif would be replaced by another. In Moscow, it is considered highly probable that the European nations will have to choose between west and east, between London and Moscow. It is possible that the weaker nations will be compelled to lean upon one of the two surviving Great Powers in Europe. Thus the struggle inside the occupied nations described above is even now taking the definite shape of a contest between orientation toward Russia on the one hand and orientation toward the Anglo-American bloc on the other. It is only natural that the Soviets are leaving nothing undone to prepare and strengthen their position for that possibly not far-off event.

In the opinion of Moscow the eight governments-in-exile in London are bourgeois governments, ready to commit treason. Because of their capitalist interests they are not active enough in their struggle against German and Italian fascism. In contrast to them, the patriotic workers of those countries are rallying around the Communists and are beginning to change their attitude of waiting to an attitude of action, to guerrilla warfare, and to open revolt. Thus, not two but three forces are involved in the struggle in occupied Europe: the foreign conqueror on one side, the intransigent, revolutionary proletariat on the other, and between them, the "national bourgeoisie," which throws its weight now on one scale, now on the other.

Such is the latest concept of Moscow about things in Europe, a concept which has developed from mere theory to actual practice in 1943.

In the foregoing account only the occupied countries have been considered. Hungary and Rumania, even Germany, have been omitted from the list. Yet in the grand postwar perspective envisaged by Moscow, Germany stands ahead of all other countries of the world. It may be said without exaggeration that for Moscow everything depends on the postwar future of Germany and her inner political development.

2. RUSSIA'S FRONTIERS IN EUROPE

After several centuries of large territorial gains achieved in rapid succession by conquest and diplomacy, the process of Russian expansion stopped at the very beginning of the nineteenth century, and Russia had made no further additions to her territory in Europe for a hundred and thirty years. World War I, once it started, became on Russia's part an attempt to break down the established limits of her frontiers and to cut through the western wall. Had she succeeded in this and expanded into the west, a grand coalition of European states, led by England, would tave taken up arms against her and brought upon her inevitable defeat and equally inevitable revolution.

This would have been so because at the end of the eighteenth century Russia had advanced into Europe to the limit of her ethnographic or, in a sense, her natural, frontiers. Russia's wars with Turkey brought her to the Black Sea. Her wars with Poland won her her western provinces, among them territories populated by White Russians and Ukrainians. The possible menace from the northwest, as represented by a once powerful Sweden, was eliminated, and the small Baltic peoples, formerly subjects of the multinational Swedish monarchy, were brought within the multinational Russian Empire which entrenched itself on the Baltic shores. But after extraordinary successes and victories, when the process of the gathering together of Slav lands and adjacent territories that had gone on for several centuries came to an end, the Empire stood at the borders of the western nations which, in cultural development and material resources, were equal to and in some cases surpassed Russia. By the beginning of the nineteenth century it was no longer Polish, Lithuanian, or Swedish troops which opposed Russian pressure to the west, but the first-rate armies of Prussia, Austria, and Hungary.

The last victorious advance westward took place in the Napoleonic era and resulted in Bessarabia, Finland, and the small Duchy of Warsaw being acquired. But the fate of these countries, especially of Finland and Poland, was symptomatic of the new position in which Russia found herself. The conquests which had preceded these gains had been quickly followed by the assimilation of the conquered lands even when inhabited by alien national groups.[14] As far as Finland was concerned, the Russian Governments realized the impossibility of assimilating this independent nation, and not until the reign of the last Czar was a policy of Russification initiated. It led to the most lamentable results as far as the Russian regime was concerned. In Poland an attempt was made at first (between 1815 and 1830) to achieve a compromise—a Polish autonomy within the framework of the Russian Empire. But after the Polish insurrection of 1830–31 this autonomy was revoked. As a result Poland never ceased to agitate for freedom, to seethe with insurrection and revolutionary activities, and to engage in European propaganda against "the great prison of nations," acting more than anything else as a source of the universal antagonism to the "barbarian Empire of the Czars."

At this point the western expansion came to an end. Russia came out of the Napoleonic wars not only with a halo of military glory. She pushed right toward the heart of Europe and, in the eyes of her neighbors, quickly became a source of military danger. There had been a time when, from the point of view of western European relationships and the European balance of power, Muscovy was a country of no importance. Now, having saved Europe from Napoleon and with her troops almost on the banks of the Oder and the Danube, she was a tremendous weight on the international scales. All the world capitals, especially London, watched her every step with tension and suspicion. Her activity called forth counteractivity. Had she been drawn into a great war she would have found a huge European coalition, with Britain, the traditional guardian of the balance of power, at its head, ranged against her. It was during that long period of east European stability, which lasted from 1815 to 1914, that the antagonism between St. Petersburg and London took form and grew.

The concept of Russia as the saviour of Europe and of the Russian Emperor as the strongest single ruler within the

---

14. The only exception were the Baltic States, which remained autonomous under the rule of German barons until the end of the 'eighties, and it was only then that Russification started.

"Concert of Powers" expressed the shift in political forces
during the early part of the nineteenth century. Russia's war
against Turkey and the promise of Russian help in saving
Central Europe from revolution still further increased Russian influence. Then, in 1849, Nicholas I made a sortie into the
west when he sent a Russian Army to suppress a revolution in
Hungary. Russian guns thundered near Budapest and this
roar echoed throughout Europe.

Within a few years there came a reaction. In 1854 a coalition of four powers, headed by Great Britain, opened war
on Russia, and the Russian defeat in the Crimea was the
result of this "encirclement." The situation was the natural
consequence of an attempt to extend the expansionist tendencies of the eighteenth century into a new international setting.

There is a small piece of land on the coast of the Black Sea
at the mouth of the Danube which may be said to symbolize
the whole situation of Russia after she had attained her
"natural frontiers" and found herself unable to push any
farther to the west. In 1812 this territory, together with
Bessarabia, was added to Russia. In 1856 Russia lost the
territory to Moldavia. In 1878 the greater part of it was
again joined to Russia. In 1918, together with Bessarabia,
it returned to Rumania. In 1940 it and Bessarabia were again
in Russian hands. This bit of land is, as it were, a symbol of
the limits of "permissible" Russian territorial expansion. It
is as if a steel wall had been raised all along the western
borders of Russia from Sweden to the Black Sea.

The international situation of the nineteenth century constituted a challenge to the entire social and political system
of Russia as it had shaped itself in the preceding centuries.
This had been a system created for war, adjusted to war
aims, and, in the eyes of contemporaries, one that was natural
and justified by military necessity. What eventually developed into a new upper class, the Russian service nobility
(*dvoryanstvo*), began as a class of military commanders
whose duty was to fight for their country at the risk of their
lives and to lead armed units made up of their own soldier-
peasants. Before the nineteenth century this was the only
method of creating big armies. As the government made
grants of land to the army commanders and thus made land-
owners of them, the duties of these commanders became more

important and responsible. The more frequent the wars, the greater became the role of the new ruling class, the stronger its power over the peasantry, and the firmer the power of the autocratic Czar, the supreme leader in the inevitable and victorious wars. The great military successes gave rise to national serfdom of a scope unprecedented in Europe, to the granting of privileges to the nobility, and to the tremendous power of the Czars.

All this changed during the nineteenth century. Great wars were no longer necessary. They lacked inner justification, deep historical significance. Because of this a new feeling gradually developed toward the upper classes, and their privileges came to be regarded as devoid of sense, as parasitic, and their authority as unwarranted. In a society, domination by any one class is tolerable only in so far as it performs some important public function, whether political or economic. But when such a function is no longer performed, the rights and privileges of the class lose their meaning and submissive obedience turns into mutiny. This was precisely the picture of Russia in the second half of the nineteenth century. Doubt penetrated even into the ranks of the ruling class. There appeared the type of "penitent nobleman," a man of stricken conscience who sought to expiate the injustices done to the people. "Simple life" and "going to the people" became the slogans of the intelligentsia. At the same time the centuries-old monarchy began to shake on its foundations. The autocratic Czardom with its fabulous magnificence, its palaces and estates, balls and banquets, diamonds and emeralds, uniforms and braid, and an authority over its subjects the most unlimited in Europe and perhaps in the entire world, showed signs of weakness, of growing deterioration.

This coincided with the change in the organization of armies. Western Europe was rejecting the old military system. New standing armies were unconnected with the social relationship between landowner and peasant. In 1874 Russia followed the other countries in introducing conscription, while the right to join the ranks of the officers was extended to other classes, although the command of the army of course remained largely in the hands of the nobility.

Against this historical background popular obedience

gradually turned into a revolt against the old masters. The revolution which finally broke out after forty years of smoldering assumed its deeply social character for the very reason that it was a popular reaction against rights, privileges, and wealth which had lost their historic justification and were continued by what seemed sheer force and usurpation. Many have sought the reason for this revolution in the growth of industrial capitalism in Russia. But the industrial development was only a contributing factor. At the base lay the radical change in the internal and international position of Russia.

For a brief moment the old traditions, interests, and aspirations came to life again in 1914, when Russia entered the World War. It appeared that the international barrier set up in the west had broken down, that fate had made Britain, the guardian of the barrier, interested in the military successes of Russia, and that a new thrust westward was, therefore, possible at the end of the war. The idea of new territorial expansion westward kindled the imagination not only of all government leaders but of the liberal opposition as well. This blindness to the dictates of history was paid for dearly by both groups during the revolution.

Russia's territorial demands in the war of 1914–17 were of course never realized. But in no sense can they be described as belonging wholly to the past. Regardless of the flag under which it is carried out, every step toward expansion on the part of Russia, if directed to the west, must inevitably proceed along almost the same routes. Neither the form of government nor the social philosophy abrogates the geographic laws and inherent political trends.

On the basis of the diplomatic (mostly secret) documents of the years 1914–17 that have so far been made public, and on the basis of public statements of responsible political figures of that period the Russian plan of territorial acquisition can be stated in these terms:

1. All the Polish territories were to be unified within the framework of the Russian Empire. This meant the addition to the former Polish territories in Russia of the Polish provinces in Austria (so-called Western Galicia) and the Polish provinces in Germany (the Poznań and Pomorze regions). The Russian frontiers in the west would have coin-

cided roughly with the Polish frontiers of 1919–39. The Russian frontier in the Polish north would have touched the Baltic Sea somewhere near Danzig-Stettin.

2. East Prussia was to be annexed to Russia. Thus all the territories lying east of the Vistula would have been brought within the borders of the Russian Empire.

3. Eastern Galicia, populated mainly by Ukrainians, was to be transferred from Austrian to Russian dominion. Together with this province, the northern section of Bukovina was to become a Russian possession, while southern Bukovina was to be joined to Rumania.

4. A Czech kingdom was to be created under a Russian protectorate.[15]

5. A strip of land lying between Austria and Hungary was to become a corridor from the western to the southern Slavs, i.e., from the Czechs to the Serbians. It would have cut off Hungary from the west.

6. The northeastern provinces of Hungary, which had a considerable Slavonic minority, were to be ceded to Russia, with the rest of Hungary, which would have lost additional territory to Rumania and Yugoslavia, being reduced to a small state within the Russian sphere.

7. Turkey was to be ousted from Europe, while Russia was to receive the major portion of her possessions in Europe, including Constantinople. The remaining Turkish territory in Europe was at first intended to be given to Bulgaria; Bulgaria, however, entered the war on the side of Germany. In addition there was to be ceded to Russia a certain area of Turkish territory on the Asiatic coast of the Straits, which would have given Russia domination of the Straits as well as of the Black Sea, and would at the same time have advanced her into the sphere of the eastern Mediterranean. The Slav states in the Balkans would thus have been brought within the Russian sphere of influence.

---

15. "It is proposed to make Czechia a monarchy. . . . A Russian dynasty in any form would be the one most favored. . . . Wishes and plans of Russia will have decisive bearing." (From the memorandum on "Independent Bohemia," prepared by the Czechs in 1915. Archives of the St. Petersburg Ministry of Foreign Affairs. Published in *International Relations*, Series 3, Vol. 8, Part 1, No. 19). The future Czech president, Thomas Masaryk, said, "the general wish of the Czechs is to have a Russian king." (*Ibid.*, p. 268.)

8. In Asia, some of the Turkish territories bordering on Transcaucasia were to be ceded to Russia.

The map (page 173) shows the proposed changes. It would be no exaggeration to say that, had they materialized, they would have been tantamount to a complete revolution in the European system. The Russian frontier would have passed near Frankfort on the Oder, within two hours' journey by rail from Berlin; and in the south Vienna would have been only thirty miles from the Russian sphere. Combined with Russian domination of the Black Sea, the new Russian province at the Straits, adjoining Bulgaria and Greece and strongly fortified, would have made Russia the master of the Balkans. Finally, her position at the Straits and in the Mediterranean would have impelled her to build a great navy and would have forced her to seek the status of a first-class sea power.

At first glance it may seem idle to consider the "iffy" question of what would have happened if history had followed different roads from those it actually traveled; if, for example, the Russian revolution had broken out later than March, 1917, or if the operations of the Allies in France in 1916 had been more successful—in short, if the defeat of the German coalition had taken place before Russia withdrew from the fight. Yet this question is natural and legitimate for everybody who wants to understand the causal regularity of European developments not only in the past but in the near future as well. The vast problem of relations between eastern and western Europe, and the vexing problems of the present period, can be understood only in the light of such an examination.

Even during the negotiations conducted by St. Petersburg with Paris and London at that time, the great restraint of the western powers was apparent. They resisted and hesitated a long time before they yielded to the Russian demands. The fact that France wanted Alsace-Lorraine and the Saar district compelled her to agree to the territorial demands of Russia. Britain was getting less territory and the new rights in Persia and Afghanistan which she reserved for herself far from counterbalanced the huge increase in Russian power in the Mediterranean and the Baltic. But Britain was conducting a war in alliance with Russia; nor did she want to push Russia in any way toward an understanding with Germany. Guided by these considerations Lloyd George yielded to the Russian demands. When later Italy entered the war, Britain and France refrained for a long time from informing their new ally about the future rights of Russia: unquestionably, a Russia entrenched in the Balkans was a grave menace to Italy.

If after an Allied victory, Russia had actually made these acquisitions, the whole of eastern and Central Europe east of the line Stettin-Trieste would have been either completely within Russian control or within the sphere of Russian influence. The Slav countries in the Balkans would have formed a natural continuation of the newly annexed Russian territory at Adrianople. Little Greece, Russia's new neighbor, would always have felt her influence. Little Hungary, situated as it would have been between Russia in the east and Yugoslavia in the south, would have been as dependent on the St. Petersburg government as Slovakia and Bohemia. In the Baltic Sea, as in the Black Sea, the Russian Navy would have enjoyed unlimited domination. Finally, the Russian islands in the Aegean would have become the bases and starting points for Russian influence in the eastern Mediterranean: in Suez, Egypt, and Asia Minor.

It is not hard to realize that in these circumstances the old Anglo-Russian antagonism would have sprung into existence almost automatically. Only this time the antagonism would have found violent expression. Russia, as the principal victor in the World War, could not have failed to become the chief rival of Britain throughout Europe, and especially in the Near East. All the traditional strong points that Britain holds in this sphere—from Athens to Jerusalem, from Cyprus to Cairo—would have been exposed to constant danger. In the north, the eyes of Scandinavia would have been turning more and more toward London; in Poland and among Polish émigrés, demands for independence would have sounded with growing force; Hungary and Rumania, too, would have been seeking the support of the west against the east. But Britain's principal allies in the new situation would have been, first, victorious Italy, whose interests would have been clashing with Russia's in the Balkans and in the Mediterranean; and second, Germany, who would have ceded to Russia her entire eastern territory and one half of her Baltic littoral, and who would have been living under the threat of Russian guns from Silesia to Stettin.

As early as May, 1915, Masaryk summed up the mood prevailing in London:

"The next war will probably be a war of England and Germany against Russia."

Thus, inevitably, a coalition, comprising Great Britain, Germany, Italy, and a number of small states of northern and southeastern Europe, would have been formed against Russia. In the main one recognizes in this coalition the familiar Hitler dream of a later period, the dream which pictured the Axis in alliance with Britain. Such a combination would have been equivalent to isolating Russia and would inevitably have led to her defeat. This new European war could not possibly have been avoided, and would probably have broken out long before 1939. It would have ended not only in Russian frontiers receding far to the east but also in the inevitable revolution. Russia could not avoid that, because for her the roads of great territorial expansion in Europe were closed.

Two attempts to break this barrier were made after the revolution, although under conditions that were entirely new. One of these has already been mentioned—the Soviet-Polish War of 1920 which was to open to Soviet Russia the road of expansion toward the west. This attempt ended in defeat. But when the end of the war was still uncertain, and at the moment when Soviet troops were crossing the Vistula, Lloyd George warned Moscow that Britain would send her navy into the Baltic Sea. This threat contained the first suggestion of the European reaction which was bound to be provoked every time Russia took a long stride westward.

The second attempt was the annexation, between September, 1939, and June, 1940, of the neighboring territories, in one case (Finland) by military force, in the rest (the Baltic States, Poland, and Bessarabia) without important military action. In the great majority of cases these were territories which before 1917 had been parts of the Russian state. Despite this fact, the policy of the Moscow government was perceived by Russia's neighbors as a revival of the old expansionist tendencies—a menace from the east; and their reaction was in accord with this view.

One distinguishing trait marked the Soviet territorial acquisitions—they have been characterized not only by political but also by social transformations. Accompanying them (differing from what had occurred in other cases of expansion) there was an immediate revolution in the economic and political life of the local population. No matter in what guise the acquisition or return of territories was presented, for the outside world the policy of those ten months signified a break with the tradition of "peaceful collaboration," an opening of the new era of state expansion.

Prior to this the impression was widespread that the small neighbors of Soviet Russia had nothing to fear from the east. Many factors must have contributed to this impression. One was probably the belief, widely held outside of Russia, that the Red Army was weak. Another was the view that in the absence of revolutions in western Europe, Moscow would refrain from violent action. Finally, the regular, methodical assurances that the Soviets were inspired solely by peaceful motives must have had their effect. "I fail to see," Stalin stated in his interview with Roy W. Howard, on March 1, 1936, "what danger the surrounding states can perceive in the ideas of the Soviet people. . . . The export of revolutions is nonsense. To assert that we want to make a revolution in other countries means saying what is untrue." Declarations of this kind, as they continued to pile up, created a definite impression. For this reason the words and deeds of the Soviet Government in the beginning of the European war appeared both as a sensational change of policy and as a definite menace.

For one year, from June, 1940, to June, 1941, there was a lull when further expansion was impossible. Finally, since 1941, the old problems have reappeared, this time, in the eyes of the outer world, as the puzzle of Soviet war aims.

— Black line: Borders of Russia, August, 1914.

▨ Territories to be annexed by Russia:
① East Prussia
② Eastern Galicia and Northern Bukovina
③ Part of Turkey in Europe

▦ Territories to be annexed to Poland, within the framework of the Empire: ④

▨ Slav countries in the Russian sphere of influence:
⑤ Czechoslovakia
⑥ Yugoslavia
⑦ Bulgaria

‖ ⑧ Corridor from the Czechs to the Serbs, dividing Austria from Hungary

▱ ⑨ Hungary ⎫
⑩ Rumania ⎭ surrounded by Russia and her sphere.

-- Broken black line: borders of U.S.S.R., Sept. 1, 1939.

3. THE SOVIET SECURITY SPHERE

This war in Europe will probably come to an end not when Germany is defeated but when there are created on the European continent at least one, and possibly two, Great Powers in addition to the Soviet Union.

Such a development is not the deliberate objective of the Allied nations at the present moment, nor does it reflect today's public mood in the Allied countries. But public opinion changes with the change in situation, and for the policy of Great Powers their real interests are the decisive consideration. In particular, the policy of Britain and America, when that conclusive stage of the war is reached, will depend, to a large extent, on the policy of the only remaining Great Power on the European continent—Soviet Russia.

Assuming that the character of the Soviet Government remains essentially the same, the policy of this government during the last stages of the war and following the war will be determined by its view of the nature of the next historical period. Will that be an era of peaceful collaboration of nations, of long years of economic prosperity? Or will it be a period of decline for Europe, an inevitable decay of the Old World? Will there be many new wars? Upon the answers to these questions will depend the course of international politics, especially so in Russia where broad ideas exercise an important influence.

It is possible, as Moscow sees it, that the European continent and perhaps even Germany will come out of the war without a revolution. It is a firm conviction in leading Soviet circles that in that case the new peace treaty will be not more but probably less enduring than the Treaty of Versailles —that it will soon become a scrap of paper, because everything in the European mechanism would remain, in general, unchanged. If the old social system survives unshaken political power will remain in the hands of the old parties whose interests will impel them, through various new and unexpected combinations, to engage in foreign conflicts and wars which will probably be more destructive of life than any the world has seen. No, there will be no enduring peace after the war—such is the conviction of Moscow, a conviction made still stronger by theoretical considerations.

It should be noted that Moscow does not accept the prevalent division of the history of the past thirty years into periods of peace and war. According to the view commonly held outside Russia World War I lasted four years. Then there was a period of peace lasting twenty-one years. Finally, beginning with 1939, a new war broke out, spreading over the entire world. Here the periods of peace and of war are sharply delineated. In Soviet Russia the facts are seen differently.

According to the Soviet view, the war of 1914–18 was first followed by a two-year war with Russia and a five-year period of revolutionary upheavals in Europe, when neither the political nor the economic life of the continent could be stabilized. Then, between 1923 and 1929, a certain measure of stability was attained, although it scarcely approached the settled conditions of the prewar period. Those five years were, Moscow asserts, the only ones in the entire span of the past twenty-nine years when it seemed that Old Europe had recovered enough strength to pursue normal development along the Versailles-capitalist lines. From the end of the 'twenties on, this stability vanished again. There came economic depression, millions of unemployed, bankruptcies, despair. Out of the deep economic crisis there developed a deeper political crisis, which in its internal manifestation gave rise to fascist movements and in its external revealed the irreconcilable nature of opposing national interests. Then came the Japanese aggression in Manchuria and the rise of Hitlerism. Finally, according to this Soviet view, as early as 1937–38 there began the second World War: in Asia from the moment Japan invaded China, and in Europe from the moment Hitler began his territorial annexations (not from the time he invaded Poland). Thus, with the exception of a few years, the entire world for almost thirty years has lived under a reign of chaos—or wars, revolution, antirevolutionary dictatorships, civil wars, militant nationalism, widespread unemployment, and abject poverty. The world tosses about, shakes and writhes in convulsion; it looks for a way out but cannot find one.

In this stylized, overcolored, and exaggerated picture of the historical events, the sharp edges of the periods of war and those of peace are blurred. War is followed by something that is half peace, half war. Everything merges into a mass of unrelieved gloom.

But why has not the world ceased to toss about and writhe since 1914? The answer to this question is a mixture of faith with theory—more faith than theory—a circumstance which endows it with great political force. As the Communist intelligentsia sees it, the system of social inequality, accumulation of wealth and poverty at the two social poles, the expansionist aspirations of states built on a basis of exploitation, have, for the several past decades, made world relations unstable and wars inevitable. The inner mechanism of civilized countries has been stalling with increasing frequency. The entire social system of these countries is visualized by Communism as the engine of a huge tank: there was a time when the engine performed marvels of efficiency; but gradually this efficiency has deteriorated—now cylinders cease to function, now the lubrication fails, now the ignition does not work. Small repairs make it run for a short time, and the tank, not without an enforced stop here and there, is able to lumber on for a few miles. But it is clear that what the tank needs is a new engine. The problem confronting history is to find a great mechanic who is able to dismantle the old engine, throw some parts onto a junk heap, and replace them with a new engine. If such a mechanic (the active minority of the oppressed classes) be found, the world will start off on the road of harmonious development. If he is not found, or is found too late, humanity will continue to writhe, bleed, and die.

This diagnosis of the possible developments determines the future policy of the Soviet Government. The latter has never put any trust in the pacifism of any other government. It has regarded skeptically, even ironically, the assurances of true friendship that have been offered it. It has in latter years become still more confirmed in this attitude. Hence, a skeptical and cautious attitude toward the pacification of the entire world after the war is only a continuation, development, and consolidation of the basic lines of policy.

As a logical conclusion from this it follows that the Soviet Government must strive to secure peace terms which will give Russia new strategic positions for the imminent new period of great world conflicts.

The Soviet Government has not the least faith in the durability of postwar alliances, in assurances of friendship, or in pacts of collective security. For this reason it seeks, and will seek even more as time goes on, to ensure its interests by means of widening its sphere of influence in Europe, in the territory which separates Russia from Germany and Italy. Recognition by other powers of Russia's right to control these territories is the first aim of Soviet foreign policy in the last stages of the present war. In this war aim the Soviet Government, as formerly, sees a combination of two ideas— the idea of defense as expressed in the so-called "strategic frontiers," and the idea of expansion of the socialist sphere in Europe. Herein lies the Soviet solution of the problem of Poland, Yugoslavia, Czechoslovakia, and Bulgaria, and next to them, of Rumania, Hungary, and Finland. At the same time, this program also presents a new modernized form of social revolution.

It is very probable that after the war a superstate organization will be set up in Europe, an organization which the Soviet Government will agree to join. But Soviet Russia will not commit the defense of her territories to a new League, nor will she agree to placing her military forces at the disposal of an international body such as an international police force or some similar organization, whatever its name may be.

In this respect the Soviet Government follows unswervingly the principles which lay at the foundation of its policy in the first period of the European war. Fearing an attack by Germany, it at that time sought to protect its interests, not so much in an anti-Nazi alliance with the Anglo-French coalition as by extending its territories in the west, in the countries which separated Soviet Russia from Germany and Italy. In August and September of 1939 it concluded agreements (which have not been made public to this day) regarding a division of "spheres of interest" between itself and Germany, agreements, by virtue of which six different territories with a combined population of over 23 million would find themselves within the Soviet sphere. The frontiers of the Soviet Union moved far into the west. In the world press they were often called Russia's "strategic frontiers," although the experience of the first weeks of the Soviet-German war hardly confirmed their strategic value.

What is known of these agreements, however, makes clear that Soviet Russia was bound to refrain from "sovietizing" certain regions in its sphere, the Baltic countries being included in that category. The Soviet Government therefore began very cautiously. After concluding Pacts of Mutual Assistance with the three Baltic States and establishing its garrison troops on their territories, it at first refrained from intervention in their internal life. The old governments were left at their posts. Many Communists remained in prison. The Red Army held back from any contact with the local labor organizations. The old system of private property continued unimpaired. So it went on for eight months until a change in the international situation permitted taking the next step: in June, 1940, the Soviet Government took measures to effect a complete absorption and sovietization of the Baltic States, extending the process to Bessarabia as well.

Acquisition of these territories was in effect an expansion of the sphere of Soviet Communism. Within the course of a few months private industry, trade, and banks were liquidated in all the newly annexed lands. The "socially harmful element" of the population, i.e., dealers, tradesmen, agents, and similar businessmen, big and small, were deported to the eastern provinces and to Siberia. The social revolution which occurred in Russia between 1918 and 1920 had its counterpart in these countries, too, but here it came as a ripened fruit imported from outside and no popular movements were required to set it in motion.

"The capitalist world will have to draw back a bit," Molotov exclaimed triumphantly before the Supreme Soviet, in August, 1940. This was a new method of expanding Soviet socialism, a substitute for social revolution. It seemed to give better, or at least quicker, results. Military force instead of popular movements, pressure from outside instead of pressure from inside—what difference did it make, the man in Moscow reasoned. What mattered was the result—the death of capitalism in a number of countries and provinces with a population twice as great as the combined population of all the three Scandinavian countries. Was not that a victory for world revolution?

Yes, a victory without a civil war, without the dangerous popular dream of combining socialism in economy with political freedom, without a protracted crisis inside the Communist ranks. The whole question was one of concrete possibilities. The recipe for the Baltic States read: 90 per cent Red Army plus 10 per cent local Communism. The experiment proved successful. In Spain, due to various circumstances, the recipe had to be different: 10 per cent military aid from Russia plus 90 per cent local forces. The experiment proved a failure. The whole question therefore boiled down to what were the real possibilities and the expected combinations in various countries.

A Soviet security sphere, or sphere of influence (these terms will probably replace the German term coined in 1939, of "sphere of interest"), as a war aim encompasses in the main the same territories which represented the aims of Russian policy in 1914–16. The map following page 173 is still accurate. The main differences between those years (1914–16) and today concern two points: the Straits, inasmuch as in World War II Turkey is not an enemy but a pro-ally neutral; and Rumania, an ally in World War I and today an enemy. Hence, the road to the Balkans now leads across Rumania and not through Turkey. Both then and now, however, the general plan of territorial changes as prepared during the war was and is inevitably approximate. A final plan will be possible only when military operations have been completed.

The close resemblance of the new war aim to the program of the last war is of course not an accident, since it is dictated by the general similarity of conditions. But it is far from being unintentional on the part of the Soviet Government. There is evidence to indicate that the People's Commissariat for Foreign Affairs has been studying closely the diplomatic material relating to the last World War, in particular the attitude of Britain and France to the territorial claims of Russia when they were put forward as purely national and not as social-revolutionary objectives.[16] The Commissariat even

---

16. Literally a few hours before the revolution broke out in Petrograd, a telegram was received from the French Government containing a formula which would have been ideal for the present Russian Government as well. It said: "The Government of the French Republic recognizes complete freedom of Russia in determining her western

seems to be using a map which closely resembles the one here reproduced.

The security sphere mentioned above comprises seven medium-sized and small states and also East Prussia. Mutual assistance pacts with these states would be a legal form of a security sphere. But of these states three non-Slav countries have been members of the German coalition. For this reason, planning for new strategic frontiers for Russia during the progress of the war has been reduced to propaganda for an alliance between Soviet Russia and the Slav countries—a new form of Pan-Slavism [17]—while the hostile non-Slav countries are to be added to the sphere after the war. The policy of the Soviet security sphere has thus been erected as a means of Slav defense against Germanism.

The new "Pan-Slavist movement" of 1941–43 has but a remote resemblance to the old Pan-Slavism of the nineteenth century. The new movement proclaims no mystic faith in the unique characteristics of "the Slav soul," recognizes no special mission with which history has charged the Slav nations, and does not subscribe to hostility to the west as a tenet of its doctrine. Ideological moments are not too conspicuous in the new movement. Rather is it an opportunist construction designed for the present political situation. It expresses more the realistic political program of Moscow than any national philosophy.

The first All-Slav meeting was held in Moscow in the very beginning of the war, on August 10–11, 1941. At that time the chief aim of the new movement had already been revealed as an appeal to the non-Communist elements in the Slav countries to give their support to Soviet Russia. At this meeting the speeches were made not by émigré Communists but by professors, writers, and artists. Alexei Tolstoy, the most prominent of contemporary Russian writers, was the first to speak. He was followed by the Polish General Januszaitis (this was the time of the Soviet-Polish honeymoon), the Czech professor Zdenek Nejedly, the Serbian professor Boz-

---

frontiers." Of course, the Russian Government also recognized complete freedom of Britain and France in determining the future western frontiers of Germany.

17. The neutrality of Bulgaria, the smallest of these countries, does not introduce any important modifications in this program.

hidar Maslarich, and others. The orators discussed the war with Germany and the German danger to the Slavs, but not a word was said about Communism or revolution. The All-Slav Committee, elected as a permanent body, was composed mainly of writers, scientists, poets, and musicians.

During the next eight months the Slav movement showed hardly any activity. At first this was due to the rapid advance of the Germans and the disinclination to stir up new conflicts with the London governments of the Slav countries. But beginning in the spring of 1942, as a result of the change in the general situation, the All-Slav Committee became more active. The second meeting took place on April 4–5, 1942. The speakers were almost the same as at the first meeting, and the meeting decided to publish a monthly magazine. It ended its appeal to the Slav nations with the words :

"Light comes from the East!
"Victory will be ours !"

The third All-Slav meeting was held on May 9, 1943, immediately after the rupture of relations with the Sikorski government. At this meeting announcement was made of the creation of a new Polish Army, and the new Polish leader, Wanda Wasilewska, referred to the Polish Government in London as "traitors who agree to serve the Germans."

The magazine *Slavyanye* (The Slavs), which began regular publication in July, 1942, was essentially an instrument of Soviet diplomacy. The history of the Slav nations served as a background for anti-German conclusions as well as an argument for the closest possible ties with Russia. Contributors to the magazine, apart from the Russians, are chosen from among those Slavs who in opposition to the policy of their governments (Polish, Serbian, Bulgarian) advocated an alliance with Moscow. The Communist writers show no partisanship in their writings, rather the opposite. The better-known Slav writers associated with the Communist International (Dimitrov, Kolarov, and others) are kept out of the magazine. On the other hand, among those who do write are officials of the Slav countries who accept the Soviet position, though perhaps paying only lip service to it (such as the Czechs, including Eduard Beneš).

Complementing the magazine, there are regular radio

broadcasts from Moscow in Slav languages, coupled with encouragement of new organizations, such as the Union of Polish Patriots, the Yugoslav guerrillas, and similar groups. The creation of the Czech Battalion and of the Polish Division (after the breaking of relations with the Sikorski government) was intended to serve the same end. This was actually a practical laying of the ground for the future security sphere. The organ of the Union of Polish Patriots, for example, pointed out the necessity for Poland not only of defeating Germany but of making a choice between the victors —in favor of the Soviet Union: "The national interests of Poland demand that after the war she lean on our great, democratic neighbor, the Soviet Union. Every policy aiming at tying up the fate of Poland to that of any imperialism . . . is bound to lead to a new national catastrophe." [18]

In the eyes of Moscow such was also, essentially, the meaning of the Yugoslav guerrilla movement. The backbone of this movement was composed of men who had taken part in the Spanish Civil War and who had won the complete confidence of the Soviet Government. Following the first successes of the Yugoslav guerrillas, Moscow was pleased to acknowledge that the most active part in the movement had been played not only by "the 33 lieutenants and 39 sergeants who returned from Spain" but also by "15 political commissars." [19] On the twenty-fifth anniversary of the Soviet revolution, "the soldiers, officers, and political commissars of the Yugoslav Partisans" sent their greetings to Stalin, while a Soviet diplomatic note to all the Allied governments (October 14, 1942), in an oblique reference to the guerrilla warfare in the occupied countries, stressed particularly the Yugoslav guerrillas. "The Partisans swear to fight for their Yugoslavia and to struggle together with the Red Army," the *Communist International* wrote in May, 1942.

The Yugoslav Government addressed the Soviet Government in August, 1942, with a diplomatically veiled request, "should the possibility be found to do so," to exercise its influence on the guerrillas in order to restrain them from hostile actions against the Chetniks. The Soviet Government replied in January, 1943, that of course there was no such

---

18. *Wolna Polska*, No. 3.
19. *Communist International*, 1942, Nos. 8–9.

possibility, and pointed out that the facts mentioned by the Yugoslav Government were not correctly stated. The aims of Soviet policy were made clear.

Soviet war aims in regard to Finland followed a similar course. Conceded by Hitler to the Soviet sphere of interests, Finland, as early as October, 1939, received a proposal to sign a mutual assistance pact, after the pattern of the Baltic pacts, with Russia. The compromise conclusion of the Soviet-Finnish War of 1939–40 failed to result in such a pact. But the new war between Soviet Russia and Finland revived the old schemes, as was revealed in the unsuccessful negotiations of the spring of 1943, in which Washington, London, Moscow, and Helsinki took part. In the early stages of these negotiations Winston Churchill, after his conference with President Roosevelt at Casablanca, met the Finnish Ambassador Yrjo Koskinen in Turkey and discussed with him terms of peace between Finland and Russia. After the Finnish presidential election (February 15, 1943) Rolf Witting, the strongly pro-German Finnish Minister of Foreign Affairs, was removed from his post and the Finnish Government began to sound out the Allies. One of the conditions of peace proposed by the Finns was "guarantee of the Finnish frontiers" by the United States.

About the same time, Finland sounded out Berlin regarding Germany's attitude toward her withdrawal from the coalition, receiving from Ribbentrop a categorical threat of dire consequences. This was enough to make Finland abandon the idea of a separate peace or a truce. The answer of the United States to this action of the Finnish Government was to recall nearly all of its Embassy staff from Helsinki.

During these negotiations, which continued from February to April, 1943, it became apparent that the position of Moscow, too, would have made the contemplated agreement impossible, since Russia's demands went beyond the treaty of 1940,[20] while her general attitude toward the Finnish question made impossible any outside guarantee, i.e., any intervention of a third power.

These positions were stated, after the Finnish presidential

---

20. On April 4, 1943, Finland inquired about Soviet peace terms. The reply included demands reaching further than the stipulations of the peace treaty of 1940. (*New York Times*, April 24, 1943.)

elections, both by the official Soviet press agency, *Tass*, and by the Moscow radio broadcasts in English on February 19. The latter spoke of the "comedy of the presidential elections," and referred to them as "a blind violation of democracy." If the elections were a breach of the law, then the new government had no legal standing.

As a result, the American State Department came to the conclusion that "the United States would not act as intermediary since there is no expectation that Russia would recede from her position." [21]

"Security sphere," as a reality and as a legal concept can assume a variety of forms, from ties with Moscow that are very close to ties that are very slight. One form of a close connection would of course be the direct inclusion of a number of territories within the body politic of the Soviet Union, in other words, a switching over in all relations with these territories from the norms under international law and foreign policy to those of public law and internal policy of the Soviets. But realization of this program will also depend on the will of the Great Powers among the victorious United Nations, and upon public opinion in Europe. For this reason the Soviet Government, which has demonstrated its flexibility, will no doubt agree to any political or legal form provided it gives Russia actual supremacy in the political life of the given sphere. For example, it will probably be willing to undertake not to sovietize these countries. It will no doubt confirm its readiness to refrain from any interference in internal politics, party struggle, parliamentary life, local self-government, and police organization. The principle of independence has already been promised in Moscow declarations. But the minimum demands which would be necessary in order to transform this collection of states into a Soviet security sphere would first of all require that the governments of the security sphere conform their foreign policies to the foreign policy of Moscow. As a natural complement to these demands there would have to be guarantees of enforcement of this obligation, including the use of armed force if and when necessary. This would be similar to the Mutual Assistance

---

21. *New York Times*, April 28, 1943.

Pacts between Russia and her neighbors concluded in 1939.

In 1942 and 1943 the Kremlin offered Mutual Assistance Pacts to all the three Slav countries occupied by the Germans. In the spring of 1942 the draft of a treaty with Yugoslavia was ready for signature, and Molotov was expected to sign it for Russia during his visit to London in May of that year. (The new treaty was construed as a development of the Soviet-Yugoslav Treaty of April 5, 1941, whose ratification was made impossible by the German invasion of Yugoslavia.) Again the treaty remained unsigned. The British Government, backed by Washington, opposed the creation of a Soviet sphere in eastern Europe. Following the failure of this Soviet attempt, the struggle of the Yugoslav guerrillas against Mihailovich entered upon its bitterest phase.

Regarding Poland, one week after the Soviet Government had broken off diplomatic relations with the Sikorski government, Stalin, on May 4, 1943, publicly offered Poland a Mutual Assistance Pact, announcing, in order to avoid intensification of the conflict with Britain and America, that conclusion of the pact would have to be deferred until after the war.

Negotiations with Czechoslovakia proved more successful, thanks to the special position taken up by the Beneš government. The westernmost of the Slav nations, the Czechs have waged a bitter struggle with the Germans throughout their history, but unlike the Poles they never had to defend themselves against "the Russian menace." Since December, 1942, the Beneš government has been cooler toward Poland, to which it was tied by the treaty of 1940, at the same time drawing closer to Russia. When it became evident that Beneš' idea of an alliance with both these countries could not be realized, the Czechoslovak government, on April 8, 1943, resolved to agree to "an alliance between Czechoslovakia and the Soviet Union." With the object of smoothing the way for this alliance, Beneš visited Washington and engaged in negotiations in London. He did not find it easy to convert either Britain or America to his views.

In Moscow his government was regarded as a loyal ally, and in anticipation of the Mutual Assistance Pact there began to appear in Moscow a fortnightly magazine, *Československe*

Listy, which stated in its first editorial (August, 1943) that "the Soviet Union is the main support in the struggle of the Czechoslovak peoples for their future."

Quite naturally all these treaties, prepared in wartime, bore the character of treaties between two equal and independent countries. Incidentally, they contained no military guarantees for the Soviet Union. They could be further expanded and augmented by clauses necessary from the Soviet point of view, only after Russia had won the decisive victories over Germany.

The extent to which the Soviet undertaking not to overstep these self-assumed limitations would be fulfilled is another question. Considering the Moscow tendency to strict unification and centralized control, it would hardly be possible for the countries in the security sphere to oppose Soviet policies freely or to reveal, which is inevitable, trends toward emancipation, without bringing upon themselves countermeasures by the Soviets. On the other hand, the preservation in those countries of the basic forms of the old economic system, deprived of extensive foreign credits and accompanied by the inevitable flight of capital and widespread unemployment, would probably provide a stimulus for a scattered and gradual *Gleichschaltung* with the norms of the Soviet Union.

Soviet war aims were a subject of discussion as early as the end of the summer of 1941. While the Soviet Government was anxious to have these questions clarified as quickly as possible (it expected the war to last not more than one year), the British Government was on the contrary inclined to avoid discussion of peace problems. Moreover, the Atlantic Charter, which was proclaimed in those months, made it difficult for the British to make concessions to the Soviet point of view. But this resistance weakened as the Red Army loomed more and more important to British public opinion. On his visit to Stalin in December, 1941, Foreign Secretary Anthony Eden discussed with him the problems of future Russian security. No agreement was reached, but shortly afterward a majority of the members of the British War Cabinet swung over in favor of some of the Soviet demands, with Winston Churchill remaining in the minority. At the same time there were voices in the British press which argued for still greater concessions to Moscow. It is hard to say how much of this was sincere and how much an emergency diplomacy.

In the meantime, the United States had entered the war and the voice of Washington grew in importance. Discussion of Soviet projects was carried on not only between Moscow and London but also between London and Washington. In America Soviet demands met with serious resistance. Discussion on the question reached an impasse, but as the result of protracted negotiations, an Anglo-Soviet Treaty, the idea of which came from Washington, was signed in London on May 26, 1942.

The treaty contained neither territorial concessions nor provision for division of Europe into spheres. On the contrary, its basic idea was that all questions of the organization of Europe, including those pertaining to the east of Europe, were to be solved only by joint decision of Britain and Russia after the war. The treaty also proclaimed "the desire of both parties to unite with other like-minded states" after the war, i.e., both Britain and Russia favored the formation of some supernational organization. If this desire should for some reason fail of realization, the Anglo-Soviet alliance (bearing in mind its decisive role in Europe) shall remain in force for twenty years. Enrollment of other states in this alliance, i.e., its conversion into a great League or Council was contingent on the consent of both primary powers, and opposition by either power was sufficient to rule out a candidacy.

The Anglo-Russian Treaty was, therefore, only a form, a plan, which could be filled with the most varied content; all the projects of frontiers, federations, national states could find a place within its framework. On the other hand, all of them could be rejected. In point of fact, after the treaty was signed a lively discussion of the same problems was continued among the governments of the United Nations, and six months later it was felt in London that although "there is a necessity of overcoming Russian suspicions," "the Anglo-Russian Treaty has not accomplished this." [22]

The only feature of the treaty which, historically speaking, seemed to have an element of sensation, was Britain's readiness not to strive for a balance of power on the continent but to recognize Soviet Russia as the only victor. Russia's domi-

22. *New York Times*, January 23, 1943.

nant position was to be balanced not by another continental power but—and this was a concession on the part of Britain —by Britain herself. The plan was certainly original but it failed to satisfy anybody either in London or in Moscow.

Thus the discussions continued, with the governments-in-exile of some east European countries taking a very active part in them. The role of Russia in the war grew in importance, while in London more voices were heard favoring recognition of Russia's right to control eastern Europe. When Soviet-Polish relations became strained and were clearly moving toward rupture, public opinion in Britain was divided. The pro-Soviet point of view was expressed by the London *Times*. If it is held by the British, the *Times* stated in an editorial, that Britain's frontier is on the Rhine, then "Russia's frontier is on the Oder." Hence, "the lands between Russia's frontiers and those of Germany" are to be held "by governments and peoples friendly to herself." [23] From this it is to be concluded that governments (such as those of Poland, Yugoslavia, and Finland) which refuse to subscribe to the latter principle must not be recognized or permitted to exist. The classic formula of Soviet sphere of influence demanded no more.

The Soviet press made much of this London *Times* editorial. Anthony Eden countered this by stating that the *Times* does not express the opinions of the British Government; while Churchill who, from the beginning of the war opposed public discussion of war aims, now deemed it necessary to make a statement bearing on this question. In a long address delivered on March 21, 1943, at the time when, under pressure from Moscow, the agreement for a Polish-Czech combination was annulled, Churchill contemplated, instead of a division of Europe into spheres of influence, a formation of "confederations of states side by side with the great powers." These confederations were to be independent members of the future "Council of Europe" which, accordingly, was to be made up "of states and groups of states."

We would have to respect and have a care to the rights of weaker and smaller states, and it will not be given to any one nation to achieve the full satisfaction of its individual wishes. . . . It is my earnest hope

23. *Times*, March 10, 1943.

that we shall achieve the largest common measure of the integrated life of Europe that is possible without destroying the individual characteristics and traditions of its many ancient and historic races.

Churchill thus postulated the creation of a European superstate organization in which the Soviet Government would be dealing not with Britain alone, as was provided for in the treaty, but with many other states. The confederations suggested by Churchill were to be alliances of smaller states united for the preservation of their independence, instead of being forced into the Soviet sphere. Furthermore, Churchill expressed the desire to see the United States in the Council of Europe, evidently in order to strengthen the position of Britain.

Naturally, Churchill's declaration did not meet with the approval of Moscow. The plan of an East European Federation found warm support among the Poles, and, in criticizing the Polish émigrés in London, Moscow aimed at the British and American governments. The Moscow magazine, *War and the Working Class,* which began publication immediately after the suspension of *Communist International,* attacked, in August, 1943, "the plan for the creation of a United States of Europe," in which Russia would have been, as she was in the League of Nations, only one element among a great number of equals. It also expressed opposition to "federations, confederations, and regional blocs of states," and especially denounced the idea of "an Eastern European Federation which is to be the political union of democratic Czechoslovakia and feudal Hungary, republican Poland and monarchical Rumania." "The project of an East European Federation is directed against the Soviet Union," the magazine declared.

Soviet foreign policy has for years been publicly pursuing the object of making impossible the formation of any alliances between Russian neighbors in Eastern Europe. Molotov's strong pressure was responsible, for example, for the failure of Finland and the Scandinavian countries to form the Northern Alliance, while the existence of the Baltic Alliance between Latvia and Estonia was one of the arguments used to justify the occupation of these states by Russia in 1940. As applied to all postwar plans, this principle would mean: alliances and pacts in this part of Europe are possible only with the Soviet Union. The threads connecting the capitals must run east and west, and not north and south.

Any such federation would represent an attempt to restore Austria-Hungary without the Austrians. In reality, because of its weakness, it would be capable only of self-defense, never of united aggressive action. Nonetheless, the project stands in conflict with the idea of the Soviet security sphere, wherefore "we would be obliged to regard every attempt to form new federations on the model of the Austro-Hungarian union as a reactionary attempt which would be harmful, and incapable of realization." [24] The project of an East European Federation as a defense barrier against the German menace no doubt also contemplates, as Moscow not unreasonably claims, the possibility of defense against the Soviet Union.

The position taken by Churchill on this question represented the traditional policy of Britain. Britain is neither willing nor able to replace continental powers by herself. So long as Britain remains undefeated she will not consent to a structure of the European continent in which one Great Power possesses great military forces while the rest of the nations remain small, weak, even disarmed. The war may end in a debacle for Germany, and for a time the Anglo-American armies of occupation will play the part of a second Great Power. They will not leave the continent, however, until they have transferred the function they will have been performing in shattered Europe to some newly created national forces. The more persistent the pressure from the east, the more rapid will be the formation of these forces. The clearer the expansionist tendencies of one power appear, the stronger will be the resistance. If only one of the victorious powers repudiates the program of pacification and disarmament, this will be enough to cause the program to founder for all the victors.

It is not likely that the solution of the problem will have to await the peace conference, since the entire situation will be cleared up during the last stages of the war. If the Allies fail to come to an agreement, the question of frontiers and spheres of influence will be resolved (not for the first time in history, not even in the twentieth century) by the actual situation on

---

24. *Wolna Polska*, August 25, 1943.

the war fronts. Defeat of Rumania will open the way to the Balkans either to the armies which will come from the south and west, or to those which will come from the east. The fate of Poland may well be decided by the national colors of the armies which will be the first to enter Warsaw. This would be a paradox as well as a tragedy. But such developments are entirely possible at the last stages of a war which lacks a common program.

It is hardly probable that Russia's chief allies would comply with her desires for a considerable expansion in any form whatever. But it is another paradox that the consequences of Soviet expansion would in both cases be almost the same, i.e., whether it is achieved with or without the consent of the powers. In both cases the world press would be full of alarmist reports from every corner of the security sphere, the diplomacy of the small countries would be working without let-up, air forces would be concentrated in the Anglo-American sphere in Europe.

This would be the "encirclement" which Soviet Russia has always feared more than anything else. This time the encirclement might involve an Anglo-German alliance, the most dangerous combination Russia could face. This process of encirclement is certain to take place after Soviet Russia crosses the Vistula, enters the Balkans, and moves up to the Mediterranean. Neither arguments nor appeals nor pacifism will be able to check the development of this conflict.

"World War III?" It need not break out immediately after the victory. The Soviet Government will spare no effort to avoid a serious and decisive conflict with the Anglo-American alliance, while trying to preserve its newly won territories, taking daring leaps when necessary and not hesitating to appear guilty of minor contradictions. Maneuvers, partial retreats, promises, diplomatic moves, assistance of Communist parties in other countries—all will be used in order to solve the problem of squaring the circle. But the tension will go on rising and the Soviet Union will be facing the greatest danger it has ever faced since its founding. Moscow will call this an offensive of world capitalism against the land of socialism. Actually, it will be the natural reaction of Europe to the expansion from the east, and it will be all the more

formidable because the Russian expansion will be fraught
with the danger of economic expropriation and specific political reprisals.

It is possible that the effect of this expansionist policy will
be not an immediate war but creation of powerful states in
Europe capable of acting as counterweights. If Germany lies
in ruins, special measures will be taken to bring her back to
life. If any chips of old Austria-Hungary exist, they will be
welded together to form an important state. France will become again a first-class military power.

In the Soviet program of a new Europe, however, there will
again be evident as in all problems of Russian policy, the
conflict of national requirements and those of Communism.

Russia as a nation does not need these huge alien territories
in any form, whether by formal annexation or inclusion in
the security sphere. Bringing these nations under Russia's
domination would create difficulties and dangers that would
outweigh all the benefits that might accrue from them. Conquest and territorial expansion do not always increase the
power of a state. Sometimes they contribute to its weakness.

It should be remembered that among the non-Slav nationalities of Russia, with her total prewar population of 170
million, the largest national groups are still rather small:
Uzbeks, 4.8 million; Tartars, 4.3 million; Jews, 3 million.
Dozens of nations which to this day stand on a lower level of
civilization have been swallowed and digested by the giant.
Others have had to resign themselves to their subordinate
status either because of geographic conditions, making them
an island in the Russia sea, or because they were too weak
numerically.[25] This is why multinational Russia (the crisis
years 1917–23, of course, excluded) had remarkably few
national-separatist movements.

The nationalities living along the western frontiers of
Russia are in a different position. The Poles, roughly 20 mil-

---

25. The questions of the Ukraine and White Russia cannot be discussed at length here. Suffice it to say that these problems, due to a
number of reasons, stand apart from the question of other national
minorities in Russia, and that, in the main, the Ukraine and White
Russia have become an integral part of the Russian state, and whatever element of separatism is manifest in them exists only on the surface.

lion strong, are the most important, both in numbers and in political strength, of Russia's western neighbors. They form a nation which will not reconcile itself to being incorporated within another state, or even to an autonomous form of dependence. Hungary, defeated and conquered, may be subdued, but that her submission cannot be lasting is hardly open to doubt. Finland's jealous concern for her national independence has been amply demonstrated. In varying degree and form this applies to the 3 million Germans in East Prussia, the 10 million Rumanians, and lastly to the Serbians and Czechs. Taken as a whole, this belt of Central Europe, with a population of roughly 100 million, would, if bound to Russia, become the focus of centrifugal forces, while its compact mass of foreign nationalities would be a source of weakness to the Protector. An alliance of all these nations with one another, which so far has been shown to be an impossibility, would become a reality when there existed a common aim of national liberation from foreign rule. The "western orientation" of these nations would resolve into a search among the Great Powers for allies against Moscow. In these countries "separatism" would flourish, and in every international conflict the opponents of Russia would find in them ready tools for their own ends.

Moscow holds a different view of all this. It believes that these dangers, when they refer to Communist Russia, are not nearly as great as they appear. It is true, this theory proclaims, that Russian Czarism, which tried to suppress national languages and national cultures, often turned the nations it conquered into its enemies and was unable to make them integral parts of its system. But the Soviets do not oppress nations as such; quite the reverse, they open the widest opportunities to the intelligentsia of these national groups. Furthermore, the Soviets appeal to certain elements of the workers among these nations and win them over to the Soviet side. Hence, the Soviet era opens the way for integrating new and great nations within the Soviet Union.

This was reiterated as late as 1943:

Formerly, it used to be held—as was proved by the experience of many countries—that the presence of different peoples and nationalities within the boundaries of one state makes that state weak and vulnerable to its enemies. But the multinational Soviet state built . . . on the foundations of Lenin's teachings, afterward developed by Stalin, upset this concept and rejected this experience.[26]

This Communist theory is not only erroneous but extremely harmful. There is not the slightest evidence that European nations would reconcile themselves to Moscow supremacy over them, least of all, to a Communist supremacy. Quite the opposite appears inevitable. It is not true that national aspirations are limited to questions of language, and it is especially not true when applied to nations with a long historical past and statehood. Ireland fought and is still fighting for independence despite the broad autonomy conceded her. The Austrian monarchy specially favored some of its nationalities, but its favors did not reconcile them to their subordinate status. Many such examples are found in history. To these considerations there is added, under Soviet conditions, an inevitable social transformation which requires stern political measures. The centrifugal national tendencies would be intensified by the results of a foreign economic system imported from the east. To these nations this would make the oppression trebly hard as compared with simple national oppression. If in the domestic life of the Soviet Union the national problem has so far held second place in comparison with problems of internal and economic policies, the reasons for this lie in the character and history of the peoples comprising the Soviet Union. The same set of causes cannot be assumed as applicable to a new situation involving great new nations.

The necessity to Communism for it to expand its sphere of influence is perfectly clear. But from the point of view of the Russian nation as a whole such an expansion, far from being merely undesirable, is actually highly dangerous. France, great power that she was and will be, would not become stronger if she were able to bring the 25 million people of Spain within her "sphere." This would become for her a constant source of wars and a cause for a defeat. Germany has not become stronger through the annexation of Czechoslovakia and Poland. On the contrary, her action is already leading her to inevitable defeat. Russia will not become stronger by subjugating great territories in the

---

26. *Communist International* (editorial), 1943, No. 1.

heart of Europe. The Tatra and Carpathian Mountains, the waters of Sava and Drava, and the rocks of Montenegro are not worth to Russia as such, the bones of a single Red Army man!

Restraint at the moment of military victory is as necessary, though sometimes as difficult, as the achievement of victory itself.

4. RELATIONS WITH POLAND

A Soviet security sphere would include Poland as its most essential component part. Poland is the largest of the states which lie between Russia and the Axis Powers. On the other hand, if these states ever realize a policy of joint action, the leading role in it will be played by Poland.

In Soviet eyes Poland is either a barrier against, or a bridge to, Germany. She was the only one of the European neighbors of Soviet Russia who joined the anti-German and not the German coalition. Conversely, she was the only European state among the United Nations which had border disputes with Soviet Russia (in 1919–20 and after 1939).

Soviet-Polish relations bore the weight of twenty years of history, influenced by the tendencies and distant aims of both governments. There was the fact that Imperial Russia, which was in possession of the greater part of Polish territory, was the principal national enemy of restoration of an independent Poland, and that as a result Josef Pilsudski was more anti-Russian than anti-German. There was the influence of the early aspirations of the new Poland to restore the frontiers of the seventeenth century, these aspirations (as professed in 1919–20) postulating the inclusion of vast Russian-Ukrainian territories within a Polish-Ukrainian state, whose combined population would have exceeded that of Germany. There was, in short, the influence of the political trend in Poland which had for its goal the transformation of the new Poland from an important state into a Great Power—in which the Poles themselves would form a minority among Ukrainians, Germans, Lithuanians, and Russians.

Traditions of Soviet policy added their weight to the other side of Soviet-Polish relations. The Soviet Government of 1920, which attempted to transform Pilsudski's war against Russia into a war for a Communist Poland, had Stalin as one of its members. The Polish campaign, terminating in Russian defeat and in the Peace of Riga, was also his personal defeat. From 1919 to 1937 Warsaw was, in the eyes of the Kremlin, an outpost of the French and British domination of the continent, and the state of prolonged antagonism between Soviet Russia and these countries added to the strained relations between Soviet Russia and Poland. There were, to be sure, trade agreements and periods of rapprochement. But all this was on the surface: the deeper realities remained intact. Even in the 'thirties, when the German menace was the chief concern and Soviet relations with France began to improve, relations with Poland were but slightly affected by the turn in the international situation. In 1939, when efforts were being made to create an anti-German coalition, Poland held uncompromisingly to its refusal to permit the movement of Soviet troops across Polish territory. Poland, which had feared and fought the weak Soviet Russia, feared even more the strong military power that Russia had become at the end of the 'thirties.

Then came the partition of Poland, the operations of the Red Army, and the Moscow declaration that "the Polish state had ceased to exist." As a result, a part of the Polish Army became Soviet prisoners of war; hundreds of thousands were deported from eastern Poland to Siberia and the Russian north; and eastern Poland was incorporated in the Soviet Union, sovietized and socialized.

Such was the political background on the eve of the war between Germany and the Soviet Union. It promised little, particularly since the political tendencies and dominant attitudes both in Poland and Soviet Russia continued in the main as before. Poland's aims in the war were: retention of the former Polish territories, addition of East Prussia and a part of German Silesia, and internationalization of the straits connecting the Baltic Sea with the Atlantic Ocean. The Soviet Government's aims embraced, first, permanent inclusion of eastern Poland in the Soviet Union, and, second, a new form of relationship for the future which would have deprived Poland of full independence in her foreign policies. The two policies were clearly irreconcilable and the differences far deeper actually than those involved in the disputes over border territories.

In the first agreement between the Soviet and Polish Governments, which was concluded on July 30, 1941, the question of eastern Poland was left open. The agreement made possible, in principle, the creation of a Polish Army in Russia, an army recruited mainly from Polish citizens deported from the territories occupied by the Red Army in 1939.

This agreement was followed, on August 14, 1941, by a military agreement which has not been made public. The military agreement set no definite limit to the size of the Polish Army; in the circumstances it could hardly have done otherwise, since it was impossible to foresee future requirements. It was supposed that the British would fit out the army, while the Russians would feed and arm it. On August 19 it was agreed that as a beginning two Polish divisions of about 30,000 men would be created. This force was to be trained in Buzuluk (the south Urals) and in Tatishchev (Saratov region), and before being sent to the front it was of course to be fully equipped and armed.

The number of recruits grew rapidly. After two months there were more than 40,000. Meantime, winter was drawing near. Accommodations for billeting of the troops were inadequate, and food and footwear were insufficient. Friction developed. In a note dated November 8, 1941, Molotov informed the Poles that the army in training must not exceed two divisions. Actually at that time only one division had been equipped and armed, though not fully.

It must be borne in mind that while in matters of war operations at the front the Polish Army was to be subordinate to the Russian High Command, in all other respects it remained an organ of its own government and retained a certain amount of autonomy in internal affairs, as, for example, in having Catholic army chaplains instead of military commissars, and in other similar privileges. The Polish Government also obtained Stalin's consent to the principle that the Poles would be sent to the front not in small units but in divisions and corps. The Polish Government wished to see a big Polish Army march into Poland when the moment of liberation arrived. But this prospect was precisely what the Soviet Government regarded as dangerous, since it foresaw inevitable political difficulties in the last stage of the war when all the questions dividing Soviet Russia and Poland would come to the fore. The Soviet Government readily sent to the front a battalion of Czechs or a group of French flyers —this was a demonstration of international unity. Likewise, a Polish force was welcome within these limits. But a big Polish Army with a certain amount of independence was a different problem.

In 1914–18 the Belgian Army fought on French soil. This was possible because there was no disagreement between France and Belgium regarding war aims. Such harmony of views is a necessary condition for coöperation of two armies on each other's territory. In this war there has been no such harmony of views between Poland and Russia.

This explains the obstinate and seemingly senseless opposition of the Soviet Government to any increase in the size of the allied Polish Army. Numerous conferences and discussions between the Polish representatives and the Foreign Commissariat, the military authorities, and the leaders of the Soviet Government, Stalin and Molotov, failed to bring results. Incidentally, Stalin was more generous with concessions than others and stressed his friendly attitude to Poland. But the results were of course the same.

On November 14, 1941, the Polish Ambassador Stanislaus Kot was received by Stalin, who confirmed that the Polish Army was not to be limited to any maximum strength, that he personally had no objection to its having five to six divisions, and that it was absurd to demand that Polish troops be sent to the front before they were fully trained and armed. On December 3 Premier Sikorski visited Stalin and again the principal subject of conversation was the Polish Army. Stalin made extensive promises to Sikorski, such as assignment of a special section of the front to the Polish Army, an adequate supply of provisions ("Why are not the Poles given sufficient provisions?" he demanded sternly of General Panfilov, the Soviet-Polish liaison officer, adding, "Are they to feed themselves on our instructions?"), and all the necessary arms and technical equipment. It was agreed between Stalin and Sikorski that the Polish troops would be transferred to a warmer district, in the neighborhood of Tashkent. Altogether, Stalin expressed himself as wishing to see "a big and strong Poland" —a statement which Sikorski made public in his broadcast from Moscow the following day. The radio listeners probably wondered what precisely was meant by "a strong Poland," seeing that for more than twenty years Stalin had regarded a strong Poland as the principal link in the *cordon sanitaire* and as a bulwark of capitalism.

To give effect to the negotiations between Stalin and Sikorski a second military agreement was signed on January 22,

1942, making provisions for raising the strength of the Polish Army to 96,000 men and guaranteeing this army complete war equipment. In the middle of March, when more than 70,000 men had already been recruited, General Anders, Commander in Chief of the Polish Army, was summoned by Stalin and told that in view of the failure of the United States to deliver the promised quantity of wheat the Soviet Government was able to supply food for only 44,000 Polish soldiers. Stalin suggested that the rest be used as farm hands on collective farms. General Anders declined the proposal, whereupon Stalin suggested sending the balance to Iran.

This was the beginning of the dissolution of the Polish Army in Russia. The transfer was pushed with great speed, and within two weeks, by the end of March, about 30,000 Polish soldiers, together with 12,000 Polish civilians were evacuated. The question of continued drafting of Poles in Russia was left hanging in the air. The Polish Government proposed compulsory drafting and transportation to Iran of all new recruits, and at first Stalin seemed to favor this proposal. Later, however, the Foreign Commissariat informed the Poles that the Soviet Government was unable to approve the project. The actual reason was that the recruits were needed for the contemplated Polish Army which was to be created later on Soviet soil on entirely different principles.

Nevertheless, little headway was being made in the preparation of the Polish troops for war service, and with the exception of a few units, their being sent to the front was out of the question. At the end of August, 1942, General Anders was again summoned by Stalin, who informed him that in view of the general shortage of food, there was "no food for nonfighters" in Russia, and that consequently the entire Polish Army had to be evacuated from Russia. In a short time the Polish Army in its entirety was removed from Soviet territory.

Another question played an important role in Soviet-Polish relations—the question of the deportees from eastern Poland. In itself this was not a problem that wise statesmanship could not solve safely and amicably. But here again the deep fissures in the very foundations of national policies made themselves felt.

At the end of 1939, when Soviet armies were occupying eastern Poland, the Soviet Government ordered deportation from the occupied territory of a great number of inhabitants, estimated by the Poles at or above 1,500,000, who were transported mainly to Siberia.[27] The deported people were those considered by the new authorities as politically or "socially dangerous." They included, in addition to the men and women active in politics, a large percentage of the propertied classes, especially small independent manufacturers and small tradesmen, who were regarded as particularly harmful.[28] About two thirds of the deportees were set free after arrival, but they were forbidden to change their district of residence. People in this category were known as *Spetspereselentsy*— "special migrants." The remaining third, numbering several hundred thousand, were placed in labor camps, in which living and working conditions were extremely hard. In numerous cases husbands were separated from their wives, and there are still many families whose members are unable to locate one another. When the Soviet-German War broke out, many of the deportees were put on trial and a number of them were sentenced to death. However, under the terms of the Soviet-Polish agreement, these sentences were set aside.

Relief measures to aid this vast aggregation of human beings produced much friction between the Polish agents and the Soviet administrative agencies, and had a dramatic ending. Release of the interned Poles began in August, 1941, and by the end of the next month the number released reached the figure of 350,000 persons. In a note dated November 8, 1941, Molotov informed the Polish Government that all interned Poles had been released, but even after that date the search for individuals and their release when found continued for some time. From the end of 1941 on, British sup-

---

27. Other authorities give somewhat different figures. Elma Dangerfield in *The Nineteenth Century and After*, July, 1943, says that the Poles deported in the autumn of 1939 numbered about one million, of whom roughly one half were women and children. She adds however that there were other mass deportations in the spring and summer of 1940.

28. Small trade in the eastern Polish cities was concentrated in the hands of the Jews, with the result that 55 per cent of the deportees were Jews.

plies for Polish relief began to reach Russia, and in the beginning of 1942 American lend-lease aid also became available.

To direct and supervise this relief work, which involved long journeys over the country, the Polish Government appointed 20 delegates (of whom 6 enjoyed diplomatic immunity) ; while among the Polish deportees agents were appointed in each colony, to the total number of 420. Thus in 1942 there was created an administrative organization of the Polish Government operating on Soviet territory. This was something wholly unprecedented in Soviet Russia, where foreigners, even when they were newspapermen or diplomats, were separated from the native population by a kind of invisible wall. This organization had not been working very long when the G.P.U. began to eye its activities, its correspondence, and its contacts with a certain amount of suspicion. In 1942, between June 29 and July 12, all the Polish "delegates," including those enjoying diplomatic "immunity," were arrested. They were soon released, however—all except one. Several had their visas for staying in Soviet Russia cancelled, among them a few secretaries of the Polish Embassy and a military attaché.

Following this, as revealed by Soviet authorities, numerous trials were held, at which, after the established custom, many of the defendants admitted the "criminal activities" (espionage and similar offenses) with which they were charged. They were charged, however, with spying not for Germany but for Britain, thus providing a unique occasion in history, when one war ally accused another of widespread espionage in favor of a third ally!

The work of the Polish representatives in Russia thus came to an end. In January, 1943, all Polish institutions, such as hospitals and schools, passed into Soviet hands. By that time nothing was left in Russia either of the Polish Army or of the independent Polish relief organization.

As the ties with the Sikorski government were breaking off one after another, the new Polish political organization, the Union of Polish Patriots in Moscow, was coming to the foreground. The Union was not officially Communist. Among its active members the majority were new people, from dif-

ferent non-Communist camps.[29] Basically, of course, it was
wholly reliable and docile. It published a magazine, *Nowe
Widnokręgi,* for the hundreds of thousands of Poles in all
parts of Soviet Russia, which competed with the magazine
of the Polish Embassy. During the entire year 1942, however, it pursued a cautious policy, refraining from attacks
on the Sikorski government, and permitting itself criticism
only of the Polish rightist opposition.

But, as has been pointed out, the situation changed materially at the beginning of 1943. The Union of Polish Patriots
came forward, more and more boldly, with its own Polish
program. The situation came to a head in February, when
the Soviet Government, partly as a result of the Stalingrad
victory, deemed the situation favorable for a change in its
policy.

Among the causes which led to an exacerbation of mutual
relations, the question of Soviet-Polish boundaries was in
itself only a reflection of differences that lay much deeper.
The Polish demand for "the frontiers of 1939" was not of
decisive importance, since the entire question was to be
postponed until after the end of the war. Moreover, were
this the only point of disagreement, there could hardly be
any doubt that a way to compose the difference would have
been found. General Sikorski made mention of a compromise
solution which, it seems, was informally discussed in Moscow
—the part of eastern Poland which formerly belonged to the
Russian Empire was to be returned to Russia, while the
southern part (eastern Galicia) was to be restored to Poland.[30] Division of the disputed territory would have been
possible if the question of boundaries had been the main
point at issue.

A fairer method of solving the problem was suggested by
the British Government, through its Ambassador to Moscow,

29. The fate of the old Polish Communists was rather pathetic.
When the Red Army occupied eastern Poland, the native Communists
were everywhere elected to the leading positions. But a month later the
Soviet military authorities handed the civil administration over to the
Commissariat of Internal Affairs (the G.P.U.), whereupon almost all
the old Communists were ousted and new men put in their places.

30. Sikorski's interview of February 22, 1943: "There has been the
belief that Russia is willing to let Poland keep the Lwow area, but
this is unofficial."

Sir Archibald Kerr, during those tense days of February, 1943. Britain proposed the method of plebiscite as it had been used between the two wars for solving a number of territorial disputes. As a condition of a free and genuine expression of the will of the people, a preliminary occupation of the disputed territory by a neutral army, neither Polish nor Soviet, would have become necessary.

Resort to plebiscite in deciding the fate of this large territory, comparable in size to many a European state and with a population of 12 million, would have the further advantage of making possible the acceptance by vote of the third solution—the deferment of annexation and the retention of the international regime for some time. It must be borne in mind that the population of this territory, non-Polish in its majority, has bad memories not only of the Polish rule of 1920–39 but also of the two years of Soviet rule preceding June, 1941. The prospect of economic revolution and political oppression made familiar by that two-year experiment might be the decisive consideration, and it would be a crime to force a regime on this population which has as much right to decide its fate as any other. Yet the British proposal was rejected by the Soviet Government.[31]

On February 20, 1943, *Pravda* published an article by the Ukrainian writer, Alexander Korneichuk (author of the play *Front*), in which the Polish émigrés were sharply attacked for advancing claims to eastern Poland. On February 25 General Sikorski declared that Poland would continue to insist on her demand for the restoration of the old Soviet-Polish frontiers, and the following day the Polish National Council confirmed the statement by a sharply worded resolution which proclaimed: "Integrity of the territory of the Polish Republic in her frontiers of September 1, 1939, and her sovereignty are inviolable and indivisible. No unilateral or illegal activities . . . can in any way alter this state of things."

---

31. The history of the Soviet Government contains a proposal made at the Vienna conference of 1924 for a plebiscite for the solution of the question of Bessarabia. When the Rumanian Government rejected this proposal, Maxim Litvinov declared that "a government refusing the method of plebiscite for solving a dispute thereby reveals both that it is wrong and that it fears the population."

In reply to this came on March 2, 1943, the official Soviet declaration through the Tass Agency which, after mentioning the prewar collaboration of Polish Governments with Germany, spoke of the right of the Ukrainians and White Russians of eastern Poland to unite with the Soviet Ukraine and White Russia, and stated in this connection that "the present Polish ruling circles do not reflect the true opinion of the Polish people on this question."

Strictly speaking, this declaration was tantamount to a breaking off of relations. "There are very great difficulties with Russia," General Sikorski stated on February 21, 1943, as he cancelled his proposed trip to Moscow. For its part the Soviet Government, having decided on a definite policy toward Poland, reassured the Czechoslovak Government, to which it was now tied by an anti-German and anti-Polish policy, by promising it restoration of Czechoslovakia within her old boundaries.

By the beginning of March the situation was quite clear. The Union of Polish Patriots, which had just then begun publication in Moscow of a new weekly paper, *Free Poland* (*Wolna Polska*)—in opposition to *Poland*, organ of the Polish Embassy—in the very first issue of its paper, dated March 1, attacked the Sikorski government and formulated its own program, an indissoluble alliance of Poland and the Soviet Union. In matters of Polish internal policy the paper promised expropriation of large landholders and other economic reforms.

It must now be clear from the foregoing that the breaking off of diplomatic relations between Soviet Russia and Poland which occurred two months later, on April 26, 1943, was only the last step, and not the most important at that, in the progress of these relations. The official reason for the break was Poland's request addressed to the International Red Cross for an investigation of the fate of several thousand Polish officers interned in Russia between 1939 and 1940. The action implied a request to verify the German assertions that those officers had been shot in Russia.

There can be little doubt that the incident was merely an excuse for breaking off relations. The Soviet Government has never taken serious political steps on the spur of a moment, impelled by feelings, considerations of prestige, or similar motives. In this it had been guided by a sense of its difference from and superiority over the capitalist world. Its attitude toward international diplomacy always has been businesslike and unsentimental.

The breach with the Sikorski government was the first step, coolly calculated if not free from risk, by which the Soviet Government attempted to organize its sphere of influence. It now had to make sure that it had chosen the right moment for it. As soon as the Soviet note of April 26 announcing the break reached London, the British and American Governments undertook *démarches* in Moscow with these ends in view: first, to restore normal relations between the two parties by persuading them to make concessions to each other; and second, to prevent the formation of a new Polish Government in Moscow. They succeeded in the second aim, but resumption of normal relations was flatly rejected by the Kremlin. On the contrary, the Union of Polish Patriots publicly announced on May 9 that it was taking steps to create its own Polish Army, and a Polish Division named after Tadeusz Kosciuszko, the eighteenth-century Polish hero, was founded, with Colonel Zygmunt Berling as its chief. It wore national Polish uniforms and retained the old banner of Pilsudski's and Sikorski's armies.

At the same time, Stalin made public his program. In an interview of May 4, 1943, he stated as his aims, first, "a strong and independent Poland," and second, "a mutual assistance pact against the Germans, if the Polish people wish to have it." In this statement he openly employed the old term, mutual assistance pact, which after the experience of 1939–40 had acquired a definite political meaning. As for the "wishes of the Polish people," the main task was to create a government which would be willing to follow the policy of an assistance pact. The Union of Polish Patriots satisfied this requirement.

The first convention of the Union, held in Moscow, opened on June 8, 1943. In his reply to its address, Stalin thanked it for "strengthening friendship between the peoples of Poland and of the Soviet Union"; and history may yet have to record these words as the first recognition of the Union in the capacity of a new government of Poland. The Congress enthusiastically acclaimed its new army and resolved to demand annexation of East Prussia to Poland. The last demand, which could have been made only with the approval of the Soviet Government, is of great importance. The program of the Union, which it published in its paper, followed the pattern of the programs announced by all similar organizations sponsored by Moscow in wartime, and was based on purely "democratic and national" principles, including even "the parliamentary-democratic system in a free Poland." At the same time the editorial of the Union's weekly suggested that "parliament would decide the future of the people and the state," thus leaving the door open for all kinds of reforms.

Moscow displayed exceptional political skill in all this difficult operation. It completely eschewed the term "Soviet Poland"; it strove to dispel the gathering anti-Soviet sentiment by the timely dissolution of the Communist International; and it succeeded, as far as the outside world was concerned, in separating the question of Poland from the general question of its future sphere of security. Concentrating its efforts on one section of the diplomatic front, it even induced a measure of moderation in the conflict in Yugoslavia and won the support of Eduard Beneš, head of the Czechoslovak Government. The skill, the timing, and the choice of methods shown in executing this very serious and perhaps politically decisive maneuver cannot be denied.

5. GERMANY—WEAK OR STRONG?

A defeat of Germany, followed by the defeat of Japan, will leave the victors far greater power in the future world than was the case after 1918.

At the end of the first World War there were five great masters of the world—Britain and America, powerful France, strong Italy, and rising Japan. The last three of these powers have lost their standing, during the course of this war, or they will have by the time the conflict is over, while the Anglo-American bloc, if there is no separate or compromise peace, will have acquired a power and an authority surpassing anything known in the past. It will be many years before the armies of other powers are restored; and during the years immediately after the war the huge navies of Britain and the United States will rule the world seas, and their air power will ensure their predominance on the continents. Whether an international military force is created or not, in actual practice for three quarters of the globe the only real force will be the combined power of the two Anglo-Saxon countries, especially since Soviet Russia will take no part in an international police system and since in the beginning the share contributed by the other states will be negligible.

Such a prospect spells grave danger for the foreign policy of the Soviet Government, since this policy conceives of no greater menace to Russia than a domination of one coalition of powers over the entire world. From traditionally Anglophile Scandinavia in the north to Turkey in the south, from pro-American China in the east to Holland and France in the west—in all latitudes and longitudes the English and American governments, with Spitfires and Flying Fortresses at their call, will have the last say. World politics has always been a tense struggle even aside from its military phases. Soviet policy if it continues on the old lines will encounter formidable obstacles.

Whether it be questions concerning the Balkans, Iran, or Manchuria, trade and loans, combinations and alliances of various neighboring states, or serious internal conflicts in other countries with a possibility of Soviet intervention in them—everywhere Soviet policy will stumble against the policy of Britain and America, a policy very different from Moscow's and sometimes diametrically opposite to it. Every attempt of Soviet Russia to tilt the new balance of power in its favor will bring a counteraction from those two powers. Under these conditions, expansion of the Communist economic system and policy will be out of the question; but even apart from that, frequent conflicts will be inevitable. Even now while striving for victory, Moscow regards with great anxiety the new combination of forces looming in the postwar period.

But what direction will Soviet foreign policy take in the case outlined? It would be natural if the direction were based on hopes of a conflict within the Anglo-American alliance, of the latter's disintegration, of the weakening of the "united front" which would be confronting Russia. But hopes of a conflict between Britain and America, which played a great role in the Soviet plans of the 'twenties and 'thirties, were belied in the past, and there are no serious reasons to expect such a conflict immediately after this war. The future rivalry of Britain and the United States in the South American market, in air transportation, or in other fields will not destroy their unity of views in regard to many questions affecting Soviet Russia.

In these circumstances attention turns anew to Germany. A broken, weak, and disabled Germany can become a pawn in the hands of the Anglo-American alliance. If Germany is weak she is likely to assume a "western orientation" in all European conflicts (as she did in 1919–21). Things will be different if Germany is to remain independent, if she will have retained her dignity, as well as military strength, if she pursues her own interests, conducts her own policy. A Germany like that may be found more useful. She will oppose her demands to the interests of the western powers. Her struggle against the west may break up the united front. Once again, therefore, there will be the traditional balance of power in European politics in which Germany will have a definite weight.

It will consequently be the policy of Soviet Russia, after the defeat of Hitlerism, to see Germany preserved as an important European power. Such a state of affairs is demanded not only by prospects—dim, perhaps—of revolutionary Communism, but by realistic policy as understood by Soviet Russia, with her tradition of choosing for herself the position of the third power, her distrust of all allies, and her satisfaction at dissension within the capitalist camp.

Stalin was therefore extremely cautious, from the very beginning of the war, in formulating his attitude toward Germany. In his conversation with Harry Hopkins in July, 1941, he laid the blame for the war on Hitler but not on Germany or even her General Staff: Hitler's invasion, Hopkins writes, aroused in Stalin "a hatred that nothing but the death of the German chancellor can lessen. As Stalin made clear to me, this was not a hatred of the German people, nor of the General Staff." [32]

Then in February, 1942, he spoke in these terms: "From time to time statements appear in the foreign press to the effect that the Red Army aims at the destruction of the German people. This is a wicked, foolish libel . . . History teaches that Hitlers come and go, but the German people and the German state remain."

In November of the same year he reiterated: "It is not our aim to destroy Germany." He went even further: "It is not our aim to destroy all military force in Germany." Stalin, of course, wants to see Hitler's armies destroyed, but after the war "the destruction of all German military force is inadvisable from the point of view of the victor!"

In the middle of 1943 the problem of the future regime in Germany assumed a concrete significance. That was the time when a promising new organization, Free Germany, was being set up in Moscow. The changed situation compelled even Ilya Ehrenburg, the passionate hater of the Germans, to reverse his attitude as expressed in all his previous articles and short stories, and to declare, no doubt to avoid being in opposition to Stalin, that "we hate the Germans not because they were born Germans but because . . . they are Fascists." [33] "We must not identify the Hitler clique with the German people," wrote a prominent Soviet personage hiding under the pen name of Malinin.[34]

---

32. *American Magazine*, December, 1941.
33. *Pravda*, June 21, 1943.
34. *War and the Working Class*, No. 3.

This problem is the crux of the postwar organization of Europe. The Atlantic Charter demands "disarmament of aggressors." This means, at least, the revival of the complicated regulations of 1919, and probably much more.

The Treaty of Versailles permitted Germany an army of not more than 100,000 men and forbade conscription as well as military training outside the army. Military aviation and submarines were banned as was the sending of military missions abroad. The size of the German Navy was severely limited. Finally, "control commissions" of the Entente and the League of Nations were given the right of constant supervision. The Versailles system of disarming Germany made provision for every small detail. Had only half of these provisions been carried out there would not have been the slightest possibility of a German war.

From the very beginning the Soviet Government strongly disapproved of the Treaty of Versailles as a whole and of its military clauses in particular. It shared the view that unilateral disarmament of Germany was unjust and that Germany's fight for equality of armament (i.e., either universal disarmament or arming of Germany up to the prevailing standard) deserved support. It deliberately pursued a policy of strengthening Germany, liquidating reparation payments, and revoking the Treaty of Versailles.

The Soviet Government now, however, prefers to proclaim and develop its program for Germany not as a new system forced upon the German people from outside but as reforms brought about by the German people themselves. The Red Army's task is to liberate Russian territory. Hence the special importance acquired in Moscow by German organizations in which émigré-Communists and war prisoners were joined in a common cause.

As in 1917–18, "the political work" among German and Austrian prisoners plays an important role in Soviet policy, in contrast to the strictly nonpolitical treatment of war prisoners elsewhere in the world. Instead of being handled by the Army, as in other countries, in Russia war prisoners are placed in the charge of the N.K.V.D. As early as October 8, 1941, there was held in Camp No. 58 the First Conference of German War Prisoners, in which 158 prisoners, officers and soldiers, took part, as well as a few leading German Communists. The adopted "Declaration of Demands of the

German People" embodied the basic ideas of Soviet policy: liberation of Germany from Hitlerism is the concern primarily of the German people; and if the latter succeed in overthrowing Hitler, this "can save Germany from another Versailles and lead to a just peace." But "woe to us Germans if Hitler is defeated without our aid, without our participation." The declaration also noted the role of Soviet Russia, "the country that has always opposed the Versailles Treaty." It concluded with the characteristic slogan: "Long live free and independent Germany."

All the basic ideas of the later Manifesto of the Free Germany Committee, which caused so much stir in 1943, were already stated in this declaration. The earlier document, however, was cast in a phraseology which bore the stamp of the time of its origin—the first months of the war when purely Communist formulas were still in use and the transition to the "national outlook" was in its initial stages. The declaration, for example, stated that "national unity can arise only after the crying contradictions between riches and poverty have been removed"; it also spoke repeatedly in rapturous tones of Socialism being built in Soviet Russia.

During the two years that followed that declaration all the organizations united in the Communist International gradually acquired a strictly national phraseology, and accordingly the Manifesto of the National Committee of Free Germany of July 21, 1943, bore a different form. Military defeat of Hitler's Germany is inevitable, the manifesto said. For the German people only two possibilities remain. The first, the worst fate that may befall the nation, would be "the overthrow of Hitler by the coalition armies," which would lead to "the end of national independence, of existence as a state, and dismemberment." The military triumph of the Anglo-American Armies would result in a new version of the Treaty of Versailles, worse than the original one—this is the leading idea of the manifesto.

But still another road lies open for Germany—the road of revolution. The new German Government is to "recall the German troops to the Reich's frontiers and embark on peace negotiations" (instead of yielding to the demand for unconditional surrender). Instead of asking for the disarmament of Germany, the manifesto declared:

"German soldiers and officers on all fronts! You have weapons in your hands! Hold on to them!

"Under the leadership of those commanders who recognize their responsibility move together against Hitler and yourselves clear the pass leading to peace."

The manifesto carried the signatures of a number of German officers and soldiers as well as German Communist émigrés. In this lay its importance. For the outside world leaders of the organization were announced as Erich Weinert, a poet-Communist, and Prince Heinrich von Einsiedel, the 22-year-old great-grandson of Bismarck. The committee presented a blueprint of a new German regime, which would save Germany from the consequences of a military defeat. It made clear once more that were a new government to form in Germany with the participation of even a few German Communists, no international treaties and undertakings could prevent an immediate termination of war on the eastern front followed by the conclusion of a Russian-German military alliance.

The probability of such a regime being set up in Germany is extremely small and the Soviet Government therefore has kept open for itself other roads as well, retaining freedom of action for other policies.

In 1914–16 the Russian program contained, as was pointed out earlier, the inclusion of East Prussia within the Russian Empire, a natural geographical consequence of uniting the whole of Poland within Russian boundaries. If at the end of this war Poland finds herself situated within the Soviet sphere, the problem of this large and rich German province will arise anew. Under a pro-Soviet Polish Government, East Prussia, which is located between Poland and Lithuania, would probably become a German "People's Republic" within the Soviet framework.

The Soviet Government has readily and frequently employed the method of national Irredenta in its foreign policy. For example, there is the small Karelian Soviet Republic on the borders of Finland, which was formed in July, 1923, as the nucleus of the future Soviet Finland, and which in 1940 received the territory ceded to Soviet Russia by Finland after the Soviet-Finnish War. A small Moldavian Soviet Republic was formed along the border of Bessarabia in October, 1924. In 1940, it was joined with the major part of Bessarabia after the latter was regained from Rumania. In October, 1939, after the Vilna district had been occupied by the Russians, it was restored to Lithuania, except for the small territory of Święciany, which was kept within the Soviet boundaries.

East Prussia could serve the same purpose. It would become an important German state organization under a Soviet banner situated right on the border of Germany and linked by historic, economic, and blood ties to the mighty organism of the former Reich—a living and constant appeal to the German people.

The final formulation of Soviet policy toward East Prussia will, however, depend on the general situation in Germany, and at present the Soviet Government keeps both doors open: either the close collaboration with a "People's Germany," without any territorial changes; or the annexation of some German territories, which will not, however, exclude a subsequent rapprochement.

But Russia also faces political factors which operate in a different—anti-German—direction.

Nowhere have the ravages of war been nearly as great as in Russia. What the countries of the Entente, and especially France, succeeded in securing for themselves by the terms of the Armistice and the Treaty of Versailles a quarter of a century ago today assumes great interest for Russia. Those 5,000 locomotives, 150,000 railway cars, and 60,000 agricultural machines which were stipulated in the terms of the Armistice long before the peace treaty was signed would be of great help to her. There would also be reparation payments and restoration of ruined territories, the handing over by Germany of her large tonnage commercial ships, plus new ones to be built, deliveries of livestock, of coal, of dyes, of gold reserves, of building materials. However vast these deliveries, they would cover but a tiny fraction of the monstrous destruction suffered by Russia. Only by keeping an army of her workingmen in Russia over a long period of years, by supplying them with all the necessary materials, and by a planned and consistent rebuilding of cities and villages could Germany compensate, and only partly at that, the damage caused by the war. Even then she could not restore life to the millions killed or bring back to health the millions of invalids. Yet for Russia to demand of Germany this vast amount of work of restoration would mean abandonment of Russia's pro-German policy.

"Germany will pay for everything," the Soviet press says today, both in prose and in verse. But this is proclaimed only by the less-known writers of pronounced nationalist sentiments who preach hatred and stern punishment of the Germans. The matter was first raised officially in August, 1943, by Prof. Eugene Varga, who read a paper on the reparations Russia needed and on Germany's duty to restore what she had destroyed. No doubt this question may become a source of serious internal differences.

Among the factors that will determine the attitude of Soviet Russia toward Germany in the final stage of the war and during the postwar period, the internal situation in Germany will be one of the most important. But this chapter of the near future remains as much a mystery for the Soviet Government as for the rest of the world, and all suppositions, expectations, and predictions under this heading are entirely arbitrary.

"The whole New Order is a volcano ready to erupt," Stalin has stated. If the victors insist on the unconditional surrender of Germany and refuse, in accord with their declarations, to have any dealings with the Hitler government, a political vacuum will be created which will have to be filled by some means or other. In that case—Moscow reasons—the defeat of Germany may become the starting point for revolutionary processes, as did the German defeat of 1918.

However, there is a substantial difference between that time and the present. Throughout World War I Germany had a number of political parties among which the most radical one (the Independent Socialists) was a revolutionary anti-war party. The contrary is true of the current war. The enemies of Germany now demand as a formal condition of peace the removal of the Nazi Government, but no anti-Nazi political parties are as yet evident inside Germany. The situation even prompts a mistaken belief that outside forces would be able to fill the vacuum in accordance with their own wishes, weaving the political patterns in any way they choose.

The contrast between the situation today and the situation in 1918 has an instructive analogy in the history of France. Entering Paris in 1814, the Allies forced Napoleon to abdicate and restored a Bourbon, Louis XVIII, to the French throne, the French people taking but a passive part in the transaction. But the defeat of the same France in 1871 resulted in a national revolution. It was this and not Bismarck that overthrew the monarchy and created the short-lived Paris Commune. Between these two extremes of a foreign intervention and a revolution range the present anticipations, hopes, and expectations.

It is natural that Moscow sees a revolution looming in Germany. But it is wholly skeptical about the possibility of a direct transformation of Nazi Germany into a Soviet Germany. The decisive factor is the absence in Germany of a revolutionary party of substantial proportions. At the moment of defeat popular discontent may turn into strikes, food riots, and mass outbreaks of violence, but discontent does not produce a revolutionary regime so long as the outbreaks, strikes, and riots lack a political program of their own, in other words, so long as there is no strong party of revolution. On the other hand, a Soviet regime cannot be "planted" in Germany even in the event of her being occupied by the Red Army. The recipe that worked so well in several other countries—a big dose of Soviet troops and a spoonful of local Communist movement—is inapplicable to a great nation such as Germany.

For all these reasons the first task to be accomplished in Germany is, from the point of view of Moscow policy, the creation of a Communist party, not of a Soviet state. All existing evidence seems to suggest that the German police, making free use of executions, terrorism, and *agents provocateurs*, have achieved greater successes in the extermination of Communists than did the Hungarians, Rumanians, and others in their respective countries. The few Communists that have survived are far from sufficient to form the basis for a revival of the party.[35]

35. Reviews of Communist movements in various countries which have appeared in the *Communist International* seldom discussed Ger-

For the immediate future, therefore, the Moscow program of internal policy in Germany requires "democracy." The principal value of democracy, from this point of view, lies, of course, in the fact that democracy provides special ways and opportunities for an unhampered building up of a Communist party—for its propaganda activity, its press, and its congresses. Not until there is formed a firm party framework will it be possible to proceed with the major tasks of the Communist program. According to the Communist view, it is because the Paris Commune was not directed by a single strong party that it collapsed after seventy-three days of existence.[36]

The Communist party is not a mechanism for conducting electoral campaigns but a ruling body for the future—the future state itself. This fact explains a characteristic of the party which would be wholly incomprehensible in other parties—the passionate concern with "organizational" questions, the endless discussions at all congresses about "the party-building work," the never-ending "purges." According to Lenin, "the revolution in Finland perished because of the absence of a Communist party." Concerning Italy, the Fourth Congress of the Communist International declared in its resolution: "After the war the objective premises for a revolution were present, only a Communist party was missing."

From the Communist point of view the chief value of the brief democratic interlude in Russia lay in the fact that it made it possible for the Bolsheviks to transform their small nucleus within eight months into a great party, which by October, 1917, counted as many as 200,000 members.

To have a strong party it is at first essential to have a democracy.

When, in June, 1940, the Soviet Government decided that complete subordination of the Baltic States was necessary,

---

many and contained only disjointed bits of information. Careful analysis of these data reveals the terrible efficiency of the Gestapo's work.

36. "Undivided dominance of a single party," wrote Stalin, underscoring the world "single," "this is what distinguishes the Bolshevik revolution to its advantage from the revolution of 1871 in France, where the direction of the revolution was divided between two parties neither of which can be called a Communist party." (*Problems of Leninism*, [11th ed.], p. 94.)

and sent its troops there, it did not proclaim an immediate Soviet dictatorship. For that it lacked an extensive and centralized organization such as a Communist party, without which a transformation of this nature was impossible. Before the Soviet occupation the Communist parties in the Baltic States were small and weak underground organizations. In the beginning, therefore, "democratic republics" were proclaimed in all three countries, and their new governments were free of Communist members. At the same time, with the financial and political aid of the Soviet Government, party organizations were feverishly built in all towns and villages. Within a month their organization had progressed so far that at the parliamentary elections the Communist party had long lists of candidates, and later the old Constitution was replaced by a Soviet system. Such is the value of democracy, according to the Moscow concepts. It explains why, during the years of this war, the Moscow radio, broadcasting in German, has been continuously addressing appeals to all classes of the German people, workers as well as farmers and artisans, Protestants and Catholics, and the entire army, calling upon them to rally in a popular movement against the Nazi Government under the slogan of democracy. The extensive propaganda work among German war prisoners was in the same vein. Stalin formulated his program—and not for Germany alone—as "restoration of democratic liberties and destruction of the Hitlerite regime."

But to him democracy is not an end in itself. Should stabilized political relations fail to be quickly established in postwar Europe, and should Germany, for instance, become a scene of stormy popular movements, then the old, cherished dreams of a great Soviet coalition from Vladivostok to Aachen are certain to awaken, and the old ideas, put aside many years ago, may be revived. Whether the events in Germany will take this turn will be revealed in the immediate future. But on the assumption that such a development is possible, Soviet policy will pursue these objectives:

First, it will resist proposals to deprive Germany of the right of maintaining substantial military forces. Destruction of the "German Fascist Army" is not identical with the disarmament of Germany. The former is a Soviet war aim, the latter is not.

Second, it will seek a common frontier with Germany and will try to prevent Poland from gaining a position which, as in 1920, would be able to keep the forces of Russia and Germany apart.

Third, it will show no kindly disposition toward the "international police force" whose task it will be in this case to restore order in Germany.

Fourth, in case of a favorable development of German domestic affairs Soviet policy will endeavor to convert the probable collaboration with Germany into a hard-and-fast military alliance.

The German problem, in its new postwar form, will be one of the decisive factors in Soviet policy and in the future attitude of the Soviet Union to its former allies of World War II.

6. POSTWAR RUSSIA

The war will pass, but Germany, the German people, the German problem will remain. No peace program does or can exist which would eliminate this problem within the next few decades. The wisest of peace treaties would not solve it. A partition of Germany into small territorial units would probably result in a great movement for national unity which no tanks or airplanes could combat. On the other hand, preservation of Germany in her old form would also preserve the German menace. Disarmament of Germany would bring about a struggle for "equal rights." But retention of military rights by her would increase the danger. Shutting off of German economic resources by force would hit the interests of other European nations. But their preservation would in a few years restore Germany to a first-class economic and (potentially) military power. Finally, Sovietization of Germany, a new form of unilateral dominance of the Old World, would be only a challenge to new wars, not at all a solution of the problem.

One hundred and thirty years ago another world conqueror suffered a defeat at the hands of the united nations of Europe. But his France, which seemed to have lost her military ardor as well as the cream of her population, only a few years after the defeat became once again a great world power and the strongest one on the European continent. And there were 27 million Frenchmen then, while there are 80 million Germans today, who occupy, moreover, the very center of Europe.

As was the case with the French expansionism of the eighteenth to nineteenth centuries, it will be many years, perhaps decades, before Germany will change from the militant and expansionist power that she is today into a peaceful and no longer dangerous member of the European community of nations. Defeat in two world wars is a powerful argument; but its effect is not likely to endure forever. As the defeat of Napoleon's France in 1815 necessitated a strong European coalition to make peace secure, so after the second World War the best guarantee of peace would be a new organization of powers, if this were possible to bring about.

A changed world will emerge from the war but certain

problems will remain, even if in new forms, and there will remain also the few definite methods of solving them. Germany's neighbors, including Russia, will be faced with a choice between the policy of strategic frontiers, i.e., of wide spheres of influence, and the policy of international alliances. The choice will have to be made because the alternatives are irreconcilable: the problem must be solved, either separately or collectively.

The separate solution, which would be no more than a continuation of the traditional trends of Soviet foreign policy, will involve the following consequences. First, it will mean political mobilization of the European east (Slav and non-Slav countries as well) under the leadership of Moscow against the danger from the west. Second, it will involve the creation of a great military force in support of this policy. Third, it will be tantamount to a flat refusal to participate in any international military body. Fourth, it will imply a controlling influence on the foreign policy of a number of smaller states, and a strong pressure exercised on their domestic life. Finally it will represent a Soviet effort to develop kindred political forces inside Germany. This course of policy will especially accord with Moscow's guiding principles, since for Moscow the potential danger will lie not only in Germany but in the other Great Powers as well.

As soon as one of the great states of Europe enters upon the course of expansion at the end of this war, whether impelled by high purposes or by base ones, and whether the expansion is open or veiled, that state will inevitably contribute to the formation of international coalitions directed against itself, which will at the same time provoke a rapid restoration of the military power of Germany. Separate methods do not solve the problem.

Lying open before Russia, however, there is another political course, which, to be sure, is in contradiction to her traditions of the last decades, but which better accords with her needs as well as with the national sentiments in the country. Russia can seek her security in the demilitarization of Germany and in an alliance with the great nations of the west rather than with the multitude of small nations in eastern Europe. This policy of stabilization of the Old World would involve a repudiation of the former pro-German orientation;

recognition of complete and genuine independence of the small nations of central and eastern Europe; renunciation of large-scale territorial expansion; and limitation of armaments corresponding to the gradual slackening of tension in the European atmosphere. The security of Russia would be assured more firmly by a lasting alliance with London-Paris-Washington than by an agreement with Prague-Warsaw-Belgrade-Berlin. This course would satisfy the interests of postwar Russia far better than large-scale expansion, involving the creation of a German buffer state, a method fraught with the seeds of new wars.

Russia has never seen a war as destructive of human lives as this war. As far as the war in Europe is concerned, she has suffered at least 90 per cent of the total of the United Nations' casualties. In World War I Russia's killed numbered 1,800,-000, and her western provinces within the theater of operations were devastated. In the present war the number of Russians killed is already greater by far than in the last war, in addition to which there have been great losses from starvation and epidemics. Whole provinces of the rich Russian south have been looted and depopulated, and where the German tanks passed they left nothing but wilderness behind them. Since the days of the Tartar invasions there has been no such brutality as that resorted to by Hitler's army in its march over the country. And so millions of children roam over Russia, dying of cold and hunger, mothers and widows move about, behind the front line and deep in the rear, half insane, only half alive, without hope, and without strength. They will be joined by millions returning from prison camps, from labor slavery, from German factories and fields, people who have seen much, suffered much, and thought much.

Nowhere in the world are home and foreign policies bound by such organic ties as in Soviet Russia. Continuity of foreign policy, regardless of internal political changes, was a principle observed in many European countries during the period between the two wars. Russia has been an exception to this rule. Her foreign policy has been always the obverse of her internal policy.

Only naïve people, however, can believe that in the mighty stream of wartime and postwar transformation the basic principles of policy can remain inviolate. Nobody can foresee the exact direction of the future political development, but profound changes are bound to come and they will reflect in a decisive fashion new political orientations and programs.

These changes may also have a great, perhaps decisive, influence on international relations. The new moods and movements described in the early parts of this volume are shared by, and find support in, the vast majority of the people and of the army. They will have a highly important bearing on the future course of both internal and foreign policies. Joined to a renunciation of social Messianism, they would instantly tell on the relations with other countries. If the mortal fear of the red specter from the east vanishes in Central Europe, many problems which were baffling up to now will find their solution made easier, among them the problem of an economic alliance with the Baltic countries, the state allegiance of disputed eastern Poland, and the Finnish border question. A new Russian policy would give Europe one of the principal conditions for a long and lasting peace which otherwise would be impossible of realization.

INDEX